To Nancy —

— with warmest
personal regards —

Tom O'Connor
Nov. 2002
—

❡ EMINENT BOSTONIANS

❧ EMINENT BOSTONIANS

Thomas H. O'Connor

HARVARD UNIVERSITY PRESS

CAMBRIDGE, MASSACHUSETTS

LONDON, ENGLAND • 2002

Designed by Annamarie Why

Library of Congress Cataloging-in-Publication Data
O'Connor, Thomas H., 1922–
   Eminent Bostonians / Thomas H. O'Connor.
      p. cm.
   Includes index.
   ISBN 0-674-00942-8 (alk. paper)
      1. Boston (Mass.)—Biography.   2. Boston (Mass.)—History.   I. Title.
F73.25.O28 2002
920.0744'61—dc21   2002068616

❡ Contents

Contents

◉ Preface: Footprints on the Sands of Time

Some years ago I was interviewing an elderly neighbor about grow-ing up in a small Irish Catholic neighborhood in Boston early in the century. Although he was well into his eighties, the old man had an excellent memory, and he sat back in his easy chair, smiling, as he reminisced about an era of gaslights, horse-drawn wagons, narrow streets, crowded pubs, parish priests, and corner cops. But he re-called with special fondness the women who had been his grammar school teachers in the local public school in those days. Severe in appearance, modest in dress, and completely dedicated to their profession—women of "significant glances and few words," as one historian has described them—they not only insisted upon such basic essentials as correct spelling, proper grammar, and legible handwriting, but also managed to convey to their young charges an appreciation of the elements of poetry, music, and the fine arts. The old gentleman remembered the way his sixth-grade teacher would start off each class with a reading of the 23rd or 24th Psalm "so that the rhythm and the ideas of those beautiful poems became second nature to us." He also took a great deal of pleasure in the fact that he and many of his old schoolmates, even fifty or sixty years later, could still recall verbatim many of the poems they had been forced to memorize—and he promptly launched into an emotional rendition of "The Charge of the Light Brigade" for my edification.

Those of us who attended the Boston schools in those days when the rigorous process of memorization was regarded as a social benefit, not an educational taboo, will undoubtedly recall Henry Wadsworth Longfellow's poem "A Psalm of Life," which reminds us that the lives and accomplishments of those who have gone before us can often provide some measure of inspiration for those who follow in their footsteps. As I am sure most readers of my generation will recall, the most memorable lines went:

> Lives of great men all remind us
> We can make our lives sublime.
> And, departing, leave behind us
> Footprints on the sands of time.

The practice of singling out notable figures as inspirational models for other generations to admire and to emulate has a long and illustrious tradition, beginning with Plutarch and his lives of forty-six Greek and Roman heroes, and extending to the early twentieth century, when Lytton Strachey revived the genre of multiple biographies with his *Eminent Victorians*. I'm afraid that my own introduction to memorable figures was neither that long nor that distinguished. I guess the first time I was aware of any kind of formal presentation of inspirational models was when I attended parochial grammar school and the nuns had us read a children's version of *The Lives of the Saints*. Apostles and disciples, virgins and martyrs, preachers and hermits, missionaries and explorers, bishops and confessors (I never really figured out who *they* were): the example of their courage and sacrifices was intended to strengthen our religious faith and improve our obviously weak characters. Later, when I went on to the Boston Latin School, I was introduced to a litany of a much more secular sainthood, men whose names were emblazoned on a frieze that ran along the edge of the ceiling in the school's large auditorium. John Adams, John Hancock, Ralph Waldo Emerson, and the like (all white males in those days), they were graduates of the oldest public school in America who had gone on to attain eminence in politics, scholarship, and science. Their grand achievements were designed to inspire in our young hearts and minds a commitment to excellence and a passion for success.

This present collection of brief lives of Eminent Bostonians differs in several respects from earlier compilations of biographies of persons whose notable careers were considered worthy of study. First of all, the people I have singled out in this volume have come from all walks of life, various economic levels, and different social classes. Their inclusion is determined by the positive contributions they have made to the life and society of their city, rather than by having been members of an aristocracy in which their eminence would be assured by the exalted nature of their birth or the social pedigree of their family. Second, not all of the Eminent Bostonians in this volume were actually born in the city of Boston, but all of them contributed in some distinctive and constructive way to the life and culture of the city. Some, like the Adamses and the Hancocks, came up from the South Shore towns of Braintree and Duxbury; others, like the Lawrences, were members of the "codfish aristocracy" who came down from the North Shore towns of Essex County. In more recent years, many persons left their original homes in various parts of Europe, Asia, and Africa, to become citizens of a new city. Their eventual importance to Boston is not where they originated, but how they came to renew and redefine the life and society of the city of which they had become an integral part.

The selection and arrangement of these Eminent Bostonians were, of course, matters of considerable discussion. Some selections are so obvious that failure to include them would arouse the collective wrath of those already well acquainted with the history of the city. Other names will be immediately recognized by readers who may recall having seen them in an earlier Harvard University Press publication called *Boston A to Z.* Some names may be vaguely familiar from early childhood memories, school lessons, family anecdotes, or newspaper gossip. And others may be completely new to readers. They are, admittedly, an odd mixture of the famous and the modest, the brilliant and the ordinary, the wealthy and the poor, the artist and the athlete, the native and the newcomer. But in one way or another, each one of them added something personal and distinctive to the continually fascinating history of the city.

As far as arrangement is concerned, there were many possibilities, but we ultimately decided on a simple alphabetical listing ranging over the almost 400 years of Boston's history. This arrangement provides both the appearance of method and the pleasures of serendipitous association: a best-selling woman novelist is found between a nineteenth-century Harvard scientist and a twentieth-century radio comedian. The story of a disabled young woman comes between the accomplishments of a colonial housewife on one side, and the life of a celebrated Boston churchman on the other. A prize-winning Olympic athlete finds himself situated between a colorful big-city mayor and a world-renowned painter. A remarkable modern scientist can be found alongside a famous musical conductor, followed by a well-known African American social reformer. And so it goes. This sometimes jarring sequence of unusual and often contradictory personalities seems to me somewhat evocative of the idiosyncratic character of Boston itself. I have always thought that one of the more lovable and distinctive aspects of Boston is the rather haphazard way in which its buildings cluster together—colonial meetinghouses, Federal townhouses, and Greek Revival market buildings side by side with Victorian mansions, Gothic Revival cathedrals, and high-rise skyscrapers. They are all separate and distinctive, and yet they all merge into a striking unity that conveys something of the distinctiveness of the city.

Actually, the choice of who is included and who is not included in such a volume will probably create much more controversy than the way in which they are arranged. The selection of some of these figures will undoubtedly upset many readers; the omission of other figures will certainly enrage others. But that kind of dissent is inevitable in any project based on personal decisions and subjective judgments. I will leave it to my readers to reflect upon the long and fascinating history of Boston, and decide for themselves which men and women would be their choice for the prestigious title of Eminent Bostonians.

Thomas H. O'Connor
Chestnut Hill, Massachusetts
April 15, 2002

¶ Abigail Adams

In an age of increasing gender consciousness and growing feminist pride, the figure of Abigail Adams has emerged from the shadows of the past to assume a much more visible and significant role in American history. Her keen observations regarding the implications of independence, the foibles of men, and the potential of women have marked her as a thoughtful, intelligent, articulate, and far-seeing woman, well in advance of her time.

Abigail Smith was born in 1744, the second child of William Smith, a Weymouth minister, and Elizabeth Quincy, of the nearby town of Braintree. A highly intelligent young woman of strong Congregational convictions, Abigail never attended school because of poor health, but her father had an excellent library and, with the guidance of her brother-in-law, Richard Cranch, Abigail and her sisters were educated beyond what was offered to most girls of that time. Abigail became politically aware, well read in the classics and in current affairs.

On October 24, 1764, Abigail Smith married a promising young lawyer from Braintree, John Adams, who had known her family for many years. While John spent most of his time traveling to court sessions in Boston, Abigail kept house and produced five children, two of whom died in infancy. In 1788 John moved his family to Boston, where they rented a house in Brattle Square. Once again Abigail concentrated on the upbringing of the children, while John was soon off to Philadelphia to serve as a member of the Continental Congress.

Over the years, John and Abigail engaged in a long, lively, and loving correspondence involving serious issues of state as well as personal expressions of love. Into the period of rebellion, and throughout the years of Revolution, Abigail proved to be a constant, brilliant, and perceptive correspondent, responding to her husband's activities and offering her wise, mature, and sometimes critical comments. She followed his involvement in the affairs of the Continental Congress, and in March 1774 advised him to carefully think through the implications of the declaration of independence on which he was working. "I desire you would remember the ladies," she famously wrote, "and be more generous and favorable to them than your ancestors!" Abigail was also concerned with the education of women, and urged her husband to see that the new nation had "learned women" as well as heroes, statesmen, and philosophers. "If you complain of neglect of Education in sons," she wrote, "what shall I say with regard to daughters."

Abigail Adams followed the course of independence closely and communicated with her "Dearest Friend" regularly. In June 1775, with her eight-year-old son, she watched from a rooftop in Boston as the smoke from the flaming houses of Charlestown blackened the sky, and a short time later reported the death of their friend, Dr. Joseph Warren, at the Battle of Bunker Hill. "The race is not swift, nor the battle strong," she wrote, confirming her faith in the future, "but the God of Israel is he that giveth strength and power unto his people." A year later, on March 17, 1776, she described the scene as the "largest Fleet ever seen in America," the occupying British, evacuated the town and sailed out of Boston Harbor. The following month she wrote to her husband about how she first heard the words of the Declaration of Independence proclaimed from the balcony of Boston's Old State House. When the reading was concluded, she wrote, the cannon was discharged, and all the people shouted "God save our American states!" After the surrender of the British following the Battle of Yorktown in 1781, she anxiously waited for John to complete his work in Paris on the final peace treaty so that at last her "dearest of Friends and the tenderest of Husbands" would return home.

When the Treaty of Paris was finally signed and the Revolution over, Abigail and some of the children joined John in London, where he was serving as ambassador to Great Britain. When they returned to America, they lived in New York City while John served as the first vice-president in George Washington's administration. In 1796 Abigail somewhat reluctantly supported her husband's decision to offer himself for the presidency, but feared that on the national scene she might not have the "patience, prudence, and discretion" displayed by Martha Washington, whom she had come to know and greatly admire. After John Adams's victory in 1796, the couple moved to the temporary capital at Philadelphia, but after two years Abigail decided to return home to Massachusetts. After a serious bout of illness that almost proved fatal, she once again returned to her husband, and became the first First Lady to occupy the newly constructed presidential mansion in Washington, D.C. John and Abigail did not remain residents of the White House very long, however, for in November 1800 John Adams was defeated by his rival, Thomas Jefferson, and the Adamses returned to Massachusetts for good.

Although Abigail Smith Adams had the pleasure of seeing her oldest son, John Quincy Adams, sworn into office in 1817 as Secretary of State to President James Monroe, she did not live long enough to see him go on to achieve the presidency. After coming down with typhoid fever, John Adams's loving wife and constant companion of fifty-four years died on October 28, 1818, just before her seventy-fourth birthday.

❧ HENRY ADAMS

Henry Adams had one of the most distinguished pedigrees of any man in American history. He was the great-grandson of John Adams, second President of the United States; grandson of John Quincy Adams, the sixth President; and son of the reformist statesman Charles Francis Adams, Lincoln's minister to England during the Civil War. His brothers, Brooks Adams and Charles Francis Adams, Jr., shared his lifelong interest in writing history and in exploring the philosophy of history.

Born in Boston in 1838, Henry Adams graduated from Harvard in 1858, and studied law at Berlin and Dresden during 1859–60. After the outbreak of the Civil War he went to Washington as secretary to his father, and then accompanied his father to London, where he continued to serve as secretary at the Court of St. James's. In this capacity, Henry learned much about the process of diplomacy, met the most famous British statesmen and scientists, and broadened the Harvard education he believed had failed him so badly. He would later write *The Education of Henry Adams,* a third-person autobiography, complaining of how his undergraduate study, with its antiquated methods and outmoded curriculum, had turned him out more suited to life in the Middle Ages than in the modern world. With what Martin Green has described as an air of "plaintive hopelessness," Adams expressed annoyance that his Harvard education had failed to instruct him in the ways of the city and the machine, and had ignored completely the major social issues confronting industrial society.

Returning to America, Adams was both fascinated and repelled by the crudeness and strength of America in the postwar years. He gave up the idea of practicing law and turned to journalism, writing critical articles about such captains of industry as Jay Gould and James Fisk, and commenting on the corruption of politics and business. In 1870 he accepted Harvard's invitation to teach medieval history, but soon added courses in early American history. By 1877 he had given up teaching and settled permanently in Washington, D.C., with his Boston bluestocking wife Marian "Clover" Hooper. He incorporated many of his observations on the machinations of Washington political life in an anonymous novel called *Democracy,* which caused quite a stir when it was published in 1880. In 1879 he completed work on an excellent and appreciative biography of Albert Gallatin, followed in 1882 by an unsympathetic study of the eccentric John Randolph of Virginia. In 1885, he was shattered by the suicide of his wife and embarked on an extended tour of Asia before returning to Washington.

By this time he was fully engaged in what would become his major work, *The History of the United States during the Administrations of Jefferson and Madison,* in nine volumes (1889–1892). Adams's *History,* given his early background, was particularly expert in diplomatic affairs, and its coverage of the War of 1812 was exceptionally well done. Although the bias of the Adams family against Thomas Jefferson and the Republican administration is apparent, Adams nevertheless displays both accuracy and thoroughness in dealing with national issues, drawing heavily upon original sources from both European and American depositories. American historians were almost unanimous in their praise of Adams's *History of the United States* when the final volume appeared in 1892, and in tribute to this outstanding work of historical research, they elected him president of the prestigious American Historical Association.

In his approach to the philosophy of history, Henry Adams bypassed the Social Darwinism that influenced so many other historians and social scientists during the late nineteenth century. He drew, instead, upon what he saw as the potential of the New Physics as a means of historical analysis. He felt that the implications of the New Physics, particularly its Second Law of Thermodynamics concerning the conservation of energy and the equilibrium of force, could eventually be reduced to a kind of mathematical formula that could be applied to the study and writing of history. Some of Adams's thoughts about a scientific philosophy of history can be seen in his study *Mont Saint Michel and Chartres* (1904), in which he speculates about the ways in which the Virgin Mary served as a powerful force in stimulating the magnificent art and inspiring architecture of the medieval centuries. In trying to find a modern counterpart, he suggested that perhaps the Dynamo might be regarded as an energizing symbol of the modern technological spirit. Adams's incessant urging of teachers and historians to seek a philosophy of history based on the New Physics left most professionals unconvinced, although his gifted brother, Brooks Adams, did use natural science as a major theme in his own historical writings.

His last major work, and the one most read today, *The Education of Henry Adams*, was privately printed and distributed to a select circle of his friends in 1906. In the early sections of the book, he recounts his Boston boyhood and muses on his Adams heritage. After Henry Adams's death in 1918, the book was published to widespread acclaim and was awarded the Pulitzer Prize.

¶ JOHN ADAMS

"Sit down, John. For God's sake, John, sit down!" sing the members of the Continental Congress to John Adams in the Broadway musical *1776*. But John Adams would not sit down and continued, in his stubborn, determined, and occasionally obnoxious manner, to insist upon a separation between the American colonies and the British Empire. And in the end, Adams had his way. He was pleased to add his own signature to those of the other American representatives on the Declaration of Independence.

Born in 1735 in the small farming community of Braintree, Mass., John Adams had Boston connections through his mother Susanna Boylston, the daughter of a Boston physician. Young John graduated from Harvard College in 1755, later studied law, and was admitted to the Massachusetts bar in 1758. In 1764 he married Abigail Smith of Weymouth, in a loving union that would be a significant influence on his public and private life.

John Adams soon became involved in the increasingly tense relations between the American colonists and the British government. In 1765 he wrote the "resolution and protest" for the town of Braintree, and came out publicly against the Stamp Act. In 1768 he moved his family to Boston and successfully defended John Hancock against charges of smuggling. In 1700, after British soldiers killed five colonials during the Boston Massacre, Adams agreed to defend the soldiers. Insisting that every accused person had the right to a fair trial, Adams achieved acquittal for the British soldiers on the grounds of self-defense.

Adams was less judicious in his reaction against the passage of the Tea Act, however. In December 1773 he wrote that the Boston Tea Party was "the grandest event" since the trouble with Britain began. The following year he was selected to represent Massachusetts in the first Continental Congress, and was reelected to the second. Early in 1776, Adams supported the idea of separation from Britain, seconded Richard Henry Lee's motion for independence, and worked closely with Thomas Jefferson in preparing the Declaration of Independence. During the early stages of the Revolution, he used his legal talents on the Board of War, as well as on several congressional committees.

Late in 1777, accompanied by his ten-year-old son, John Quincy, Adams went to Europe as a commissioner to France. There he found that France had already extended recognition to the new United States of America and was working on a treaty of alliance. Adams continued to serve his country overseas until Great Britain, following the defeat at Yorktown in 1781, agreed to negotiations. Adams was dispatched to Paris to assist Benjamin Franklin and John Jay in working out a final peace treaty that recognized the independence of the United States and ceded the new nation all territory east of the Mississippi River.

Adams served three years as ambassador to Great Britain before returning to the United States in 1787 to become George Washington's first vice-president under the terms of the new Constitution. Always his own man, with his own strong and stubborn views, John Adams clashed with Secretary of State Thomas Jefferson over questions of national policy, as well as with Secretary of the Treasury Alexander Hamilton, a member of his own Federalist party, over foreign policy issues. After Washington completed two terms in office, in 1796 John Adams was elected President of the United States, although he had to accept Thomas Jefferson as his vice-president. The most important controversy of his administration came with his fellow Federalist, Alexander Hamilton, over the question of war with France. Relations between the United States and France had deteriorated so badly that French and American ships were already firing on one another on the high seas. Although Hamilton and his supporters argued strongly in favor of a declaration of war, Adams stubbornly held out for a peaceful settlement. To Adams's good fortune, Napoleon Bonaparte came to power in 1799 and agreed to peaceful negotiations with the United States.

Adams may have preserved the peace (something he regarded as his greatest accomplishment), but his split with the Hamilton wing of the Federalist party proved fatal to his political future. In the election of 1800, Adams was defeated by Thomas Jefferson in a political turnover that ushered in the Democratic party and began the eventual decline of the Federalists. Out of office at the age of sixty-five, Adams returned to Braintree, where, like Jefferson at Monticello, writes Van Wyck Brooks, "the patriarch cheerfully sat for the painters and sculptors, and studied the greater art of growing old." His beloved wife, Abigail, died in 1818, but Adams himself lived long enough to see his son, John Quincy Adams, elected President of the United States in November 1824. On the evening of July 4, 1826, John Adams died, only a few hours after the death of Thomas Jefferson—the two Founding Fathers passing into history on the same date, July 4, on which they had given to the nation, and indeed to the world, the Declaration of Independence.

❡ SAMUEL ADAMS

Arms folded, legs planted firmly apart, his brow furrowed in a frown, Samuel Adams stands in front of Faneuil Hall and looks across at the new City Hall and the city whose freedom he helped to forge. And it is an appropriate location for his statue, as it was in Faneuil Hall that Adams spoke out resolutely against the Grenville Acts and the Townshend Duties, advocating the overthrow of British rule and the creation of an independent nation.

Born in Boston in 1722, Samuel Adams was the son of a wealthy ship owner also named Samuel Adams. Young Samuel attended Harvard College, studied theology and law, and presciently enough wrote his senior thesis on the subject of resistance to political authority. After Samuel's graduation in 1740, his father suffered financial reverses, upon his death leaving to his son a brewery business which soon slipped into bankruptcy. Samuel went into politics, held several minor offices, and in 1756 was elected town tax collector. He proved so ineffective at collecting taxes that appreciative voters elected him to nine one-year terms. By 1769 Adams had become a member of several local political clubs, most notably the powerful Boston Caucus. After the end of the French and Indian War in 1763, he supported James Otis in his attacks against the writs of assistance that allowed British officials to search for unspecified cargo while looking for smuggled goods. The following year Adams argued against the Sugar Act, claiming that Parliament had no authority to use taxes to raise revenue, and he persuaded the Massachusetts assembly to adopt a petition calling for the act's repeal.

But it was the passage of the Stamp Act in 1765 that propelled Adams to the leadership of the radical movement in Massachusetts. He supported mob violence against both the person of the local tax collector and the property of Lieutenant-Governor Thomas Hutchinson. Although the Stamp Act was repealed the following year, Adams continued to participate in the Sons of Liberty and other local patriot groups. The Townshend Act of 1767, which set up duties on a series of imported commodities, reactivated the radical movement in Boston and provided Adams with more ammunition in his fight against British authority. Under his direction, the Massachusetts House of Representatives circulated a letter to the other colonies denying Parliament's right to introduce such taxes. In response to this so-called Circular Letter, merchants in other colonial cities organized non-importation associations. Smuggling increased, and tensions heightened as Britain sent military reinforcements to Boston. The explosion came on the evening of March 5, 1770, with the confrontation that came to be called the Boston Massacre, an event Samuel Adams repeatedly exploited in his efforts to enlarge the scope of opposition to the Crown.

For a short time, the repeal of the Townshend Duties appeared to have deflated the radical movement. The passage of the Tea Act in 1773, however, granting the British East India Company a monopoly on tea, generated fierce local opposition that led to the Boston Tea Party in December 1773. The response of Parliament came in the form of the Coercive Acts, which closed the port of Boston, suspended the Massachusetts charter, and established military rule throughout the colony. When the Massachusetts legislature met in session, it was Samuel Adams who locked the doors of the council chamber so that the assembly could not be dissolved. Despite Governor Gage's denunciations, the House remained in session. Both

Samuel and his cousin John were elected as representatives to the Continental Congress in Philadelphia. As the sessions of the Congress continued, it was John Adams the lawyer, not Samuel Adams the politician, whose voice became more prominent. Samuel eventually retired from the Congress in 1781, just after adding his signature to the Articles of Confederation.

Although Samuel Adams recognized that there were serious flaws in the Articles of Confederation and spoke in favor of making whatever changes and revisions were necessary, he still hoped that the Articles would be kept as the permanent framework of government for the new nation. For that reason, he came out early in opposition to the new Constitution of the United States that had been created at Philadelphia during the summer of 1787. Adams greatly feared that his precious state sovereignty would be overwhelmed by the strong central government that had been established by the Constitution. Despite his reservations, however, at the ratification convention held in Boston in February 1788, Adams finally agreed to support the new government. He cooperated with John Hancock in formulating a series of "Conciliatory Proposals" to safeguard the rights of the states—proposals that were later included among the first ten amendments to the Constitution.

During the 1790s Samuel Adams succeeded John Hancock to serve three terms as governor of Massachusetts. In 1797, at the age of seventy-five, Adams announced his withdrawal from political life, and passed quietly away in 1803. A stubborn, inflexible, and self-righteous man, with a brilliant mind for politics and an uncanny skill for propaganda, Samuel Adams laid the groundwork for the revolutionary movement that led to American independence.

❧ Louis Agassiz

Some persons come to Boston—from other parts of the United States or from countries throughout the world—with wealth, talent, power, and influence, and yet are never truly accepted as part of the community. There are other persons who, for whatever reasons, are quickly and quite easily accepted into the Boston culture regardless of cultural differences and personal eccentricities. Louis Agassiz would seem to be one of those outsiders who found a home in the city.

Born in Switzerland in 1807, Jean Louis Rodolphe Agassiz studied medicine at the universities of Zurich, Heidelberg, and Munich. In 1829, at the age of twenty-two, he published *The Fishes of Brazil,* an important account of a fish fauna that established his scientific reputation. As a professor of natural history at Neuchâtel, he continued his extensive research on fossil fish, and eventually became a leading authority on the glacial movements of the early Ice Age.

Agassiz came to America in 1846, made several trips on coastal surveys, and in 1848 accepted the chair of natural history at Harvard University. With his dark eyes, long hair, and appealing French accent, he proved to be a popular and charismatic lecturer both in the classroom and on the public lecture circuit. In 1848 his wife died in Germany; two years later he married Elizabeth Cabot Cary, the daughter of a wealthy lawyer with connections to the Lowell textile industry, and moved into the higher echelons of Boston society. His three daughters from his first marriage moved to Boston, and each of them married into a prominent Boston family: the Shaws, the Higginsons, and the Russells. Agassiz was a founding member of the prestigious Saturday Club, and became such an integral part of its literary and social activities that it was often referred to as "Agassiz's Club."

In 1848 he led groups to explore the shores of Lake Superior, and three years later explored the Florida reefs, assembling materials for what would become a multivolume work called *Contributions to the Natural History of the United States.* Through the 1850s Agassiz not only continued his writing, his lectures, and his explorations of glacial formations in such widely separated regions as Brazil and the Rocky Mountains, but also found time to conduct a successful fund-raising campaign for a Museum of Comparative Zoology in Cambridge that opened in 1860.

As a result of his hypotheses relating embryonic changes to the succession of geological ages, Louis Agassiz came out against the evolutionary theories of Charles Darwin, and many Bostonians followed his lead. Darwin saw the various species of life as evolving out of a single original source ("monogenism"). Agassiz, however, based on his study of fossils and skulls, concluded that all differences were attributable to "the will of the Creator" who created distinct and separate forms of life ("polygenism"). Although he personally deplored slavery, Agassiz's views were surprisingly and disturbingly similar to many of the pseudo-scientific arguments used in the antebellum South to classify Negroes as members of an inferior race and thereby justify racial segregation.

In addition to his prominence as a scientist and zoologist, Louis Agassiz also became well known for his enthusiasm to reform current teaching methods and educational practices in the United States. He was convinced that the dominance of theology in the curriculum had held back scientific education in American colleges. He insisted on the independence of scientific inquiry and discounted the traditional importance of rote memorization. Rather than deriving the laws of nature from scripture or from abstract principles, Agassiz insisted that individual investigation and personal observation were the primary means of intellectual development and scientific knowledge.

Agassiz's heavy work schedule eventually took a toll on his health, resulting in a physical breakdown that led to a succession of debilitating illnesses. In October 1873, shortly before his death at the age of sixty-six, Louis Agassiz gave his final course of lectures at what was now called the Agassiz Museum, and wrote his last article concerning current trends in biological research. Today his legacy continues in Harvard's Museum of Comparative Zoology, a world-renowned center for research and education—although one where Darwinism has prevailed.

❡ Louisa May Alcott

There was scarcely a home in late nineteenth-century America that did not know the name of the writer Louisa May Alcott, and that did not look forward each year to purchasing the latest volume of her seemingly endless stream of popular, family-oriented novels. *Little Women* and *Little Men,* certainly her most famous works, not only captivated American readers with their moving narratives and engaging characters, but later provided the scenarios for several twentieth-century motion picture productions that found a receptive audience for the wholesome work of a noted American writer.

Born in Germantown, Penn., on November 29, 1832, Louisa May Alcott was the second of four daughters of Amos Bronson Alcott, a schoolteacher and educational innovator, and Abigail May, the descendant of an old-line Boston family. While the idealistic eccentricities of Bronson Alcott made for a happy and creative home environment, they also kept the family in continuing financial difficulty. This was particularly true after 1840, when Alcott had to close his Temple School in Boston for lack of students and suffered the failure of his utopian Fruitlands community in 1843.

To help support the family, at the age of eighteen Louisa did some "schoolmarming" in Boston, as well as taking other jobs as seamstress, maid, and governess—experiences she would later draw upon in her novels. During this period she also experimented with a career in writing, turning out a variety of thrillers, poems, and juvenile stories she submitted to many popular magazines. With the outbreak of the Civil War she served briefly as an army nurse in crowded Washington military hospitals, recording her experiences in 1863 in a book called *Hospital Sketches.* Its favorable reception by well-known American literary critics quickly established Louisa May Alcott as a serious professional writer.

In 1865, a visit to Europe provided Louisa with material for future travel pieces. After her return to America she moved to Boston and had started editing a juvenile magazine when Thomas Niles, Jr., of the Roberts Brothers publishers, urged her to write a popular novel for girls. Encouraged by her family, she turned out *Little Women,* the story of the four March girls (Meg, Jo, Beth, and Amy) in a middle-class American household generally reminiscent of her own. The instant success of *Little Women* on its publication in 1868—it sold 13,000 copies in two weeks—surprised everyone, including her publisher; Louisa was soon under pressure to produce more books and repeat her initial success. In 1870 she published *An Old-Fashioned Girl,* another popular novel that sold 27,000 copies in its first year, and in 1871 she published *Little Men,* which took its place among Alcott's best-loved works about nineteenth-century American family life.

For the rest of her career, Louisa May Alcott found herself hailed as a national celebrity. The demand for her books was incessant, and she turned them out at an incredible pace of at least one a year—in addition to a succession of stories, articles, and sketches she did for popular juvenile magazines of the day. She produced so much not just because of the urgings of her publisher and her own constant need for money, but also because of her own sense of obligation to her loyal readers, who waited avidly for the next work from her pen. The heavy work schedule took a serious toll on her health, however, and her final years were filled with sickness, loneliness, and sorrow. Wasted and fragile, she paid a last visit to her dying eighty-nine-year-old father on March 4, 1888; two days later, on March 6, the day of her father's funeral, she died at the age of fifty-five, and was buried in Sleepy Hollow Cemetery in the town of Concord, Mass., not far from Orchard House, the setting for *Little Women.*

❧ FRED ALLEN

During the 1930s and 1940s, when radio was America's most popular form of home entertainment, a young comedian named Fred Allen became perhaps the nation's best-known Bostonian. A poor boy who grew up in one of the city's small working-class neighborhoods, this local humorist rose to become one of the most famous and admired entertainers in the nation. Many families felt that the *Fred Allen Show* helped them laugh their way through the dark days of the Great Depression and World War II.

Fred Allen, whose original name was John Florence Sullivan, was born in North Cambridge in 1894, the elder of two sons of an alcoholic father who was a bookbinder. When John was three years old, his mother died and the family moved to nearby Allston to live with his mother's aunt Lizzie, to whom he became deeply attached. Living in an Irish Catholic neighborhood, surrounded by aunts, uncles, nieces, and nephews, he had "a poor boy's childhood," according to the historian Sam Bass Warner, Jr., but Allen himself recalled it as a parade of colorful characters "each one associated with a little story" that he would later incorporate into his comedy routines. Every morning, John walked the six miles from Allston to the High School of Commerce in Roxbury. After school he walked to the Boston Public Library in Copley Square, where he ate a cold supper and shelved books until 9 P.M., when he often walked back to Allston. In 1908, when he was fifteen, his father remarried, taking one son with him, and left John with his aunt Lizzie, who moved into a smaller apartment in the Savin Hill section of Dorchester. Although he was not an outstanding student in school, he was a reliable worker, enjoyed performing in school plays and local church pageants, and went to vaudeville performances to watch the jugglers and memorize their patter. After graduation he took a job at the Colonial Piano Company on Boylston Street, continuing to attend the vaudeville shows in Boston's Scollay Square area, which featured colorful comics along with singers, dancers, and burlesque queens.

In 1912, using the name Johnny Sullivan, the aspiring entertainer made his debut as a juggler on "Amateur Night" at the Hub Theater in the South End. He gave up his job with the piano company and joined a troupe appearing at local amusement parks and summer resorts under the name of "Freddy James, the World's Worst Juggler," brushing up his act and gaining valuable experience. In 1922, after eight years traveling the vaudeville circuit and settling on the stage

name of Fred Allen, he played the Shubert theater circuit as a comedian in the musical *The Passing Show of 1922*. For five years he
courted one of the chorus girls, Portland Hoffa, whom he eventually
married and worked into his act, first on stage and then when he
began his radio career. They lived, worked, and raised their family in
New York City, while creating a series of weekly comedy shows that
soon became one of the most popular features series on radio.

The 1930s were the golden age of radio, when the entire nation
would huddle around the radio each night listening to their favorite
comedy performers—Jack Benny, Amos 'n' Andy, the Goldbergs,
Fibber McGee and Molly, Edgar Bergen and Charlie McCarthy.
Fred Allen was a little different, however, making his reputation not
so much as a stand-up comedian, but as the creator of a series of
comedy routines that drew upon the great diversity of people in
America's cities and towns. His humor was dry, sarcastic, irreverent,
and occasionally outrageous. From week to week, audiences followed the raspy-voiced comedian as he walked through "Allen's Alley," knocking on doors, interviewing the various characters, and
asking their views on the news of the day. Uninhibited by the views
of a later time that would regard it as politically incorrect to poke
fun at ethnic foibles or to use foreign accents as a source of humor,
Allen capitalized on the ethnic and regional characteristics of his personalities. Senator Claghorn came across as a blowhard Southern
politician with an exaggerated drawl; Titus Moody was a skinflint
farmer from Maine with a distinctive nasal twang; Mrs. Nussbaum
talked about her family and friends with an unmistakable Jewish accent; and Ajax Cassidy was a professional Irishman with a stereotypical brogue. Allen used these and similar characters to satirize what he
saw as the faults and the shortcomings of contemporary American
society.

But the days of Allen's Alley came to an end. By the late 1940s and
early 1950s a younger and more sophisticated generation was no
longer responsive to Allen's critical satire, or amused by his use of
ethnic humor. In addition, after writing, producing, and acting in
his own show for eighteen years, Allen was burning out. During the
1948 season, a brand-new radio show called *Stop the Music!* became

an instant success and all but destroyed Allen's mass audience over-night. But it was the advent of television in the early 1950s that proved to be the final blow. Fred Allen was never able to make the comedic transition to television—nor did he really want to. In his autobiography, *Treadmill to Oblivion*, he made it clear that he de-spised the new medium, calling it "a device that permits people who haven't anything to do to watch people who can't do anything." Nor was he any kinder to television network executives, whom he de-scribed as people "who walked around their offices backwards so they wouldn't have to face an issue." When he was stricken with a fatal heart attack in March 1956, "a certain kind of humor went with him," wrote David Halberstam.

❦ George Thorndike Angell

In Mount Auburn Cemetery, in Cambridge, Mass., there is a monu-ment with an emblem in the form of a shield shaped like a star, sym-bolizing an organization called the Bands of Mercy. On the shield are the words "Glory to God, Peace on Earth, Kindness, Justice, and Mercy to Every Living Creature." This monument marks the final resting place of George Thorndike Angell, the man who made the nation conscious of the importance of the humane treatment of animals.

George Thorndike Angell was born on June 5, 1823, in the town of Southbridge, Mass., the son of a Baptist minister who died when George was only four years old. George went to stay with various rel-atives and friends who lived on farms, and at an early age developed a love for animals. At the age of fourteen he moved to Boston, where he worked as a bookkeeper until his mother sent him to a prepara-tory school in New Hampshire. From there he went to Brown for one year, and then transferred to Dartmouth, where he received his undergraduate degree.

After college, George moved back to Boston and began teaching

school, studying law during evenings and summers. He passed the
bar examination in 1851 and joined the law office of the antislavery
activist Samuel Sewall. It was not until after the Civil War that
George Angell turned his attention to the protection of animal
rights. On February 22, 1868, he heard about two horses that had
been raced to death during a local Washington's Birthday celebration. He sent a passionate letter to the *Boston Daily Advertiser* denouncing the heartless mistreatment of animals and calling on his
fellow citizens to protect them from such cruelty. His appeal caught
the attention of Emily Appleton, a prominent Bostonian who had
similar concerns, and within a month they had filed legislation in-
corporating the Massachusetts Society for the Prevention of Cruelty
to Animals (MSPCA).

Angell supplied both direction and organization for the new society, engineering the passage of several anticruelty laws, raising funds,
and expanding membership. To further increase public awareness,
he created a unique publication titled *Our Dumb Animals* to "speak
for those who cannot speak for themselves." Published the first Tues-
day of every month, the magazine was sent to animal-welfare organizations in every state, as well as to similar societies in England and
Europe. Angell turned out circulars, posters, notices, and articles for
publication in newspapers, and established a network that included
associations across the country as well as influential local reformers.
He also gained support for his humane cause from churches of all
denominations. And with his own considerable legal skills, George
Angell was able to draw up legislation that mandated fines and imprisonment for anyone who would beat, mutilate, overwork, or otherwise abuse an animal. He installed some twenty iron drinking-
fountains in various parts of the city for the hard-worked horses that
served as the major source of mobile power and transportation.

In 1871 Angell retired from his law practice and, at the age of
forty-nine, married the widowed Mrs. Eliza (Mattoon) Martin, who
became a devoted wife and companion. Angell traveled widely,
speaking to civic, religious, and educational groups about the importance of humane education. In 1882, following the English model of
youth auxiliaries, he organized what he called the American Band of
Mercy. Groups of school children would engage in essay contests,

reading programs, and classroom activities directed at decreasing crime and cruelty, after signing a pledge stating "I will try to be kind to all harmless living creatures, and try to protect them from cruel usage." Convinced that it was vitally important to impart his message to children, but also conscious of the sensitivity of their parents, in 1889 Angell founded the American Humane Education Society to further advance the moral principles of respect and compassion for all forms of life.

George Angell continued to play an active role in the MSPCA, still editing his magazine *Our Dumb Animals* from his home until his death on March 16, 1909. In an appropriate tribute, thirty-eight elegant horses, arrayed in double file, followed his hearse to Mount Auburn Cemetery. Today his work still continues, with the MSPCA offering programs to counter pet overpopulation, promote conservation of wildlife, and safeguard animals from natural disasters. The well-known Angell Memorial Hospital, located on Huntington Avenue in Boston, carries out the mission of George Thorndike Angell by advancing the practice of veterinary medicine and surgery throughout New England.

❧ MARY ANTIN

As a young Jewish immigrant, Mary Antin came to Boston from Russia at the end of the nineteenth century without any money and without any knowledge of the English language. She used the opportunities offered by the city's educational system to become a well-known writer, a public lecturer, and a national personality. Later in her life, when a virulent wave of anti-Semitism was sweeping over the world set in motion by the Nazi ideology, she joined with members of the Committee of American Unity and used her considerable influence to foster "common citizenship" and to "uphold the freedom to be different" in what she saw as the best Jewish American tradition.

Mary Antin was born in 1881, of Jewish parents who left their home in the town of Polotzk, in the wake of the Russian anti-Semitic laws of 1879, to seek a new life in America. The family settled in the poor industrial city of Chelsea, and in the fall of 1895 her father enrolled her in the local public school, where she found herself in classes with other Jewish immigrant children. Devouring in a voracious manner whatever learning she was offered, the little girl proved to be such an exceptional student that teachers encouraged her efforts and gave her extra attention to develop her literary skills.

Mary's success in school, however, was offset by her father's successive failures in his small grocery business. The family was forced to move from Chelsea to the congested slums of Boston's South End, where Mary and her siblings were crowded into one apartment with "meals in the kitchen and beds in the dark." Despite her depressing home conditions, the girl continued with her books and her studies, and in 1897 graduated from the Winthrop School with many honors and awards.

After a summer mostly spent at the Boston Public Library, Mary entered Girls' Latin School. Isolating herself from the social activities enjoyed by the other girls, Mary applied herself to her academic studies with single-minded diligence, winning many more honors but making few close friends. After interviews with her appeared in the newspapers, she was befriended by the well-to-do, college-bred ladies who operated the settlement houses. They saw this accomplished young girl as a hopeful sign that with encouragement and support other European immigrants from deprived backgrounds could become educated and patriotic Americans. At the age of thirteen, while still a high-school sophomore, Mary Antin began telling the story of her rise from immigrant obscurity to social acceptability. First in 1898, in a series of reminiscences in the Jewish weekly *American Hebrew*, and then in a book titled (inaccurately) *Plotz to Boston*, Mary Antin quickly established her reputation as a national literary figure.

Instead of going on from Girls' Latin School to Radcliffe College, as many of her admirers had expected, in 1901 Mary Antin married Amadeus Grabau, a doctoral student in geology at Harvard, and moved with him to New York City when he took a post at Columbia

University. Mary took classes at Columbia and at Barnard, but spent most of her time meeting members of liberal Jewish circles. She adopted Josephine Lazarus, sister of Emma Lazarus, as her mentor, trying to reconcile Jewish religious traditions with the secular influences of modern America. The death of Josephine Lazarus in 1910 provided the impetus for Mary Antin to write a mature narrative about her life in America. In her new book, *The Promised Land,* she made an appeal for sympathy for her fellow immigrants, especially Jewish immigrants, as well as testifying to their ability to become loyal and productive American citizens. Parts of her autobiography first appeared in serial form in the *Atlantic Monthly;* when the whole work was published in book form in 1912, it was an immediate success, and for years remained a classic work on immigrant Americanization. Mary took to the lecture circuit and, at a time when a new wave of nativism was opposing the entry of "inferior races," appealed for America not to close its doors but to remain open to refugees.

About 1918, Mary Antin seems to have experienced some kind of personal crisis that produced a loss of self-confidence she herself described as a nervous breakdown. After the breakup of her marriage, she returned to Boston, and in 1923 moved into a religious and convalescent community in western Massachusetts called Gould Farm. In the face of growing anti-Semitism from Nazi Germany, Antin joined with her liberal friends from settlement house days and drew on her lifetime of experience in America to combat intolerance and discrimination in every form.

❡ GEORGE APLEY

To omit George Apley, that stereotypical figure of the Boston Brahmin caste, from a volume of Eminent Bostonians, would seem unthinkable, if not unconscionable. That Mr. Apley is a fictitious character who made his appearance in John P. Marquand's Pulitzer

Prize–winning novel of 1927, *The Late George Apley,* is completely
irrelevant to his ability to personify the qualities of a social class that
contributed so much, and for so long, to defining the distinctive
character of Boston.

George William Apley, we are informed, was born on January 25,
1866, on Mount Vernon Street, in the Beacon Hill area that supplied
the frame surrounding "his portrait as a man." George could trace
his ancestry back to the Apleys who left Sussex, England, for
Roxbury in 1636, and started sending their sons to Harvard College
as early as 1658. By the eighteenth century, the Apleys had moved to
the town of Boston, made their fortune in the West Indies trade, and
had their portraits painted by John Singleton Copley. After the Revolution, several of the Apleys married into North Shore families,
adding to their wealth by expanding into the lucrative China trade
before going into the manufacture of textiles at the Apley Mills on
the upper Merrimack River. It was a long, distinguished, and productive family ancestry of which George Apley was inordinately
proud as he prepared to take his place in the changing world of the
post–Civil War era.

George Apley came of age during the latter part of the nineteenth
century, and was acutely conscious of the responsibilities his distinguished ancestry imposed upon him to maintain the high moral and
ethical standards of the past. The product of Puritanism, privilege,
and prosperity, he saw it as his personal obligation to uphold his
family's principles against a modern industrial society that promoted
self-aggrandizement and the values of the marketplace, as well as an
open-door policy that was flooding the city with Irish Catholics,
Jews, Italians, and other members of inferior races who had little
knowledge of or appreciation for the city's distinctive heritage. The
advent of this new world was an appalling prospect; resistance to it
required constant vigilance and dedicated work on the part of those
like George Apley and his colleagues who considered themselves
guardians of the past.

With conscientious regularity, Apley attended to those things of
importance to his family and his class—inspecting the family plots
in Mount Auburn cemetery, deciding who would inherit the

Chinese bronzes, attending concerts of the Boston Symphony Orchestra, listening to scholarly papers after dinner at the Club, slowing down the process of bringing "new blood" into Harvard, and opposing plans to dam the Charles River Basin. These were serious matters, and he would occasionally become upset when his son did not seem to be devoting the same amounts of time and attention to his civic duties. "You do not understand, and I fear you will never understand, that affairs will always be controlled by a small group," he wrote to his son in obvious exasperation. "It is not a pleasant thing for me to feel that the Irish are going to run the affairs of this city, and I do not see anyone in your generation who has the force and skill to guide them."

Although it is clear through his correspondence with his friends and relatives that Apley considers himself a compassionate, progressive, and tolerant man, he unconsciously reflects the values of his own class in the decisions he makes in the face of new ethnic and cultural forces that he fears are threatening to bring about fundamental changes in his beloved city. George Apley is not at all opposed to change or unaware of modernization—he simply wants to control it and direct it in the best interest of those values and principles to which he had always subscribed. He and the other members of his class regarded themselves as the self-appointed guardians of a Boston whose rapid changes were already making Mr. Apley and his circle begin to feel like relics of an earlier time.

❡ ANTHONY ATHANAS

Amid the glitz and the glamour of the "New Boston," with its bright lights and high-rise buildings, it is easy to forget the depressed and dilapidated condition of the postwar city during the 1950s and 1960s. With a failing economy, a declining population, and a deteriorating infrastructure, Boston suffered from the lack of both government funding and private investment. It was quite surprising, then, that in 1963 a fifty-two-year-old immigrant named Anthony Athanas would mortgage his own insurance policies when local banks refused to lend to him, in order to open a restaurant among the broken piers of Boston's deserted waterfront. It was an inspired act of faith and determination that produced remarkable results.

Anthony Athanas emigrated from Albania in 1915 at the age of four. After arriving at Ellis Island, the Athanas family moved on to New Bedford, Mass., where the father peddled fruits and vegetables from a pushcart. In order to help with the family budget, young Anthony dropped out of school at the age of thirteen to find work shining shoes, hawking newspapers, and firing up the wood and coal ovens in local restaurants—a task that first aroused his interest in food services.

At the age of sixteen, Anthony traveled to New York to work in his uncle's restaurant and gained additional experience in the hotel and restaurant business throughout the Northeast. The death of his father brought him back home to care for his three sisters and one brother, while he continued to work in various restaurants. In 1937 he opened his own restaurant, Anthony's Hawthorne, in the North Shore town of Lynn. The beginning was slow and the difficulties many, but Athanas gradually expanded his enterprise through hard work and creative marketing. He named special dishes for local celebrities, offered weekly credit cards, and purchased a GE air conditioner (GE was the local employer in Lynn) to attract more customers. Business was so good that in 1946 Athanas opened a second restaurant, Hawthorne by the Sea, in the North Shore town of Swampscott. In 1957 he opened the General Glover House, also in Swampscott, and in 1975 he established Anthony's Cummaquid Inn in the Cape Cod community of Yarmouth Port.

But it was Anthony's Pier 4 Restaurant that skyrocketed Anthony Athanas into restaurant fame. Opened in 1963, at a time when Boston's old waterfront area was suffering from abandonment and neglect, the new undertaking was given little chance of survival by local businessmen. Within three years, however, with its Early American and seafaring décor, its brick and barnboard paneling, its fine seafood menu, and its spectacular view of the Boston skyline, Pier 4 had become one of the highest-grossing restaurants in the country. And Athanas displayed a remarkable sense of marketing by advertising the rich and famous celebrities who patronized Pier 4 whenever they came to Boston. On the walls of the restaurant and along the grand staircase leading to the second floor are photographs of popes and presidents, cardinals and congressmen, singers and musicians, movie stars and stage actors, politicians and businessmen, all testifying to the national and international popularity of Pier 4.

Over the years, Anthony Athanas has participated in many professional associations and has received numerous awards and citations. He has been a director of the National Restaurant Association, president of the Massachusetts Restaurant Association, and a founding member of the American Institute of Food and Wine. He has received the Horatio Alger Award, the NRA's Restaurateur of the Year Award, several honorary degrees, and the Golden Door Award, presented to Americans of foreign birth who have made outstanding contributions to the United States. These awards and honors have served to make Anthony Athanas even more conscious of the debt he owes to his country and to his community, and over the years he has been active in numerous benefits and charitable events. "There is not a charity in our community that has not found a friend in Anthony Athanas—every parish in South Boston, every social agency, public or private," said his longtime friend and admirer, William M. Bulger, president of the University of Massachusetts and former president of the Massachusetts Senate.

A devoted family man, married more than fifty years to his wife, Esther, whom he met at an Albanian American picnic, Athanas has gradually turned the day-to-day operations of his restaurant over to his four sons. But Anthony himself is still there at Pier 4, every morning, noon, and night, impeccably dressed, smiling, greeting patrons, obviously still in love with an America that made it possible for an immigrant from Albania to achieve so much wealth and happiness in a single lifetime.

❧ Samuel Adams

❧ Fred Allen

◥ Laura Bridgman and
Samuel Gridley Howe

◥ Phillips Brooks

❧ CRISPUS ATTUCKS

During the colonial period, when slavery was still legal in New England, it was not at all unusual for a Boston newspaper to carry an advertisement like this, calling for the apprehension of a runaway slave:

> Run away from his master William Brown of Framingham, on the 30th of September last, a Mulatto fellow, about 22 years of age, named Crispus, 6 feet 2 inches high, short curled hair, his knees nearer together than common . . .

This advertisement was for an African American slave who would eventually be listed in the pantheon of Boston's Revolutionary heroes—as a patriot who lost his life at the Boston Massacre.

In the course of the legal investigation that was conducted following the bloody encounter between Boston townspeople and British soldiers on the night of March 5, 1770, it was discovered that the man known as Crispus Attucks was originally named Michael Johnson, and had been the property of William Brown of Framingham. Some years earlier, Johnson had run away from Brown, settled in Boston, and changed his name to Attucks. While there seems no question that Attucks had been a slave, there appears to be some question as to his specific racial origins. Some writers refer to him as a "Negro" of African extraction; others are convinced that Attucks may have been of Algonquin blood, a "Native Natick Indian"; still others say his father was African and his mother a member of the Natick tribe. In the notes John Adams kept during the trial of the British soldiers, during which he served as defense counsel, he refers to Attucks as either "the Indian" or "the Mulatto."

According to the trial records, Attucks had just finished eating his supper on the evening of March 5, and was described by one observer as walking toward the Custom House on King Street carrying a stick "about the width of a man's wrist." In the ensuing melee between the civilians and the British soldiers, Attucks was one of five men to die, as the redcoats fired into the ranks of the mob attacking them from all sides. He and the other victims (except Patrick Carr, a Catholic) were given a public funeral at Faneuil Hall and then buried together at the Old Granary Burying Ground.

For many years, Crispus Attucks remained in the historical background, but his story appears to have been rediscovered by Boston's African American community during the 1850s. The passage of the Fugitive Slave Act of 1850 had made it possible for federal marshals to apprehend alleged fugitive slaves in any state in the Union without either trial or personal testimony. This law, along with several highly publicized cases of black people being seized on the streets of the city and sent back to the slaveholding South, caused local African Americans to seek out role models to dramatize their opposition to the new law and reenergize their demands for emancipation. As a runaway slave, as a fighter against tyranny, and as a patriot who gave his life for freedom, Crispus Attucks was the ideal figure.

William C. Nell, a prominent leader of Boston's African American community, wrote two books during the early 1850s describing the heroic service of black Americans in the Revolutionary War. In each of these works, Crispus Attucks emerged not only as a leading figure of black liberation but also as an African American only—with no mention of his Indian heritage. Historians have pointed out that in a popular and widely distributed lithograph of the Boston Massacre, done by J. H. Bufford in 1856, the figure of Crispus Attucks is clearly depicted as an African American. Not only that: Attucks is depicted in the very forefront of the confrontation, grasping the soldier's musket, taking the full volley into his own breast. Just the kind of brave hero the community was looking for!

It is hardly a coincidence that on March 5, 1858, the anniversary of the Boston Massacre, and almost exactly one year after the promulgation of the controversial Dred Scott decision, the first annual Crispus Attucks Day took place in Boston. The celebration was held in Faneuil Hall, where the slain body of Attucks had originally lain in state, and appropriate hymns were sung by the Attucks Glee Club, which had been founded expressly to keep alive the name of "the first Boston martyr." Dr. John Rock, a highly respected black resident, appealed to history to illustrate the courage of such African American heroes as Crispus Attucks and suggested, as the clouds of civil war gathered on the horizon, that American slaves might soon have the opportunity to strike a blow for their own freedom. "Sooner or later," he declared prophetically, "the clashing of arms will be heard in this country, and the black man's service will be needed."

¶ RED AUERBACH

Visitors come to the Quincy Market area to see Faneuil Hall, to shop in the market, and to soak up the atmosphere of old Boston. As they make their way along the walkway between the market and the warehouse, they come across a life-size bronze statue of a middle-aged man, seated in a casual and somewhat pensive posture. Most people stop for a minute, look at the figure, and think: "He looks familiar," or "I think I've seen him before." And then they see the big trademark cigar in his right hand, and exclaim: "Oh, it's Red Auerbach!" And indeed it is—it's the man who made the Boston Celtics famous.

Arnold "Red" Auerbach (few people ever remember hearing him called Arnold) was born September 20, 1917, in Brooklyn, N.Y. After graduating from George Washington University in 1941, he served in the United States Navy for three years, and then became the first coach of the Washington Capitols basketball team. In 1950 he was hired by Walter Brown, president of the Boston Garden, to take charge of the Boston Celtics, a basketball team he had founded in 1946 that was already on its last legs. Brown was clear: Auerbach had one season to achieve success; if he didn't, the team would likely be sold or go out of business. Red went to work right away. He drafted Chuck Cooper, the first African American player in NBA history; he selected Bob Cousy, a nifty local player from Holy Cross; and he brought in "Easy" Ed Macauley from the St. Louis Bombers.

Although Auerbach's team lost their first three games, they went on to win the next seven, made the playoffs, and finished the season in second place. Red not only had rescued the season, but he also had saved the franchise. Basketball caught on in Boston; attendance rose by 40 percent; and fans flocked to see the passing wizardry of Cousy, the "Houdini of the hardwood." Over the course of thirteen seasons, Auerbach and Cousy never missed the playoffs. They led the Celtics to eight consecutive NBA world championships, establishing the most successful franchise in Boston basketball history.

Auerbach brought another Holy Cross alumnus, Tommy Heinsohn, into the Celtics organization in the fall of 1956, to be joined by Bill Russell from California, fresh from the 1956 Olympics. Both rookies played spectacularly in the NBA finals against the St. Louis Hawks, a series that became so volatile that during one altercation Red Auerbach punched the Hawks' owner in the nose, after which the Celtics team broke a 3-3 tie and went on to win its first championship. With Bill Russell, Red Auerbach had acquired the powerful rebounder he needed for the Celtics, and in a short time young Russell was dazzling basketball fans with his energetic style of play, hauling down rebounds and blocking shots with such power that he won standing ovations. The winning momentum was sustained well into the 1970s, as players like John Havlicek, Don Nelson, Paul Silas, Jo Jo White, and Dave Cowens helped bring the Celtics into the 1976 NBA finals and win championship number 13 for Red Auerbach.

By the end of the 1978–79 season, however, the Celtic dynasty had run out of steam, Havlicek had retired, the organization was coming apart, and the team finished out of the playoffs. But Red Auerbach was not finished. He used his sixth pick in the 1978 draft to select a fourth-year junior at Indiana State University named Larry Bird, and Bird helped the Celtics fashion the most sensational turnaround in league history. With Bird on the parquet floor, Celtics home attendance increased by more than 45 percent, and most games sold out in advance as it became clear that the team was only one or two players away from championship caliber. In the NBA draft that summer, Red picked Robert Parish for center, and then brought in Kevin McHale as his third pick. Within a year, the Celtics were celebrating their fourteenth NBA title behind the play of Parish, McHale, and Bird, who captured three NBA Most Valuable Player awards, and appeared in eleven NBA All-Star games.

For his remarkable accomplishments over the years, Red Auerbach was named Coach of the Year in 1965; named All-Time NBA Coach by the National Basketball Association in 1970; and inducted into the National Basketball Hall of Fame in 1969. But he was also honored by Bostonians, too, receiving the Arch McDonald Achievement Award in 1962 and Boston's Distinguished Achievement Award in 1965. In 1985 the bronze sculpture of Auerbach by Lloyd Lillie was positioned near the information pavilion of the Quincy Market. On the night of April 21, 1995, the seventy-seven-year-old Red Auerbach joined with Bob Cousy, Bill Russell, and Larry Bird to bid farewell to the old Boston Garden, before it was torn down and replaced by the new Fleet Center, and to thank the loyal Boston fans who had done so much to support the Celtics over the years and create the legend of "Celtic Pride."

¶ EMILY GREENE BALCH

In 1946, Emily Greene Balch became the second American woman, and the first Bostonian, to receive the Nobel Peace Prize. Unable to travel to Norway for the official ceremony in December 1946, the seventy-nine-year-old woman received the medal in her Wellesley home the following spring. The award was a tribute to a woman who had devoted a lifetime to charitable works, teaching assignments, and political activism in attempts to foster those human relationships she hoped would lead to world peace.

Born in 1867 to an upper-middle-class Boston family, Emily Balch lived in a fashionable house on Prince Street in Jamaica Plain. She attended a private girls' school in Boston's Louisburg Square, and in 1886 went to Pennsylvania to attend Bryn Mawr College, where she studied issues of work, wages, and employment with the sociologist

Frank Giddings. She completed her work in three years, graduating first in her class, and then traveled to Paris to further her studies in economics. Returning to Boston, Balch decided to experience social issues at first hand by doing volunteer work with delinquent and neglected children. In December 1892 Balch and some of her colleagues in settlement-house work founded Denison House in the depressed area of Boston's South Cove. In this environment, she came to know Robert Woods, Joseph Lee, and other leading social workers and reformers of the period.

Emily Balch continued to study sociology, first at the Harvard Annex (the forerunner of Radcliffe College), later at the University of Chicago, and then at the University of Berlin. On her return to America in 1896, she served as an assistant to Katherine Coman at Wellesley College until 1913, when she was appointed a professor of economics. During her years at Wellesley, she served on several state commissions, including the first minimum-wage board in the United States. Balch undertook a study of immigration, concentrating on the newest arrivals from the Austro-Hungarian Empire. Her book *Our Slavic Fellow Citizens* (1910) explored the European background and Old World culture of these peoples in order to appeal to Americans for a more understanding and compassionate reception of the newcomers.

In 1914, with the outbreak of World War I, Balch joined with many of her fellow social workers in forming the Women's Peace Party, and sailed with Jane Addams and forty-two other American delegates to a peace conference in The Hague. In an attempt to find a solution to war, they voted to establish a permanent women's peace organization, and adopted the so-called Wisconsin Plan calling for neutral nations to promote negotiations among the belligerents. During 1916 Balch traveled to Stockholm to further her work in international mediation. As a socialist, she declared herself an opponent of war and a committed pacifist, with the result that after 1919, Wellesley College voted not to renew her teaching contract.

Supported by the generosity of her friends and colleagues, Emily Balch worked for the Women's International League for Peace and Freedom (WILPF) for the next twenty years, seeking to develop issues of common interest, like world health, that might generate cooperation among nations. Advocating total pacifism, she promoted universal disarmament and continued to study ways by which international conflicts could be adjudicated without resorting to war.

With the outbreak of war in 1939, Balch found herself forced to choose between the evils of war and the unchecked spread of a virulent fascism she had confronted in Europe in the early 1930s. To the disappointment of some of her friends, she decided to support American participation in World War II, and concentrated on helping Jewish refugees and pleading the cause of interned Japanese American citizens.

In 1946, in recognition of her lifelong efforts on behalf of peace, Emily Greene Balch was awarded the Nobel Peace Prize. Her honor came at a moment in history, just before the outbreak of a prolonged period of Cold War, when, as Sam Bass Warner, Jr., has observed, "the distortions of publicity and the passage of time" were about to obscure "what Balch experienced and learned."

❡ George Bancroft

For a good two hundred years, Americans were so busy settling in the New World, struggling to gain their independence, and trying to forge a new nation, that they had little inclination to reflect upon their origins or write their own history. By the middle of the nineteenth century, however, a number of Boston scholars were beginning to search the American past to uncover the tangled roots of the democratic experience. One of these writers, George Bancroft, emerged as perhaps the most prolific as well as the most popular of early historians, producing a series of patriotic, flag-waving histories that earned him the title of the "Father of American History."

Born in Worcester, Mass., in 1800, George Bancroft was the son of Aaron Bancroft, a liberal Congregational minister who later became the first president of the American Unitarian Association. George graduated from Harvard College in 1817, and then went abroad to acquire a doctor's degree in theology and philosophy from the University of Göttingen in 1820, and later attended lectures at the University of Berlin. After four years in Europe, Bancroft returned to Cambridge, where he spent an unsatisfactory year as a tutor at Harvard before helping to establish a progressive boys' school at Round Hill, in Northampton, Mass.

Increasingly, however, George Bancroft was pulled in the direction of a career in history and public affairs. An outspoken Jacksonian Democrat at a time when most New England literati were members of the conservative Whig party, Bancroft rose rapidly in Democratic party councils. Service to the party won him the post of Customs Collector of the Port of Boston, an important source of political patronage. Later, after working for the presidential nomination of James K. Polk in 1844, he was rewarded by a Cabinet appointment as Secretary of the Navy. During his eighteen months of service, he established the Naval Academy at Annapolis, promoted the work of the Naval Observatory, and supported Polk's policies of Manifest Destiny. In 1846, while serving in London in his new post as Minister to Great Britain, Bancroft used every opportunity to do research in French and English archives in order to gather additional material for his historical writings.

Throughout this period of active public service, George Bancroft was also in the process of achieving a national reputation as a historian that would eclipse his political career. In 1834, he turned out the first volume of what would eventually become a ten-volume *History of the United States.* Drawing upon the "germ theory" of history he had acquired during his early years of study in Germany, his narrative traced the development of what he regarded as clearly superior American political institutions out of the earlier Teutonic and Anglo-Saxon traditions. After returning to the United States in 1849 from his post in England, he published six more volumes between 1852 and 1866, in which he carried the narrative of colonial history up through the American Revolution. The outbreak of the Civil War drew his attention once more to public affairs, and although at

first he considered Abraham Lincoln inadequate to the task of preserving the Union, he gradually came to admire his leadership and
support his administration. After Lincoln's assassination, Bancroft
was on friendly terms with President Andrew Johnson, and served as
a ghostwriter in the preparation of his 1865 Annual Message. Johnson appointed him Minister to Berlin in 1867, where he not only
demonstrated considerable diplomatic ability but also continued to
work on the tenth volume of his *History*, published in 1874.

In 1876, Bancroft reworked the *History* into a six-volume cente-
nary edition, in which he corrected factual errors and toned down
some of the more florid passages. He did not, however, modify his
strong Jacksonian philosophy, his ardent support of democratic
government, or his continuing belief in the inherent goodness and
wisdom of the common man. The voice of the people, he still insisted, was the voice of God. Strongly nationalistic and proudly
democratic, Bancroft's *History of the United States* was immensely
popular with an American public that believed it demonstrated the
superiority of American life and institutions. This was the kind of
patriotic history book that American families were only too happy to
purchase for their children to read.

❦ BERNARD BERENSON

Jewish immigrants began to arrive in Boston for the first time in
great numbers during the late 1880s and early 1890s. A great many of
the Jews who settled in Boston's North End came from the city of
Vilna, located at that time near the junction of Lithuania, Poland,
and Russia. Jews across Europe generally held Vilna in high regard as
a center of literary and cultural achievement; the Vilna Jews who
came to this country developed a particular affection for the city of
Boston because of its commitment to learning and education. Bernard Berenson, destined to become the world's foremost expert on
Italian Renaissance art, was a member of a Jewish family that had
come to Boston from Vilna.

Bernard Berenson was born June 26, 1865, to Albert Valvrojenski and Julia Mieliszanski, who lived in humble circumstances near Vilna. Faced with the violent anti-Semitism of Czarist Russia that followed the Crimean War, Albert changed the family name to Berenson, left for America, and in 1874 settled in Boston. A year later he was joined by his wife, his ten-year-old son, Bernard, and two other children. For a time Bernard was educated at the local synagogue, where he learned Hebrew, but he followed his father's example and gradually abandoned the Jewish religion.

Bernard was a highly intelligent and obviously precocious child, whose parents encouraged his omnivorous reading, and who was said to have taught himself Greek. He attended the Boston Latin School, entered Boston University in 1883, and was then able to arrange a transfer to Harvard, where he studied ancient languages and medieval literature. After his graduation in 1887, he received encouragement and support from the Boston socialite Isabella Stewart Gardner, which enabled him to spend the fall and winter of 1887–88 studying in Paris and London, as well as at Oxford University. The following spring he made his first trip to Italy, where he discovered his lifelong vocation to immerse himself in the study of Italian art.

During the 1880s and 1890s Berenson turned out an impressive number of articles, monographs, and books dealing with the painters of the Renaissance, the art of Florence, and the nature of Italian art itself. In these writings, he established new criteria for determining the authenticity of artworks, placing more emphasis on the characteristic mannerisms and details of individual painters than on documentary evidence outside the paintings themselves. Berenson's growing reputation as a leading connoisseur of Italian art caught the attention of newly rich Americans who were seeking to purchase Italian Medieval and Renaissance paintings to decorate their expansive mansions and estates. In a short time Berenson was in great demand by such collectors as Benjamin Altman in New York. In his association with Isabella Stewart Gardner, he spent millions of her dollars for artworks to adorn her celebrated "Fenway Court" palazzo in Boston. In time, however, Berenson found that he could earn much greater fees by serving as a consultant to international art dealers, such as Lord Joseph Duveen. Soon the poor Jewish immigrant youth from Boston's North End, originally scorned by local German Jews for his Lithuanian origins, was an enormously wealthy man who moved in stylish circles, married the wife of a prominent Anglo-Irish lawyer, and purchased Villa I Tatti, near Florence, as a place to work and to preserve his priceless collection of books, photographs, and artworks. In 1885 he was baptized an Episcopalian in Boston's Trinity Church; five years later, in Italy, he converted to Catholicism.

Throughout the Nazi occupation of Italy during World War II, Bernard Berenson remained in seclusion at Villa I Tatti, and after the war returned to his influential critical essays on Renaissance painters as well as embarking on autobiographical works. In his declining years, he appeared to rediscover the cultural and intellectual roots of the Jewish traditions of his youth that he had rejected so long ago. Berenson died in Italy at the age of ninety-five, bequeathing Villa I Tatti, together with its contents, to Harvard University, establishing in Florence the Harvard Center for Italian Renaissance Studies.

❧ LEONARD BERNSTEIN

It was like the scenario of a 1930s Busby Berkeley movie: the young understudy is rushed onstage to fill in when the leading actress becomes too ill to go on. The youngster is a hit, the audience roars its approval, and the Broadway critics announce that a new star is born. But this time it was the New York Philharmonic Orchestra that had lost its conductor, Bruno Walter, to illness, and called upon a twenty-five-year-old assistant conductor to take his place. Without even time for a rehearsal, Leonard Bernstein mounted the podium, and ended his first concert to a standing ovation from the Carnegie Hall audience.

Born Louis Bernstein in Lawrence, Mass., on August 25, 1918, the son of Samuel and Jennie Resnick Bernstein, Bernstein started playing the piano as a child. He graduated from the Boston Latin School in 1935, and at the age of seventeen went on to Harvard University, from which he graduated in 1939. After graduation, despite attempts by his father to keep him in the family beauty-supply business, he attended the Curtis Institute in Philadelphia, where he studied conducting with the legendary maestro Fritz Reiner. As a conducting student at Tanglewood in the summers of 1940 and 1941, he became a protégé of Serge Koussevitzky, who was then music director of the Boston Symphony Orchestra, and was named assistant conductor of the New York Philharmonic in 1943. It was in that position that he became an overnight sensation when he stepped in at the last minute for the ailing Bruno Walter.

After his dramatic debut, Bernstein continued an active career as a guest conductor and occasional pianist during the 1940s, composing several symphonies as well as turning out the Broadway musical *Fancy Free* in 1944. In 1952 he wrote the music for the Broadway production *Wonderful Town;* in 1954 he provided the orchestral score for the prize-winning motion picture *On the Waterfront;* in 1956 he composed the delightful music for *Candide.* It was in 1957, however, that he achieved national recognition with his spectacular musical *West Side Story.* The following year he began an eleven-year tenure as conductor of the New York Philharmonic, and during the same period employed his flamboyant conducting style in a series of televised productions called "Young People's Concerts."

In 1971, Leonard Bernstein was invited to return to his alma mater, Harvard University, to become the Charles Eliot Norton Professor of Poetry, a one-year post previously held by such notable musical figures as Igor Stravinsky and Aaron Copland. Bernstein took the required lectures quite seriously, and because of a heavy schedule of composing projects and conducting engagements, he postponed his six lectures from the spring of 1973 to the fall so that he could prepare properly, knowing that each lecture would be presented twice— once live at the University; then in a subsequent taping session for television. What Bernstein eventually produced was a coherent series of six lectures organized around the linguistic theories of Noam Chomsky in his book *Language and Mind,* intended to help a general audience understand the universality of music. In the first lecture he focused on the structure and meaning of the music of the early Classical period; in the fourth lecture he drew from the harmonic development of the Romantic period; in the fifth lecture he stressed the atonality of twentieth-century music; and in his sixth and final lecture he concentrated on the way Igor Stravinsky maintained tonality in his music. Bernstein's Norton Lectures were widely praised as a fresh and original way of analyzing music and interpreting music history.

Leonard Bernstein continued a multifaceted artistic career as both composer and conductor, and in 1971 produced a theater piece for singers, players, and dancers entitled *Mass* for the opening of the Kennedy Center in Washington, D.C. During the 1970s, he also became the spearhead for the revival of the works of Gustav Mahler, while finding time to turn out his own compositions, including *Divertimento for Orchestra, Halil, Jubilee Games,* and *Arias and Barcarolles.* When the Berlin Wall fell in November 1989, Bernstein was invited to conduct two performances of Beethoven's Ninth Symphony to celebrate the joyous occasion. The Christmas Day concert was telecast live to an audience of more than 100 million viewers in more than 20 countries around the world. In Schiller's text for the "Ode to Joy" in the last movement, Bernstein substituted the word *Freiheit* ("freedom") for *Freude* ("joy"), assuring his listeners that Beethoven himself "would have given us his blessing." He returned to the United States to conduct his final performance at Tanglewood on August 19, 1990, leading the Boston Symphony Orchestra in Britten's *Four Sea Interludes* and the Beethoven Seventh Symphony. On October 14, he died of a heart attack at the age of seventy-two at his home in the Dakota apartments in New York City.

The recipient of numerous awards, medals, and citations, Bernstein was formally recognized by his alma mater, the Boston Latin School, as one of its most eminent graduates. On Friday, May 10, 1996, his name was officially unveiled on the frieze along the ceiling of the school's auditorium, alongside the names of other notable graduates of that prestigious institution.

❧ WILLIAM BLACKSTONE

The origins of the town of Boston can be traced to the day when a clergyman named William Blackstone (or Blaxton) staked out for himself a small and secluded spot where he could live in peace and quiet. Perhaps the fact that he had grown up with ten brothers and sisters had something to do with his lifetime search for an out-of-the-way place where, without interruption, he could read his impressive library of books, tend his garden, and cultivate his orchard.

William Blackstone was no ordinary recluse, however. Born March 5, 1595, in Durham County, England, he went off to Emmanuel College, Cambridge, to begin twelve years of study for the Anglican priesthood. In May 1621 he was ordained in the Church of England; two years later he and his brother Nathaniel sailed for the New World. Nathaniel went off to the colony of Maryland, while William headed for New England and landed in the Wessagusset community that later became known as Weymouth. In 1625, however, Blackstone packed up his belongings, headed for what would become Boston Harbor, and settled on the peninsula the native people called Shawmut, an Indian name meaning "Flowing Water." On the slopes of one of the nearby hills, he discovered an excellent spring of fresh water and there this "bookish recluse" built himself a small house, traded with the local Indians, planted a garden, and cultivated the first apple orchard in the Bay Colony.

The Reverend Blackstone was able to enjoy his idyllic solitude for about four years, until one day he heard about the plight of a group of dissenting Puritans from England, led by John Winthrop, who had recently arrived and settled on the smaller peninsula across the river to the north—a place later called Charlestown. The newcomers soon discovered that the location they had chosen did not have an adequate supply of drinking water. The absence of fresh water, the shortage of food, and the effects of the long weeks at sea caused great suffering among Winthrop's people, some of whom were beginning to drift away from the group in the search for a new and better location. Although he was not a Puritan himself, Blackstone was sympathetic to the newcomers, and offered to share his own peninsula with John Winthrop and his unhappy English settlers. He invited them to move south across the river to the Shawmut peninsula and avail themselves of the fresh water from the spring there. Winthrop accepted Blackstone's invitation, and negotiated a purchase of the land on which his people would settle. Church records say that members of Winthrop's group "chiefly removed" to the new location early in August 1630.

The Reverend Blackstone was to regret his hospitality. Within a short period of time, more and more Puritans arrived, and the population of the small peninsula grew to such a size that he felt his privacy was endangered. With all state and church affairs now dominated by the Massachusetts Bay Company and its governor, John Winthrop, Blackstone had had enough. "Could ye not leave the hermit in his corner?" he asked. Seeking a less crowded location and more quiet atmosphere, he decided to move elsewhere. Before leaving, however, he sold to the town his hut, his orchard, his spring, and a large tract of land on the slope of a hill that became known as the Common. That having been done, in 1635 Blackstone bought some additional cattle, loaded their backs with pots, pans, tools, clothing, and his precious books, and set out south toward Rhode Island—riding out of town, legend has it, mounted on his own great white bull.

William Blackstone settled near the little town of Rehoboth, Mass., in what is now the town of Cumberland, R.I., to enjoy the life of a cultured recluse, browsing through his library of 186 books, and apparently at ease with the local Indians who were his neighbors. In 1659, according to the records, he returned to Boston and married a widow, Sarah Stevenson, and took her back to his isolated home, where they had a son named John. Blackstone continued to live his quiet existence until his death about 1675 at the age of eighty. Later, during King Philip's War, his house and library were destroyed by fire.

¶ NATHANIEL BOWDITCH

In an age when most New England sailors used dead reckoning by the compass and the log as the traditional method for finding their position at sea, one man provided a major treatise on navigation that virtually revolutionized sailing. Described by one historian as a "little, nimble man with burning eyes, with silky hair prematurely white, who darted around rubbing his hands with excitement," Nathaniel Bowditch was responsible for saving countless lives, and made it possible for Yankee ships to become the swiftest that ever sailed.

Born in Salem, Mass., in 1775, Nathaniel Bowditch was the son of a poor cooper and mechanic. He left school at the age of seven to help his father, and when he was twelve years old became an apprentice to a ship-chandler where he worked until he went to sea for the first time in 1795 at the age of twenty-two. During these years he read voraciously, and with his retentive memory stored up all kinds of information on numerous subjects. He constructed an almanac, studied French and Euclid, and learned Latin so that he could read Sir Isaac Newton's *Principia*.

Between 1795 and 1803, Bowditch made five voyages to all parts of the world, the final voyage as master and supercargo—the business agent of the owners on shipboard. Watching the stars from the deck of his ship, and studying the books he carried with him in his berth, he mastered the intricacies of astronomy and trained his sailors in the science of navigation. Although there are some who maintain that the story is apocryphal, old-time mariners still tell the tale of a Christmas night, in the middle of a blinding snowstorm, with not a single landmark in sight, when Bowditch sailed his vessel straight into his Salem wharf as if it had been a sunny day in June.

At the suggestion of a publisher in Newburyport, Bowditch investigated the accuracy of a popular English work, *The Practical Navigator*, found some eight thousand errors, and proceeded to make revisions that were published in a 1799 American edition of the work.

So many revisions followed that the third edition was issued in 1802 with the title *The New American Practical Navigator*. This work has been translated into a dozen languages, passed through countless editions and, according to the maritime historian Samuel Eliot Morison, still remains the standard American treatise on navigation. Along with Noah Webster's *Dictionary*, Bowditch's *Navigator* stood as a monument to New England learning in the early nineteenth century, and led to Bowditch's election to the American Academy of Arts and Sciences as a tribute to his transformation of the ancient art of navigation into a science.

In addition to his work on navigation, Bowditch also made a valuable chart of the waters and harbors of Salem, Beverly, and Manchester, as well as proposing and solving a dozen problems in Adrain's *Analyst*, a mathematical journal. Far more important, however, were the papers he published in the American Academy's *Memoirs* (1804–1820) and the preparation of the translation of the first four volumes of Laplace's *Mecanique celeste*, which were published in 1829–39. So elaborate were the notes he supplied in bringing the books' subjects up to date that the final translation was more than double the size of the original work. This accomplishment has been described as creating "an epoch" in the history of American science by "bringing the great work of Laplace down to the reach of the best American students of his time."

Upon the death of Nathaniel Bowditch in Boston in 1838, the Boston Marine Society hailed his accomplishments and expressed its appreciation for "the excellence and utility of his labours." The members of the Society praised him roundly as an astronomer, a mathematician, and a navigator, "a friend and benefactor to the navigator and seaman."

❡ JAMES BOWDOIN

In 1685, King Louis XIV of France revoked the Edict of Nantes, causing large numbers of French Protestants, known as Huguenots, to leave the country in the face of renewed religious persecution. Many Huguenots found refuge in Boston, where their strict Puritan views and their conscientious work ethic met with a sympathetic reception. One of them was Pierre Baudoin, a well-known physician and a member of an old and distinguished family from La Rochelle.

First settling in Casco, Me., Pierre Baudoin moved to Boston in May 1690, where he became a leading member of the French Protestant Church on School Street. He remained in Boston until his death in September 1706. His eldest son, James, who changed the spelling of the family name to the English phonetic form of Bowdoin, became a very important merchant of the town. When he died in 1747, he left what was reported to be the largest estate ever willed by any resident of Massachusetts.

His son, also named James, was born August 7, 1726, graduated from Harvard in 1745, and, with the aid of his father's inheritance, took up residence in a substantial estate on Beacon Street. His political career began in 1753 with his election to the General Court. Serving three terms in the house, in 1757 he was chosen a member of the Council. While this body generally favored the British point of view, Bowdoin's influence was important in bringing it more into line with colonial interests. In 1774, after the passage of the Coercive Acts, the new military governor, General Gage, refused to authorize Bowdoin's election to the Council. The General Court, however, elected him delegate to the Continental Congress, but poor health forced him to decline in favor of John Hancock. In August 1775 the Provincial Congress appointed him first member of its executive council, but once again he was forced to resign, in 1777, for reasons of health. Elected to the state constitutional convention in 1779, he was chosen president of the convention and served as chairman of the subcommittee that drafted the instrument. John Adams wrote most of the final document, but Bowdoin exercised much influence in its development.

After John Hancock retired as governor in 1785, it became apparent that Massachusetts was faced with serious social and economic problems. Bowdoin ran for governor against Thomas Cushing, candidate of the "popular" interests, winning the election after it was thrown into the legislature, which was dominated by the leading commercial and property interests. Bowdoin was reelected in 1786, just as an insurrection of debt-ridden farmers in the western counties broke out—known as Shays's Rebellion. Bowdoin's handling of the crisis was prompt and vigorous, and he helped stabilize both the state and ultimately the new nation by his insistence on law and order. He had previously urged increasing federal powers to permit control of commerce, which he believed essential to national prosperity, and had shown early support for a new Constitution. Although Bowdoin's suppression of the insurgent debtors by the use of military force was widely approved outside Massachusetts, he was criticized by many within the state for not having taken the necessary steps to reform the financial situation and prevent the uprising in the first place.

Bowdoin retired from the governorship in April 1787. His last public service came in January 1788, when he was a delegate to the Massachusetts convention to adopt the new Federal Constitution. He died in Boston in 1790 at the age of sixty-four. During his active public career, James Bowdoin also displayed a decided interest in science and literature. He was the first president of the American Academy of Arts and Sciences and wrote a number of papers on physics and astronomy for the Academy's *Transactions*. His chief memorial, appropriately enough, is Bowdoin College, which was chartered in Maine in 1794, four years after his death.

❦ ANNE BRADSTREET

Despite the general Puritan aversion to the study of such things as literature and art, considered a waste of precious time, a good number of the Bay Colony's learned ministers applied themselves rather diligently to turning out verse as an inspirational means of instructing their followers in the divine plan. There was one person in the Bay Colony, however, who appears to have written poetry simply for poetry's sake, merely to give expression to her own thoughts and aspirations, with little expectation that her verses would be read by anyone except her immediate family and friends. This "Tenth Muse," who identified herself as "a Gentlewoman in these parts," was Mistress Anne Bradstreet, daughter of Thomas Dudley, who would succeed John Winthrop in 1634 as governor of the Massachusetts Bay Colony.

Born in England in 1612, where her father Thomas was steward to the Earl of Lincoln, Anne Dudley grew up as a typical young woman of a staunchly Puritan family of the period. Thomas Dudley was a loving and indulgent father who provided his daughter with an extensive education and an appreciation of literature that led to her experimenting with writing in various poetic forms. Anne referred to her father as a "magazine of history," and attributed to him her lifelong love of books. At the age of sixteen, she married Simon Bradstreet, "in whose loving and grave companionship she passed the remainder of her life." Simon was the son of a nonconformist minister, a recent student at Emmanuel College, and successor to Dudley's stewardship. In 1639, two years after her marriage, she accompanied her husband and her father aboard the *Arbella* to Massachusetts Bay, where she was to find "a new world and new manners." Anne and Simon started out first at Charlestown, but a few months later moved to Newtowne (Cambridge), where they settled in a house near her father's, facing what would later become Harvard Yard. Thomas Dudley brought with him to America his 300-volume library, thus providing his daughter with an unusual opportunity for her to continue her reading and develop further her remarkable intellect.

Anne Bradstreet did not enjoy a strong physique. Delicate as a child, she fell into an unspecified "lingering sickness," was often laid low with fits of pain and weakness, and not long after she arrived in Massachusetts was afflicted with a "lameness." She did not become a mother as quickly as she would have liked, but eventually produced eight children, four girls and four boys, who grew to be "useful" men and women. Anne Bradstreet was often discouraged because of her frail condition, and sometimes depressed to the point where she questioned the true nature of her Puritan God, at one point wondering whether other people's views of God might not be as correct as hers. Indeed, during one period of extreme pain and distress she even speculated about whether or not the "Popish Religion" might not be the right one—but it was a thought that did not linger long.

Anne Bradstreet proved to be both a fervent Puritan and a strong-minded woman, with a superior intellect and an exalted social position that allowed her to accommodate both faith and reason. In one particularly bold poem, she displayed a brief flash of feminist wit by praising the late Queen Elizabeth for having "wiped off the aspersions of her sex / that women wisdom lacked / to play the Rex." Despite the quiet objections of Governor John Winthrop, who did not approve of women reading and writing when they should be attending to household affairs, Anne Bradstreet continued her writing. A collection of her early poems, under the title of *The Tenth Muse, Lately Sprung Up in America,* was published without her knowledge in London by her admiring brother-in-law, John Woodbridge, who brought with him to England one of the manuscript copies of her verses that were being circulated among her friends and relatives. Anne was thirty-eight years old when her book came out in 1650, but for the remaining twenty-two years of her life she would turn out her own style of lyrical poetry, instead of the more derivative verses that had constituted most of her early efforts.

Although early American critics generally treated the works of Anne Bradstreet with what Samuel Eliot Morison called "almost offensive condescension," later writers took her work much more seriously, agreeing that she was, in many ways, superior to most of the English minor poets of the period. She drew upon the New England background for much of her material as well as for her inspiration, but it was her strong Puritan religious faith that provided her underlying philosophy of perseverance and accomplishment. She confronted long periods of pain and suffering without weakness or complaint, convinced that whatever happened came about as the inscrutable decree of a just God. Anne Bradstreet died on September 16, 1672, of a wasting consumption—a Puritan mother whose son wrote that she had been "translated to Heaven." She left to her children many unpublished poems and a little manuscript book consisting of seventy-seven "Meditations, Divine and Morall." Anne

Bradstreet and her sister, Mary Woodbridge, are the only two women to be listed among the many known American poets of the seventeenth century. Not until the days of Emily Dickinson, the belle of Amherst, would Massachusetts have another woman poet of equal standing and comparative merit.

¶ LAURA BRIDGMAN

During the 1840s, most visitors to Boston from Europe and from all parts of the United States arrived with a list of things they were determined to see. These included not only Faneuil Hall, Bulfinch's State House, the Boston Common, the Harvard Observatory, and the Public Latin School, but also the Perkins Institution for the Blind, where Dr. Samuel Gridley Howe was experimenting with the education of a pupil named Laura Bridgman, who was deaf and blind. On special exhibition days, visitors would stand behind a barrier and watch the girl at work, neatly dressed, sitting erect, a green ribbon covering her sightless eyes. When he visited Boston in 1842, the writer Charles Dickens marveled at her, and included an account of her in the *American Notes* he published in England the following year.

Laura Dewey Bridgman was born on December 21, 1829, in the town of Etna, near Hanover, N.H. She was the third daughter and eighth child of Daniel and Harmony Bridgman, farm people of comfortable circumstances. Laura was apparently normal at birth, but at the age of two was stricken during an epidemic of scarlet fever that caused the death of her two sisters and left her without sight or hearing. As she grew older, her disabilities made it increasingly difficult for her parents to communicate with her or control her occasional outbursts of violent behavior.

In the spring of 1837, Dr. Samuel Gridley Howe, the well-known reformer and director of the Perkins Institution for the Blind, read an account of Laura Bridgman in a local newspaper and traveled to

Hanover to see the girl for himself and to get her parents' consent to bring her to Boston. The parents agreed that their daughter needed special attention, and on October 4, 1837, Laura Bridgman, not yet eight years old, arrived at the Perkins Institution. In establishing contact with Laura, Dr. Howe decided to teach her the alphabet by labeling common objects such as a pin, a knife, a spoon, or a cup with raised lettering. After several weeks of frustrating experimentation, in a sudden flash of understanding, Laura discovered the relationship between the objects and the letters. Letter by letter, the young girl learned the entire alphabet, and was then taught how to communicate by tapping into the hands of others the alphabet in manual form. The process was slow and tedious, but over the years Laura Bridgman learned to read as well as to write, by using specially grooved paper.

The formal education of Laura Bridgman at the Perkins Institution ceased when she reached the age of twenty, and she returned to her home in Hanover. After so many years away from her home and family, however, she found herself unable to adjust to normal life, and soon returned to Boston to stay at the Perkins Institution for the rest of her life. She maintained an extensive correspondence that took up much of her time, but she also performed such simple chores as knitting, crocheting, sewing, cleaning, and making beds. She even occasionally assisted in teaching some of the younger pupils how to sew. At the time of his death, Dr. Samuel Gridley Howe left Laura Bridgman a trust fund that provided her with a modest income that she augmented by selling examples of her handiwork to visitors and tourists.

Laura Bridgman died at the Perkins Institution of pneumonia at the age of sixty, and was taken home for burial at Hanover, N.H. Throughout her life she was perhaps one of the most studied and analyzed individuals in the nineteenth century. But in addition to her importance to physicians, psychologists, and scientists of all kinds, she had even greater significance to those men and women whose physical and mental handicaps had for so long prevented them from being recognized and accepted as thoughtful and responsible human beings. Laura Bridgman had become an international phenomenon who challenged preconceived ideas about the mental and physical abilities of disabled people.

¶ PHILLIPS BROOKS

It came a little bit late in the development of the nineteenth-century city landscape, but when Trinity Church went up in Copley Square in 1877, it was almost immediately accepted as an integral and permanent part of the Boston scene. In its towering size and massive weight, the impressive Romanesque structure personified the Reverend Phillips Brooks, the man who helped design the church and who was an influential ecclesiastical figure in Boston for many years.

Phillips Brooks was born in Boston on December 13, 1835, to parents of modest means. After graduating from the Boston Latin School and Harvard College, he entered the Virginia Theological Seminary, and upon completion of his studies, accepted the rectory of the Church of the Advent in Philadelphia. Taking up the duties of a young clergyman and developing his skills as a preacher, Brooks remained at his post until November 1861, when he accepted a call to Holy Trinity Church in Philadelphia. During the Civil War, he offered his services to the Sanitary Commission, and in July 1863 he helped tend the wounded on the Gettysburg battlefield.

After the war, Brooks traveled extensively through Europe, enjoying the pleasures of England, visiting places in Germany associated with Martin Luther, and traveling to the Holy Land, where he wrote his famous Christmas carol "O Little Town of Bethlehem." Upon his return to Philadelphia in September 1866, he settled back into his work at Holy Trinity, until in July 1869 he accepted the rectory of Trinity Church in Boston.

Brooks began his new ministry at old Trinity Church on Summer Street in downtown Boston at a time when the changing nature of the city had already demonstrated the necessity for a new location. By the end of 1871, a site had been purchased in Copley Square, and

Henry Hobson Richardson was selected to construct a new and much larger church. The decision to move was precipitated by the Great Fire of 1872, which devastated most of the downtown area of the city and consumed the old Trinity Church itself. Despite the unique technical difficulties of constructing so great a church on filled land in the newly created Back Bay, the building was completed and Trinity Church was formally consecrated on Friday, February 9, 1877, in an impressive ceremony before civic and ecclesiastical leaders. The charismatic Phillips Brooks drew thousands to see the new church as well as to hear the famous preacher. A magisterial figure six feet four inches tall and weighing nearly 300 pounds, Brooks was a spellbinding preacher whose sweeping oratorical style attracted overflow audiences.

Although he was invited to accept a chair at Harvard University, Brooks decided to remain at Trinity Church and serve the interests of his parishioners. After taking a year abroad during 1882–1883 to renew his religious studies in Germany and to expose himself to new religious experiences in India, he returned to Boston, where he proved more popular than ever. He was in great demand not only by churches and universities, but also by various humanitarian organizations who wanted him as a spokesman for such causes as prison reform and women's suffrage. Brooks constantly emphasized the positive nature of Christianity, preaching a practical and sensible approach that saw religion at its best when applied to human needs.

In 1886 he declined to be considered for election as Bishop of Pennsylvania, but five years later he agreed to have his name considered for the same post in his home state. Despite the opposition of some clergymen who felt that he was not a strong enough supporter of traditional orthodoxy, Brooks was elected to the post, and on October 14, 1891, consecrated Bishop of Massachusetts.

Phillips Brooks's episcopy demonstrated an orderly sense of executive management, but it was to last only two years. Early in January 1893, while consecrating a new church in East Boston, Brooks caught a cold in the freezing temperature. His condition rapidly worsened, and on January 23, he died. Brooks's funeral was a day of mourning throughout the city. The cortege left Trinity Church, crossed the Charles River into Cambridge, passed by the Harvard campus as the college bell tolled, and brought the great preacher to his final resting place in Mount Auburn Cemetery.

In a short time, a fund was raised for a suitable memorial, with the commission assigned to Augustus Saint-Gaudens, who had recently completed the Robert Gould Shaw monument on Beacon Hill. Learning of Brooks's lifelong interest in the life of Jesus, the sculptor placed the figure of Christ directly behind a likeness of Phillips Brooks, who stands in his accustomed pose at the pulpit, hands upraised, preaching the Word of God. In 1909 the memorial was completed and placed on the Boylston Street side of Trinity Church.

❧ ORESTES BROWNSON

Boston has always been well known for its unorthodox thinkers, its eccentric personalities, and its persistent do-gooders. Orestes Brownson was someone who fit into all these categories: a sort of permanent gadfly, he provoked commentary and controversy with his nonconformist views about such things as social structures, economic systems, and religious institutions. Not even his closest friends were always sure where Brownson stood at any one issue at any particular moment—or how long he would stand there.

Born September 16, 1803, into a poor family in Stockbridge, Vt., Orestes Brownson worked as a teacher and a preacher in upstate New York before coming to Boston, where he met Ralph Waldo Emerson and became a charter member of the Transcendental Club. Late in 1837 he began to publish his own journal, the *Boston Quarterly Review,* as a means of broadcasting his controversial views on the need for social reform in the United States. Alarmed at the way the new industrial system was oppressing the working classes, Brownson called for substantive changes in the whole economic structure to create greater equality between labor and management.

In addition to his outspoken views on social change, Brownson

was always seeking a religion that would satisfy his intellectual demands as well as his spiritual needs. In rural Vermont, he had started
out as a Congregationalist; at the age of nineteen he changed over to
Presbyterianism; two years later he adopted the principles of Univer-
salism. During the late 1820s he seems to have become something of
a skeptic or an agnostic, but his break with organized religion did
not last long. In the early 1830s the humanistic views of Boston's
William Ellery Channing led him into Unitarianism. During this
same period he was also influenced by several European philosophers who provided him with new insights into Christianity as a
gospel of social reform.

As American society failed to reform in the way he envisioned,
Brownson became disenchanted with Protestantism and turned to
the Roman Catholic Church. An institution that combined a strict
religious orthodoxy with a sympathetic view of social responsibility
such as the Catholic Church, he thought, could help establish a new
"Christian community." Working with Bishop John Fitzpatrick of
Boston, the erratic forty-one-year-old Transcendentalist studied theology and read the works of St. Augustine and St. Thomas. Despite
the differences in background and temperament, Fitzpatrick and
Brownson remained on good terms, and Brownson continued as an
active member of the Catholic Church until his death in 1876.

Once he became a Catholic, however, Brownson followed his
usual practice of inventing his own version of whichever sect he belonged to. Continuing to publish what he now called *Brownson's
Quarterly Review,* he urged members of the church hierarchy to take
a greater interest in social reform; advocated a more "American"
character for the institution itself; and criticized the growing
influence of Irish immigrants, whom he regarded as "the most
deficient class of our community," behaving "more like Irishmen
than Catholics." During the violent tensions of the Know-Nothing
movement of the mid-1850s, Brownson urged Catholics not to pro-
voke trouble, to keep a low profile, and to behave like "guests" in
someone else's home. Brown's outspoken views were not at all acceptable to Bishop Fitzpatrick; their difference of opinion sent

Brownson to New York, where the more belligerent Archbishop Hughes gave him even less encouragement.

Brownson quickly regretted his move and wrote Fitzpatrick lamenting that he had ever left Boston—his "only home"—and expressing regrets that he was no longer under the bishop's spiritual direction. Soon, however, tensions again arose between them, when Brownson criticized Chief Justice Taney's ruling in the Dred Scott case as inhuman and immoral, at a time when the Catholic bishop was anxious to maintain the status quo and avoid having his church get drawn into the slavery issue. During the Civil War, Brownson further alienated so many of his Catholic supporters by supporting emancipation that by 1864 he was forced to discontinue his journal. After the war he published *The American Republic,* a treatise that deplored secularization and the appearance of a "political atheism" he believed would destroy American culture.

Orestes Brownson was perhaps the one American Catholic who was most knowledgeable about mid-nineteenth century philosophical currents both American and Continental. In his attempts to work out a satisfactory explanation of the communion of God with human beings and human culture, however, he failed to find a receptive audience—remaining that singular Bostonian who was too Protestant for the Catholics, and too Catholic for the Protestants.

❡ CHARLES BULFINCH

Thanks to the untiring and inspired efforts of a self-taught architect named Charles Bulfinch, the old, wooden, colonial seaport town of the eighteenth century took on a new elegance in brick and granite that marked the transition of Boston into a stately federal metropolis of commerce, banking, and business at the opening of the nineteenth century.

Charles Bulfinch, the son of a Boston physician, graduated from

Harvard College in 1781. On the obligatory Grand Tour of Europe, he found architectural inspiration in France and England that persuaded him to take up designing buildings when he returned to Boston. Bulfinch's first efforts came as a number of wealthy merchants were moving out of the overcrowded waterfront section of town into the open spaces of the West End. In 1792 he constructed a three-story brick house for his relative Joseph Coolidge, who had moved into the Bowdoin Square area; four years later he built a handsome three-story house for Harrison Gray Otis on the corner of Cambridge and Lynde Streets, today maintained as a historical site by the Society for the Preservation of New England Antiquities. In 1815 the young man designed a pair of double houses between Cambridge and Green Streets for Samuel Parkman.

Bulfinch also tried his hand at the construction of churches. After building the Hollis Street Church, with its two domed towers and domed ceiling, in 1800 he drew up, free of charge, the plans for the town's first Roman Catholic church, on Franklin Street. In 1804 he constructed a red-brick church on Hanover Street in the North End, for the New North Religious Society, a structure that eventually became St. Stephen's Catholic Church. In 1805 Bulfinch enlarged the original two-story Faneuil Hall, adding a third floor, doubling the width of the building, and moving the cupola from the center to the front.

With some of Boston's wealthiest citizens now his patrons, Bulfinch was a natural choice for the design of a new State House. After the United States had achieved its independence from Great Britain in 1783, the citizens of Boston wanted to replace the old British Town House with a State House of their own. In May 1795, a special committee authorized the purchase of the old Hancock property on Beacon Hill, and then selected Charles Bulfinch as the architect. Drawing upon what he had learned during his European travels, Bulfinch provided the Commonwealth with an impressive building on the crest of Beacon Hill, with tall white columns and trim, a red-brick façade, a long flight of steps, and an imposing dome that was subsequently gilded and that continues to remain a distinctive landmark of Massachusetts.

In addition to designing homes, churches, and public buildings, Charles Bulfinch also developed complexes of apartments and townhouses. On Franklin Street, for example, he proposed what became known as the Tontine Crescent, after an English scheme of selling shares of stock in an investment enterprise known as a "tontine." He arranged a series of sixteen individual brick houses, designed as a single unit, in a graceful curve along Franklin Street with an archway in the center (later called Arch Street) that allowed pedestrians to pass through to Summer Street. Along the opposite side of the street was a straight line of eight more houses. Between these facing lines of houses was an oval grass plot, with trees and bushes, in the center of which was a large urn in honor of Benjamin Franklin, highlighting the name of the complex as Franklin Place.

Although he was an imaginative architect, however, Charles Bulfinch was not always a successful businessman. When subscriptions for the Tontine Crescent did not come in fast enough to meet expenses, in 1796 he went bankrupt. Despite his financial reverses, in 1799 he became a selectman, and in May 1799 he was appointed Superintendent of Police at an annual salary of $600, which helped pay off his debts. Unfazed by his money problems, in 1810 Bulfinch undertook the development of a complex of nineteen elegant houses along Tremont Street called Colonnade Row. For many years this was a fashionable residential complex from which residents could look out across Boston Common to the western view of distant hills and sunsets. Once again, however, Bulfinch's bills grew faster than his income, and in July 1811 he spent a month in jail for debt.

Bulfinch's brilliant reputation survived the vagaries of his fortunes, though. His most nationally significant commission came in 1818, when he was appointed to oversee the redesign and reconstruction of the Capitol building in Washington, D.C., which had been burned by British troops in 1814; it was completed in 1830.

Only a small number of persons in the history of Boston have had such a profound influence on the shape and form of their city. As the eminent historian Walter Muir Whitehill so aptly expressed it: "Few men deserve to be held by the citizens of Boston in more grateful remembrance than Charles Bulfinch."

❡ Vannevar Bush

Until recently, American scientists tended to explore the practical and applied aspects of science rather than the theoretical and speculative. In many ways, Vannevar Bush of Boston followed earlier American inventors like Eli Whitney, Cyrus McCormick, Samuel Colt, Elias Howe, Alexander Graham Bell, and Thomas Edison, who saw the value of science chiefly in its ability to improve a person's health, home, farm, or business and, in the process, bring progress to all aspects of American life.

Vannevar Bush was born in 1890 in the small industrial town of Everett, just across the harbor from Boston. He was the only son and youngest of three children of Richard Perry Bush, a Universalist minister who moved his family to the blue-collar suburb of Chelsea where, for the next thirty years, he served as minister to the Church of the Redeemer. Vannevar attended Chelsea High School and then worked his way through Tufts University in Medford by tutoring fellow students in mathematics and physics. Although he was a brilliant mathematician, he felt that an engineering career would not only be more profitable but would also give him the opportunity to engage in the pleasurable pastime of tinkering with mechanical gadgets.

Bush graduated from Tufts in 1913, worked briefly as an electrical engineer in Schenectady and Pittsburgh, and then returned to Tufts to teach mathematics. Eventually he got a Ph.D. in the joint MIT-Harvard engineering program, writing his dissertation on the application of mathematics to problems in electrical engineering. After finishing his doctoral work and getting married, Bush did consulting work for a small Medford firm, American Radio & Research Corporation (ARRC), which manufactured radio equipment. At this company he met an ingenious machinist named John A. Spencer, who had invented a thermostatic switch that operated with the application of heat. Bush left ARRC and turned to a former Tufts roommate, Laurence Marshall, a visionary engineer, to help him form a new company called Spencer Thermostat to manufacture and market the new device. The success of this new company attracted more investors, and eventually produced in 1925 a new company in Cambridge called Raytheon that announced sales of $1 million in its first year of operation.

Meanwhile, Vannevar Bush was in great demand throughout the country as a specialist in scientific research and a frequent consultant to contractors and electrical power companies. In 1932 he was appointed dean of the School of Engineering and a vice-president at MIT. Since 1924 he had also served as a consultant to the United States Navy and in 1939, with the outbreak of a new war in Europe, he assumed the chairmanship of a panel of experts called the National Advisory Council for Aeronautics that reported directly to the President of the United States. Concerned about reports that the Nazis were experimenting with atomic energy, Bush persuaded President Roosevelt to establish the Office of Scientific Research and Development that helped develop the atomic bomb, radar, proximity fuses, and various anti-aircraft and anti-submarine devices.

Persuaded that the collaboration of the nation's scientists, technologists, and engineers, along with their businesses, laboratories, and universities, had helped win World War II, Vannevar Bush carried these same convictions into the Cold War. In 1949, in his popular book *Modern Arms and Free Men,* he presented a vision of the world divided between Soviet totalitarianism and American democracy, and looked to the lessons learned in the pursuit of science—research, knowledge, teamwork, competition—that he believed would lead the nation to ultimate victory.

❡ SARAH CALDWELL

Henry Lee Higginson provided Boston music lovers with a first-rate symphony orchestra and a magnificent concert hall where they could listen to fine music. Opera lovers of the city, however, have not been so fortunate. Several attempts to form a separate opera company for Boston were made, but the companies failed to survive, and in 1958 Eben Jordan's lovely Opera House on Huntington Avenue was demolished. Not until Sarah Caldwell appeared on the scene was there a serious attempt to revive grand opera as a permanent Boston institution.

Sarah Caldwell was born March 6, 1924, in Maryville, Missouri, and graduated with a major in psychology from the University of Arkansas. Music was Sarah's passion, however; as a child prodigy she had begun taking violin lessons at the age of four, and by the age of ten she was giving concerts. As a schoolgirl, she attended performances of the Kansas City Philharmonic Orchestra as well as stage presentations by the Kansas City Repertory Theater. After graduation from college, she moved to Boston to attend the New England Conservatory of Music, where she studied violin with Richard Burgin, concertmaster of the Boston Symphony Orchestra. She also worked with Boris Goldovsky, head of the opera department, who instructed her in all elements of opera from stage management to orchestral conducting. Indeed, Caldwell might well have made a career solely as a performer and conductor. On January 13, 1976, she became the first woman to conduct at the New York Metropolitan Opera, and seven months later she conducted the Chicago Symphony Orchestra at the Ravinia Festival in a special opera program featuring Beverly Sills. She also appeared with the New York Philharmonic Orchestra, the Pittsburgh Symphony Orchestra, and the Boston Symphony Orchestra.

Although music was Sarah Caldwell's world, opera was her life. Early in her career she participated in the annual summer Tanglewood Music Festival, and so impressed Serge Koussevitzky, conductor of the Boston Symphony Orchestra, that he recommended her for a faculty position at the Berkshire Music Center. Her success there led to her appointment in 1953 as director of Boston University's Opera Workshop, where she promoted her vision of opera as a truly dramatic artform and undertook to produce unfamiliar and unperformed works for American audiences. With the help of supporters, in 1957 Caldwell founded the Boston Opera Group (re-

named the Opera Company of Boston in 1965) to stage full-scale opera productions. Caldwell's dramatic productions attracted many
notable performers who were willing to accept lower fees for the opportunity to work with innovative repertoire and unconventional
staging. In 1962, for example, Beverly Sills performed in *Manon,*
while Joan Sutherland made her Boston debut in *I Puritani.*

Caldwell's group had no permanent location until 1971, when
funding from the Ford Foundation and the National Endowment
for the Arts made it possible for the Orpheum Theater, off Washington Street, to become the home for the Opera Company of Boston.
It was there that Caldwell directed Kurt Weill's *Rise and Fall of the
City of Mahagonny* in 1973, as well as Sergei Prokofiev's *War and
Peace* in 1974. In 1978, the Opera Company of Boston moved into its
first permanent home in the Savoy Theater, formerly the B. F. Keith
Memorial Theater between Washington and Tremont Streets, now
renamed the Opera House. Here Caldwell put on Puccini's *Madame
Butterfly,* as well as offering the first American performance of Bernd
Alois Zimmerman's *Die Soldaten* in 1982.

By the 1980s Sarah Caldwell's artistic reputation had expanded far
beyond Boston. She was appointed director of the Wolf Trap summer music festival in Virginia, and asked to participate in special
cultural exchange programs in Manila and in Tel Aviv. In 1982 she
traveled to China to meet with the Central Opera Theatre of Peking,
and returned to America with authentic costumes and sets for her
Boston production of *Turandot.* Recognized for her lifelong dedication to grand opera, and praised for her ability to create imaginative
productions without lavish budgets, Sarah Caldwell was the first recipient of the Kennedy Center Award for Excellence. In 1996 she was
also awarded both the Rodgers and Hammerstein Award and the
National Medal of Arts.

Unfortunately, the Opera House off Washington Street was not
maintained properly, and a combination of neglect and water damage caused it to be shut down in the late 1980s. Nearby condomin-
ium residents have opposed the building's renovation and, as a result, Sarah Caldwell's dream of a major opera house for Boston
remains unfulfilled.

❡ Melnea Cass

For over sixty years Melnea Cass fought vigorously for the improvement of services and the expansion of resources for African American residents in Boston. First concentrating her efforts at improving
social conditions for black women in the South End, she eventually
became such a vocal and effective advocate for civil rights and social
justice that during the Bicentennial she was recognized by city leaders as a "Grand Bostonian."

Born in Richmond, Virginia, on June 16, 1896, Melnea Agnes
Jones was the eldest of three daughters. Her parents brought the
family to Boston to improve their employment opportunities and
provide an education for their children. After the death of her
mother, Melnea stayed with an aunt, moved to Virginia to complete
her high school education, and then moved back to Boston. Melnea
married Marshall Cass in 1917, and when he went into the army in
World War I she lived with her mother-in-law, Rosa Brown, and
gave birth to a son. After Marshall returned from the service, they
moved into their own house to raise their children, adding two
daughters to the family. During this period Melnea became involved
in various community activities through the influence of her
mother-in-law. She also joined the NAACP, became involved in the
club movement, and helped raise money to support William Monroe Trotter's newspaper, *The Guardian.* In 1930, Melnea Cass and her
husband moved from the South End to Roxbury, where she worked
as a housekeeper during the Depression years.

Through her involvement with her own school-age children,
Melnea Cass helped establish a Kindergarten Mothers' Club, and
was soon working with other women to expand nursery services, create choral groups, and organize athletic events at the Robert Gould
Shaw House. She became vice-president of the Harriet Tubman
Mothers' Club, an organization whose members tried to "mother"
young women who had just arrived from the South; she also served
as secretary to the Sojourner Truth Club, an organization of middle-

class black women; and she became chairwoman of the Social Action Committee of St. Mark's Congregational Church.

As the size of Boston's African American population increased during the 1940s, residents like Melnea Cass became more vocal in their demands for racial justice. During the Depression years she had helped A. Philip Randolph in his work with the Brotherhood of Sleeping Car Porters in Boston, and during World War II Randolph called upon her again to press for more jobs for African Americans in the nation's defense industries. Along with Muriel and Otto Snowden, Mrs. Cass was among the sixteen co-founders of Freedom House in 1948, an organized effort to keep Roxbury a multicultural neighborhood with clean streets, good lighting, adequate police and fire protection, and effective parental supervision of children. As the struggle for civil rights became more intense, Mrs. Cass took a leadership role in public protests and demonstrations, resigning from her position on the YWCA Boards in protest because African Americans were restricted from using the pool. By 1976, however, Melnea Cass had lived to see the Clarendon Street YWCA named in her honor. During the 1950s she marched at the head of a picket line at Woolworth's Five & Ten Cent Store on downtown Washington Street. A longtime member of the NAACP, Mrs. Cass became president of the Boston branch from 1962 to 1964, and played an active role in many of the protests, sit-ins, and boycotts surrounding the desegregation of Boston's public schools during the 1960s and 1970s.

Toward the end of her life, Mrs. Cass received many honors and awards. In 1966, the Roxbury community celebrated her many achievements by establishing Melnea Cass Day; in 1970, the Eastern Chapter of the National Association of Social Workers honored her "outstanding lay contribution to social welfare." In 1976, Mayor Kevin White included Melnea Cass in his list of seven distinguished "Grand Bostonians," and during that year's Bicentennial celebrations the First Lady of Roxbury, as she had become known, was among the local dignitaries introduced to Queen Elizabeth II on her visit to Boston.

Although she was in her late seventies, Melnea Cass continued to work for the residents of Roxbury. She served several years on the

Roxbury Council of Elders, which developed educational, nutritional, and social programs for the elderly. A short time later, she accepted an appointment as chairperson of the Mayor's Advisory Committee for the Elderly, and later received an appointment to the National Council of Senior Citizens. A few years after her death in 1978, at the age of eighty-two, Melnea Cass was honored with a new thoroughfare bearing her name. In 1981, Melnea Cass Boulevard, in the lower Roxbury section of Boston, was officially opened to traffic. This boulevard had the unusual distinction of being exempt from the traditional city regulation that any street that crosses Washington Street must change its name, in honor of the country's first president. Previously, only Massachusetts Avenue and Columbus Avenue had been exempted. The new exemption was a tribute to a truly distinguished Bostonian.

¶ WILLIAM ELLERY CHANNING

During the early nineteenth century, the new spiritual ideas of Unitarianism superseded the darker Calvinistic theology of predestination and eternal damnation. The Reverend William Ellery Channing of Boston emerged as perhaps the most eloquent and persuasive spokesman for a more enlightened view of Christianity, as well as a more confident belief in the perfectibility of human beings. Channing's grandfather had signed the Declaration of Independence; Channing himself, as a boy of seven, was present when Rhode Island ratified the Constitution. His optimistic view of human nature, therefore, was based in great part on his personal witness of the astounding success of the American experiment.

Born in the seaport town of Newport, R.I., in 1789, William Ellery Channing was descended from the best New England stock. Graduating from Harvard College in 1798, he spent a year and a half as a tutor for a family in Richmond, Virginia, during which he acquired habits of overwork and ascetic discipline that eventually did serious damage to his health. When he returned to Newport, Channing decided to turn to theology, and came to Cambridge to work on his religious studies while he served as a proctor for undergraduate classes.

Ordained to the Congregational ministry in 1803, Channing was installed as minister of the Federal Street Church in Boston, where he remained until his death forty years later. Despite the strictness of his theological training, Channing was described by one writer as a "Broad Churchman" who accepted Christianity as a way of life and wanted only to persuade others to follow in the same manner. He "breathed into theology a humane spirit," according to the inscription on his statue in the Boston Public Garden. In his own reading of the Christian scriptures, Channing could find no justification for the old Calvinist-Puritan belief in a jealous and judgmental God, a debased and iniquitous humanity, or a predestination that limited salvation only to the members of the elect. Instead, Channing preached a gospel that emphasized the beneficence of God, the essential goodness and perfectibility of human beings, and the ability of all souls to attain salvation. Because they insisted on upholding the unity of God, Channing and his supporters were called Unitarians.

Although Channing at first hesitated to form a new denomination, the popularity of his new and more liberal ideas, and the speed with which they circulated, led him to adopt the new movement and become its leader. In 1820 he published an article, "The Moral Argument against Calvinism," in which he defended his concepts as an essential part of the Christian tradition. He made clear that the debate over the Trinity was not so much about the nature of God, but more about the Calvinist doctrine of the depravity of human beings—a belief that Channing rejected entirely. By 1820 nearly all the Congregational pulpits in and around Boston had been taken over by Unitarian preachers, and in 1825, the American Unitarian Association was formed

As a preacher, William Ellery Channing was noted for the arresting quality of his voice, the sweetness of his style, and the charm of his manner. In 1822, poor health caused him to take a prolonged sabbatical in Europe, where he had further opportunity to refine his ideas and explore the thoughts of various European theologians and philosophers. Boston's great literary figures of the period—Ralph Waldo Emerson, Henry Wadsworth Longfellow, William Cullen Bryant, James Russell Lowell, Oliver Wendell Holmes—were influenced by Channing's "deep spirituality and his beautiful optimistic nature," according to Alice Felt Tyler, and they never failed to acknowledge their indebtedness to his ideas. In his *Remarks on American Literature* (1830), for example, Channing urged American writers to find inspiration in the characteristics of their own country rather than imitating English models. Only seven years later, in his famous Phi Beta Kappa address, Emerson renewed Channing's theme, calling upon American intellectuals to stop imitating "the courtly muses of Europe" and to derive their inspiration from nature. Channing also took an increasing interest in the welfare of his fellow man, particularly education. In 1838, in a work called *Self-Culture,* he made a plea for adult education, advocating a policy of setting aside funds from the sale of public lands to support public education—an idea incorporated twenty-five years later in the Morrill Act that established the basis for land-grant colleges.

When William Ellery Channing died in 1842 at the age of sixty-two, Theodore Parker claimed that "no man since Washington had done so much to elevate his country."

❡ Jean de Cheverus

In 1808 Boston was named as one of four new Roman Catholic dioceses in the United States, and a young French émigré priest named Jean de Cheverus was designated its first bishop. The news of this appointment was greeted with much delight by the town's citizens, Catholic and Protestant alike. This support from members of a community with a long-established Puritan tradition was a mark of Cheverus's distinction.

Born January 28, 1768, in the parish of Notre Dame de Mayenne, Jean-Louis-Anne-Madelaine Lefebvre de Cheverus was the eldest of six children. His high school performance was so impressive that in 1779 he was awarded a scholarship to the prestigious Collège de Louis-le-Grand in Paris. After graduation, he went on to the seminary, was ordained a priest in December 1790, and returned to his home parish. As a devout Catholic and a loyal monarchist, young Cheverus refused to take the oath to support the Civil Constitution of the Clergy demanded by the French revolutionary government, and fled his native land in fear of reprisal. Traveling in disguise, he crossed the Channel to England, where he spent nearly five years teaching French and mathematics at a small school.

In 1796 Cheverus responded to an appeal from a former professor, Fr. François Matignon, to come to Boston and help him with a diocese that extended all the way from Nantucket Sound to the Canadian border. On October 3, 1796, Fr. Cheverus arrived in Boston to join Fr. Matignon in ministering to a small local Catholic community, mostly Irish and French immigrants, as well as to several tribes of American Indians in the northern regions of Maine.

The cheerful and cooperative spirit of the two French priests, especially their heroic work during a virulent yellow fever epidemic in 1798, did much to disarm the traditional anti-Catholic prejudice of the Puritan town. Cheverus came to be fondly regarded and kindly treated in a town where, not too much earlier, a Roman Catholic priest could be jailed, exiled, and even executed. Reverend William Ellery Channing, the well-known Unitarian minister, later recalled "this good man, bent on his errands of mercy," hurrying through the crooked streets of Boston in all sorts of weather "as if armed against the elements by the power of charity." In this small colonial town, Cheverus earned the respect and friendship of prominent Bostonians who regarded him as a learned and cultivated gentleman. "He was friendly to our literary associations," commented the *Boston Monthly Magazine,* observing that the bishop helped organize the Boston Athenaeum, and provided it with "liberal donations from his extensive library."

For the most part, Bishop Cheverus carefully avoided political disputes and partisan issues, appearing to accept the constitutional parameters of the new American republic. He saw clearly the limitations imposed on Catholics in America by traditional Anglo-Saxon prejudices, but with Gallic realism worked within these limitations, in the expectation that they would gradually lessen. In 1820, for example, when Maine separated from Massachusetts, Cheverus rejoiced that in its new state constitution Catholics were no longer prevented from holding public office. "Now," said the bishop with obvious satisfaction, "Catholics, Jews, and Moslems can hold office here."

Early in 1823, Bostonians were disturbed to learn that Cheverus had been named bishop of Montauban, France. A letter signed by two hundred of the town's leading Protestant citizens attempted to explain to the French authorities how much they loved and admired the prelate and wanted him to remain in Boston. "We hold him to be a blessing and a treasure in our social community, which we cannot part with," they wrote, "and if withdrawn from us, can never be replaced."

But it was to no avail. Bishop Cheverus bowed to the inevitable and returned to his native France, where he became one of the most popular prelates in the country by virtue of his efforts on behalf of the poor, the homeless, and the needy. He was named Archbishop of Bordeaux and in 1836, three months before his death at the age of sixty-eight, he was named to the College of Cardinals.

¶ JULIA CHILD

In the early days of television, Boston viewers gathered around their sets to watch their favorite programs on small black-and-white screens. Many local performers, comedians, dramatic artists, and commentators had their moments of fame and then faded away with the advent of color television and national programming. There was one television personality, however, who took local audiences by storm, launching a national career that was to last for an incredible forty years. With a breezy exuberance and an unmistakable flair for publicity, Julia Child created a cooking show that established her reputation as one of the most creative and best-liked personalities in Boston.

Born Julia McWilliams on August 15, 1912, in Pasadena, Calif., the eldest of three children, Julia was educated at San Francisco's fashionable Katherine Branson School for Girls where, at 6 feet 2 inches tall by her senior year, she towered over the other students. In 1930 she enrolled in Smith College in Northampton, Mass., and after graduation moved to New York City to work in an advertising firm.

During World War II, Julia moved to Washington, D.C., where she worked as a research assistant for the Office of Strategic Services (OSS), and was then sent to Ceylon, an island off the coast of India, to process secret intelligence documents. In 1945 she served in China, where she met a fellow OSS employee, Paul Child, whom she married. In 1948 the couple relocated to France when Paul was assigned to the U.S. Information Service in Paris. While there, Julia developed an interest in French cuisine, attended the Cordon Bleu cooking school, and then joined with fellow students Simone Beck and Louisette Bertholle to form their own cooking school, L'Ecole de Trois Gourmandes. Later, this trio collaborated on a two-volume, 800-page cookbook, *Mastering the Art of French Cooking* (1961), that helped introduce French cuisine to the American culinary community.

After moving back to America and settling in Cambridge, Julia was asked by Russell Morash, a producer at WGBH, the Boston public television station, to appear on a book-review program. Instead of simply sitting down and talking, she proceeded to cook an omelet for the interviewer on camera and captivate the viewers with her delightful commentary. Morash was inspired to produce *The French Chef*, a program featuring Julia Child displaying her cooking techniques in the kitchen. *The French Chef* debuted in 1963 and was eventually syndicated to 96 stations throughout the United States. Morash later produced several *Julia Child & Company* shows for the same public broadcasting station. In 1965 Julia Child received the

❧ *Julia Child*

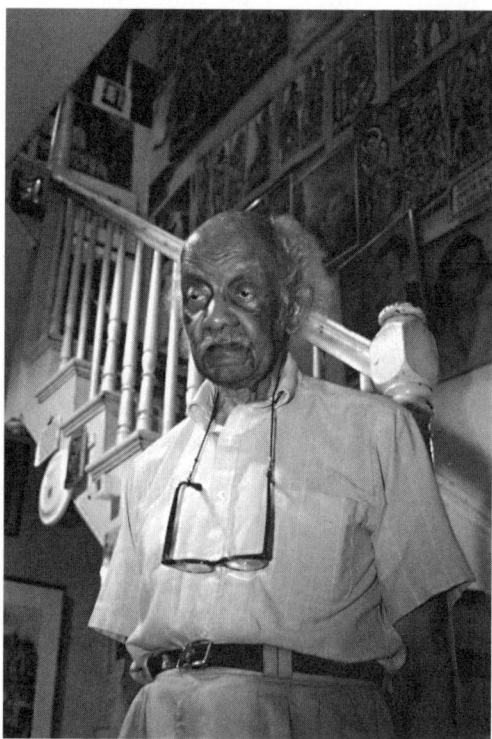

❧ *Allan Crite*

❧ James Michael Curley

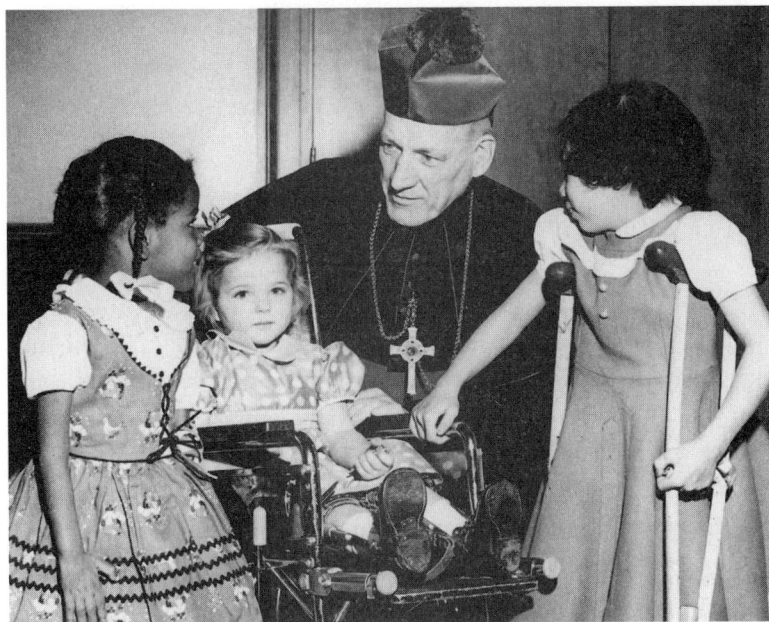

❧ Richard J. Cushing

prestigious George Foster Peabody Award, and in 1966 she was awarded an Emmy for her television work.

Throughout the 1970s and 1980s, Julia Child made regular appearances on ABC's *Good Morning America,* continued her popular cooking shows on public television, and produced a number of best-selling cookbooks, some of the most recent of which are *Baking with Julia* (1996), *Julia's Delicious Little Dinners* (1998), and *Julia's Kitchen Wisdom* (2000). In 1993, Child was the first woman inducted into the Culinary Institute Hall of Fame, and in November 2000 she received France's highest honor, the Legion d'Honneur.

In November 2000, at the age of eighty-nine, Julia Child decided it was time to escape the harsh Boston winters and retire to the warm climate of her native California. She willed her house on Irving Street in Cambridge to her alma mater, Smith College, and deposited her papers at the Schlesinger Library at Radcliffe ("a library that takes food seriously," she quipped). But the famous kitchen she has used for forty years will go—pots, pans, and all—to the Smithsonian Institution in Washington, D.C., where it will be a reminder of a talented woman who brought pleasure into the lives of several generations of Boston television viewers with her hearty salute with a glass of French wine and her chirrupy "Bon Appétit!"

❧ PATRICK COLLINS

In the seemingly endless struggle between the native and the newcomer, the Yankee and the Celt, the Protestant and the Catholic that characterized the course of nineteenth-century Boston history, one man finally emerged as an acceptable representative for both sides. Patrick Collins was that rare figure in the give-and-take of modern Boston politics—a statesman of personal integrity who could reconcile different points of view in the interests of the city as a whole.

Patrick Andrew Collins was born in Ballinafanna, near Fermoy, County Cork, Ireland, on March 12, 1844. After the death of his father in 1847, Collins and his mother emigrated to America and settled in Chelsea. He attended the local public school where, as one of only ten "Paddy boys," he was so often harassed by the other boys that he "had to fight to get to school, at recess, to get home—in fact, to go anywhere." He experienced at first hand the intolerance of the Know-Nothing movement when a half-crazed evangelist who called himself the Angel Gabriel led a mob through the Catholic section of town, smashing doors, breaking windows, tearing the cross off the church, and beating up young Collins in the process.

In 1856, at the age of twelve, he took a job as an office boy for Robert Morris, the only African American lawyer in Massachusetts. A year later, however, times were so hard that his family moved to Ohio, where young Collins labored on a farm, in a coal mine, and in a mill. In 1859 the family moved back to Boston, where Collins learned the upholsterer's trade and joined the local union. In the evenings he would walk from his home to the Boston Public Library to read the classics and improve his mind, having conceived the ambition to become a lawyer. He read law in the office of James M. Keith and then, in 1869, entered Harvard Law School. He received his law degree with honors in 1871, passed the bar, and opened his own law office on Washington Street.

Early in his career, Collins was active in the Fenian Brotherhood, an Irish American organization devoted to Irish independence, but withdrew in 1867 when the Fenians advocated violent methods. He continued to take an interest in Irish affairs, however, and in 1881 was elected president of the Irish Land League of America, whose goal was to keep the Irish farmer on the land. Meanwhile, Collins seriously applied himself to political developments in his own country. In 1867 he was elected to the Massachusetts House of Representatives, and in 1870, at the age of twenty-six, he became the youngest member, and the only Irish Catholic, ever to serve in the state Senate up to that time. Collins served as chairman of the Democratic City Committee from 1873 to 1874 and chaired the Democratic State Committee from 1884 to 1891. In 1875 he became Judge Advocate General on the staff of Governor William Gaston (after which he was always referred to as "General"), and in 1882 he became the first

Bostonian of Irish descent to be elected to the U.S. House of Representatives.

As a national figure, Collins was named permanent chairman of the 1888 Democratic National Convention, and in 1892 he seconded the nomination of Grover Cleveland as the Democratic candidate for president. In gratitude for his support, President Cleveland offered Collins either a Cabinet post or an ambassadorial position but, having left his law practice, Collins could not afford the expenses associated with either of these positions. Cleveland finally appointed Collins as consul general in London, a prestigious position that also provided a substantial income from fees, contracts, and licenses. After the election of the Republican President William McKinley in 1896, Collins returned to his law practice in Boston, but almost immediately was asked by city Democratic leaders to run for mayor. In 1899 Collins reluctantly agreed, but lost the first race to the Republican candidate, Thomas N. Hart. Collins ran again in 1901, however, and this time defeated Hart by the largest majority ever given a mayoral candidate, becoming Boston's second Irish-born mayor.

Patrick Collins ran an honest, efficient, and businesslike administration at City Hall, and won the admiration of all ranks of Boston society. When he ran for reelection in 1903, he carried every ward in the city except East Boston. As he was moving toward the completion of his second two-year term, with every expectation of reelection to a third term, Mayor Patrick Collins died suddenly on September 14, 1905, at the Homestead in Hot Springs, Va., where he had gone for a brief rest. He was sincerely mourned throughout the city and eulogized by newspapers in all parts of the country as well as in Ireland.

Immediately after his death, Richard Olney, secretary of state and attorney general in the Cleveland cabinet, organized a committee of prominent Bostonians to raise funds for a suitable memorial. Within a month, the money had been collected, and a memorial was erected on the Commonwealth Avenue Mall, between Clarendon and Dartmouth Streets. The memorial is a massive shaft of granite, topped by a bust of Collins, flanked by two female figures—one representing Erin, the other representing Columbia—symbolic of the two great loves of Collins: Ireland and America. The inscription, written by Harvard president Charles W. Eliot, praises Collins as "a talented, honest, generous, serviceable man."

❡ JAMES BRENDAN CONNOLLY

The first American athlete to win a gold medal in the modern Olympic Games was a Bostonian. A statue of James Brendan Connolly, sculpted by Thomas Haxo, was dedicated on October 31, 1987, in Columbus Park, South Boston, by Boston Mayor Raymond L. Flynn as a tribute to the scholar-athlete from the peninsula district. "A memorial to James Connolly," said the mayor, "is a testament to our highest aspirations in academics, in sports, in life, for our children."

Born in South Boston on October 28, 1868, James Brendan Connolly grew up in what he called a maritime environment. His parents were of seafaring stock from the Aran Islands, and he later boasted that he had "the sea blood of the Connollys and the O'Donnells" in his veins. At the age of seven, young Jim made his first trip to the offshore banks aboard his uncle's fishing schooner, a journey that sparked a lifelong relationship with the sea and the men who sailed it.

In 1892 Jim joined his older brother, Michael, in Savannah, Ga., where he took a job as a clerk in the office of the U.S. Engineer Corps, which was working on river and harbor improvements. In his spare time, he earned extra money writing a sports column for a local newspaper, while also competing in local track events—his other passion besides writing. Although he enjoyed his time on the river, in the summer of 1895 Connolly left Savannah to enroll in an engineering program at Harvard College.

In April 1896, while Connolly was in his freshman year at Harvard, the first modern Olympic Games were held in Greece— reviving the tradition after some 1,500 years. Although the college refused him a leave of absence to participate in the games, Connolly, a member of the Suffolk Athletic Club, traveled to the Greek capital as part of a group of Boston athletes who would dominate the international games that year. James Connolly became America's first Olympic champion, winning the gold medal for the United States in the first event—the hop, step, and jump, later called the triple jump. After victorious performances by other members of the Boston Athletic Association, Connolly and his teammates returned home to a tumultuous welcome. They were given a reception at Faneuil Hall, a formal greeting from Mayor Josiah Quincy, and a special triumphal ode set to the strains of "Fair Harvard."

Following this exhilarating experience, Connolly began earning a living by writing articles for various Boston newspapers. When the Spanish-American War broke out in 1898, Connolly enlisted in the 9th Massachusetts Infantry Regiment—the Fighting Irish of Civil War fame—and saw action in Cuba at the Battle of Santiago. His notes to a friend at home were published by the *Boston Globe* as "Letters from the Front in Cuba." In 1900 Connolly participated in the second Olympic Games at Paris, this time winning the silver medal in his track event.

Back from France, Connolly turned to writing in earnest, publishing a collection of short stories as well as his first full-length novel, *Jeb Hutton: The Story of a Georgia Boy*. In 1905 he published a second novel that continued the Jeb Hutton story. After a brief tour of duty in the U.S. Navy in 1907–1908, he ran for Congress (unsuccessfully) on the Bull Moose ticket in 1913, and the following year covered the landing of American troops at Vera Cruz, Mexico, for *Collier's Magazine*. In 1914, he won the *Collier's* short story contest (Theodore Roosevelt was one of the judges) with his powerful story "The Traveler." During World War I Connolly was the European naval correspondent for *Collier's,* and after the war he went to Ireland to cover the Troubles. His series of forty-five articles, titled "Tortured Ireland: The Black and Tan Warfare in Ireland," was published in the *Boston American* as well as in other Hearst newspapers.

During his long and varied career, James Brendan Connolly wrote twenty-five books and several hundred short stories and articles, which earned him an international reputation; Joseph Conrad called him "the best sea-story writer in America." His stories of the sea celebrate the traditional virtues of courage, loyalty, honest, justice, and sacrifice demonstrated by ordinary fishermen and sailors who battle against the forces of nature and the evil of men. Although Connolly and his literary works faded into a period of obscurity, before his death in 1957, at the age of ninety-one, he witnessed the beginning of a resurgence of interest. In recent years, critics rediscovered the distinctive qualities of his writings, scarce editions of his works became quite valuable, and collections of his maritime novels were established at such major academic institutions as Colby College, Stanford University, Princeton, and Villanova, while his major works and papers are housed in the special collections of the Burns Library at Boston College. In 1944 he published his autobiography, called *Sea Borne,* and in 1948 he was the recipient of the gold medal of the Eire Society of Boston, a fitting tribute to a remarkable Bostonian.

¶ JOHN SINGLETON COPLEY

Bostonians are understandably proud of the numerous portraits of prominent Revolutionary patriots that make up a significant part of the holdings of the Museum of Fine Arts. More than sixty of these portraits—including John Hancock, Sam Adams, Joseph Warren, and the often-reproduced study of Paul Revere gazing pensively at his silver teapot—are the works of John Singleton Copley. These paintings capture the distinctive personalities of the Bostonians who helped create the new and independent town of post-Revolutionary Boston—a town that Copley himself would never see.

John Singleton Copley was born in Boston in 1738, and studied drawing with his stepfather, Peter Pelham, a colonial artist and engraver. Copley began to produce serious paintings of his own when he was only fifteen years old. At first he did a few historical subjects based on earlier engravings, but soon he was specializing in portraits for the families of Boston's growing mercantile class. Largely self-taught, Copley drew his ideas and techniques from other engravers, as well as from English prints. He was specially influenced by a Scots artist named John Smibert, who arrived in Boston in 1730 and who painted such prominent colonial figures as Edmund Quincy and Peter Faneuil. Copley's portraits were very realistic, with an uncanny way of revealing the distinctive character and personality of his subject. Although he painted some full-length portraits, he favored half-length or quarter-length views.

In 1769 Copley married Susannah Clarke, the daughter of a wealthy Boston merchant, and was able to purchase a twenty-acre farm with three houses along Beacon Hill, facing the Boston Common and only a short distance from John Hancock's elegant mansion. In an effort to move beyond the small town of Boston where, as he put it, "were it not for portraits, art would be unknown in this place," Copley decided to project his talents across the Atlantic. He started out by sending a painting of his half-brother, Henry Pelham, *Boy with a Squirrel,* to be exhibited by the Society of Artists in London. Although it received mixed reviews, the painting attracted the attention of the influential Pennsylvania painter Benjamin West, who urged Copley to come to London to study.

Partly as a result of West's appeal, and partly to escape the tensions of the growing Revolutionary crisis—he had close friends and family members in both the Loyalist and Patriot camps—Copley sailed to England, where he was soon joined by his wife and family. He started a new career in England, continuing to paint portraits but also developing a realistic style of portraying scenes from recent history. His haunting marine painting *Watson and the Shark* (1771) was an example of his emerging flair for depicting dramatic action.

When the Revolution was over, Copley sold his Boston property to a group of real estate developers called the Mount Vernon Proprietors, who were developing the south slope of Beacon Hill at the time the new Bulfinch State House was being constructed. Complaining that because he was far away in England the entrepreneurs had taken unfair advantage of him, Copley initiated a lawsuit in an effort to obtain what he regarded as a fairer price for his valuable property. The painter's claims were denied, however, and he spent his remaining years in England with a dwindling income. Debt-ridden, ill, and enfeebled, John Singleton Copley became a lonely expatriate who never returned to his native land. He died of a stroke in London in 1815.

❡ ALLAN CRITE

Boston's South End was generated out of the filled-in land along the southern shores of Boston Neck. Originally developed as a fashion-able residential area, it was eclipsed by the Back Bay and became instead a lively multicultural community, before it was transformed by the urban renewal projects of the 1950s and 1960s. The best and most enduring artistic record of the pre–World War II South End can be found in the drawings and paintings of Allan Crite, a highly celebrated African American artist.

Allan Rohan Crite was born in Boston in 1910. His father, Oscar Crite, an engineer who had attended Cornell College and the University of Vermont, suffered a serious industrial accident in 1927, and died in 1937. His mother, Annamae Palmer Crite, was profoundly dedicated to the importance of education. She was an important influence on the academic and artistic progress of her talented son as he made his way through the Boston public schools and studied at the School of the Museum of Fine Arts, located within walking distance of his home in the South End.

In 1910 Mrs. Crite started taking classes at the Harvard Extension School, the year of her son's birth and one year after the adult-education program was founded by the Harvard president A. Lawrence Lowell. In 1937, after her husband's death, she literally dragged her son Allan over to Cambridge—"by the ear!" he later recalled—so that he too could enroll in the Harvard extension program. For the next thirty years, Allan Crite took a variety of courses in the liberal arts along with his mother ("she studied everything") until, in 1968, he graduated as First Marshal in his class, with a Bachelor of Arts degree in Extension Studies.

While he was expanding his academic knowledge, Allan Crite was also perfecting his artistic skills. In 1936, at the age of twenty-six, he made a name for himself in the art world when he exhibited a number of his paintings and drawings at the Museum of Modern Art in New York City and at Harvard University's Fogg Art Museum. His pencil drawing *Busy Street,* and his many other works of art depicting the vitality and diversity of the African American community of Boston's South End, remain a permanent reminder of what that part of Boston was like during the 1930s and 1940s. While he was attending Harvard, he worked in the Grossman Library in Sever Hall, where the librarian allowed him to continue with his sketching and drawing in between tasks.

During his lifetime, Allan Crite's portraits of African American community life, of the ordinary and often extraordinary people he encountered, and of scenes from biblical and religious history would be widely exhibited and reproduced. His prints and paintings are part of the permanent collections of the Museum of Fine Arts, the Fogg Art Museum, the Boston Public Library, the Boston Athenaeum, the Corcoran Gallery and the Smithsonian Institution in Washington, D.C., and the Museum of the National Center of Afro-American Artists in Boston. Volumes of his writings covering some fifty years have also been published, from *Were You There* and *Three Spirituals,* published by Harvard University Press in the 1940s, to his illustrations in *The Revelation of Saint John the Divine* published by the Limited Editions Club of New York in 1994. Mr. Crite has exhibited and lectured in galleries, schools, college, and churches throughout the United States as well as in the People's Republic of China. He has been awarded numerous honorary doctorates, and received the 350th Harvard University Anniversary Medal.

In recent years Allan Crite has concentrated on biblical subjects and religious themes, providing drawings for weekly church bulletins at St. Stephen's Episcopal Church, altarpieces and paintings for a variety of religious institutions, and illustrations for collections of

African American spirituals. In 1986, Crite's neighbors in the South End persuaded the Boston City Council to name the intersection nearest his house at 410 Columbus Avenue "Allan Rohan Crite Square"—the only square in Boston named for someone other than a military hero. Allan Crite maintains his home as a virtual museum, designated the Allan Rohan Crite Research Institute, filled with paintings, prints, etchings, and altarpieces, as well as books, journals, files, and artistic memorabilia of all kinds, all witness to a significant piece of Boston history.

❡ JAMES MICHAEL CURLEY

In the fascinating saga of America's big-city political bosses, there is probably no more colorful and controversial figure than Boston's James Michael Curley. To his many critics, Curley was a crook and a scoundrel who practiced the fine art of patronage, trading favors for votes in the city's Irish wards. To his many admirers, Curley was a hero, a lovable and incorrigible Robin Hood who took the spoils of government from the hands of rich Yankees to improve the lives and fortunes of poor immigrants.

Born November 20, 1874, in Boston's Roxbury section to immigrant parents from Galway, James Michael Curley grew up in the mudflats behind the Boston City Hospital. When his father died suddenly, the ten-year-old Jim worked at a variety of odd jobs while attending school, but spent most of his evenings at a local cigar store listening to old-timers swapping stories about Ward 17 politics. Although he continued to study, to broaden his reading and improve his public speaking skills, young Curley had already decided on a life of politics.

Jim Curley worked his way up the echelons of ward politics, winning a place in the Common Council in 1899 and a year later taking over control of the Ward 17 Democratic committee. In 1901 he served a single term in the state legislature, and in 1903 ran for a seat on the Board of Aldermen. Despite being sent to the Charles Street Jail for taking a Post Office examination for another person ("I did it for a friend," he explained), he won his seat on the Board. In 1910 Curley was elected to the U.S. Congress from the Tenth Congressional District, and moved his family to Washington, where he served two uneventful terms.

In 1914 Curley decided to return to Boston and run for mayor. Deliberately bypassing the two major nominating channels—the Yankee Good Government Association and the Irish Democratic City Committee—Curley used a combination of wit, bravado, and charisma to win his first mayoral contest. The only way his enemies could slow him down was to pass a state law in 1918 prohibiting the mayor of Boston from succeeding himself.

Despite such tactics, James Michael Curley moved in and out of City Hall with remarkable regularity. Through the power of his speaking voice, the loyalty of his working-class supporters, and his personal control of citywide patronage, Curley provided the immigrant population of Boston with the economic benefits and social amenities he felt they deserved. During the Depression years, he launched a series of public works projects to provide jobs for unemployed workers. He improved numerous beaches, bathhouses, parks, and playgrounds; he built branch libraries, health centers, and municipal buildings; he repaved streets, widened roadways, and constructed bridges.

After three separate four-year terms as mayor of Boston, Curley served a single two-year term as Governor of Massachusetts, from 1935 to 1937. After that, his political career went into a decline: in 1936 he was defeated in a U.S. Senate race by Henry Cabot Lodge, Jr., and the following year was beaten by young Maurice Tobin in the city's mayoral contest. In 1938 he lost a governor's race to Leverett Saltonstall, and in 1941 he lost out to Tobin in another bid for the mayor's office. Although he won another term in the U.S. Congress in 1943, it appeared that Curley's career in Boston was over.

When Maurice Tobin decided to retire as mayor and run for governor, however, Curley came back from Washington and ran for the vacant office. Despite being under indictment for mail fraud, the seventy-year-old politician swept the field and took office in January 1946. A year later, however, he was sentenced to a 6-to-18-month term in the federal prison at Danbury, Conn., leaving Boston in the hands of the City Clerk, John B. Hynes, who was appointed temporary mayor. Thanks to a pardon by President Harry Truman, Curley served only five months of his sentence and returned to Boston to resume his office. After his first day back at City Hall, he boasted to the press proudly: "I have accomplished more in one day than has been done in the five months of my absence."

Curley's offhand remark so infuriated the temporary mayor that Hynes decided to challenge him in the 1949 election. Although he had no money or political organization and had never run for public office, John Hynes went on to defeat Curley in November 1949 in a close race that was decided by the small margin of only 11,000 votes. Despite the close count, it was clear to most Bostonians that the 1949 election was Curley's "Last Hurrah."

The rise of federal patronage, the ravages of old age, the transformation of the old ethnic neighborhoods, and the advent of a new generation in Boston politics made it evident that the days of "Old Jim" were finally over. James Michael Curley died on November 12, 1958, and thousands of his devoted followers stood in line to view his body as it lay in state in the rotunda of the State House on Beacon Hill.

❡ FRANCES GREELY CURTIS

In 1920 the passage of the Nineteenth Amendment gave American women the right to vote and to run for public office. The record of female candidates in Boston politics during the following two decades, however, was far from impressive. Although by the end of the 1920s women outnumbered men in Boston by nearly twenty thousand, only three women had been elected to the School Committee, and only one woman managed to get elected to the City Council.

When a woman named Frances Curtis announced herself a candidate for mayor of Boston in 1926, therefore, it was a matter of considerable surprise and consternation.

In 1926, James Michael Curley was unable to run again for mayor of Boston because of a recent state law that prevented an incumbent mayor from succeeding himself. Frances Greely Curtis sought to take advantage of this law and become the first woman mayor of Boston. A member of the prestigious Women's Club of Boston and an elected member of the Boston School Committee for fourteen years, Curtis saw the absence of Curley as a candidate in 1926, along with the fact that the votes would be divided up among some seventeen rival male candidates, as a heaven-sent opportunity to capitalize on the women's vote and win the election.

Frances Curtis ran a simple campaign, acting as her own campaign manager and working out of her own home. Her prospect for victory was based on the fact that she had polled 79,139 votes when she won a place on the School Committee in 1921, while James Michael Curley had received only 74,261 votes that same year in his campaign for mayor. She obviously hoped that those voters who supported her in 1921 would help her achieve her goal in 1925. Running on a platform of frugality and simplicity, she said she could not understand why anyone would spend more than $40,000 (the salary for four years as mayor of Boston) on a campaign for the job, and refused to pay thousands of dollars for colorful posters and fancy automobiles because she felt that such trappings had no place in a serious political campaign. She wanted her campaign to be a contest of "character," measuring up to the high standards of political decency held by the good people of Boston.

Frances Curtis saw the job of mayor as essentially large-scale housekeeping, in which any woman who knew the importance of managing a household on a strict budget could be successful. Having brought up a family of nine brothers and sisters, Curtis insisted she was fully qualified to run the city, which she saw as little more than a large extended household. "With women in office," she declared, "there will be no graft. Women will not stand for graft." While men might earn the money, she noted, it was always the woman's job to use the funds effectively and to best advantage. She thought that, as a woman, she would be able to bring this idea of small-scale budget management to the large-scale needs of the city.

Unfortunately for Frances Curtis, her opponents' flashy campaigns, torchlight parades, and machine politics prevailed over her idealistic and simplistic approach. She failed to get the number of signatures required to get her name on the ballot, and the election went to Malcolm Nichols, who served as mayor from 1926 to 1930. Even though she did not become mayor, Frances Curtis achieved a place in history as the first woman to run for the office of mayor of Boston, and inspired a future generation of Boston women to hope that political opportunities were open to anyone who wanted to take a stand for political equality and democratic principles.

❧ RICHARD J. CUSHING

Some leaders achieve eminence simply by virtue of their official position or their administrative title. Others achieve eminence as a result of their personal virtues or their public accomplishments. As Archbishop of Boston and a member of the College of Cardinals, Richard J. Cushing became a memorable part of Boston's history both as a prince of the church and a man of the people.

Richard James Cushing was born in 1895 in the working-class neighborhood of South Boston, the third child and only son of Irish immigrant parents. He lived with his family in a three-decker house not far from the Boston Elevated Railway car barn where his father, Patrick, worked. Young Dick attended the local public schools, enrolled in the Jesuit-run Boston College High School, at the time still located in the South End, and in 1913 entered Boston College, which had recently moved to suburban Chestnut Hill. At the end of his second year, he transferred to St. John's Seminary to become a priest. Although he was selected by Cardinal O'Connell to study at the North American College at Rome, the outbreak of war in Europe caused the seminary to cancel the ocean voyage.

After six years of study, Richard Cushing was ordained to the

priesthood by Cardinal O'Connell on May 20, 1921. After serving
briefly in several parishes, he asked to be sent off to the foreign missions; instead, he was assigned to the office of the Society for the
Propagation of the Faith in Boston, encouraging vocations, publiciz-
ing foreign missions, and raising money. In recognition of Cushing's
efforts, in 1939 Pope Pius XII made him a monsignor, and two
months later named him an auxiliary bishop. When Cardinal
O'Connell died in April 1944, the forty-nine-year-old Richard J.
Cushing was named Archbishop of Boston.

Gruff, affable, down-to-earth, and unpredictable, the new archbishop was a dramatic contrast to his more formal and austere prede-
cessor. Aware of the changing times, Archbishop Cushing worked in
the spirit of modern ecumenism and preached the doctrine of universal brotherhood. By the late 1950s, he was already preaching in
Protestant churches, speaking before Jewish audiences, and promoting feelings of good will among all religious groups. In addition to
promoting ecumenism with various non-Catholic groups, Cushing
also promoted a spirit of inclusion for many of his own Catholic
parishioners he felt had been marginalized or ignored. He said Mass
for inmates at Walpole State Prison; he attended Thanksgiving dinners for elderly persons; he dedicated himself to improving the lives
of mentally retarded and disabled children. A creative and indefatigable fund-raiser, Cushing not only continued to support the foreign missions but also launched a prodigious building program of
churches, schools, and hospitals for a large and vigorous Catholic
population that was growing by 250,000 to 300,000 every five years.
On November 16, 1958, Richard J. Cushing was informed that because of his "glowing charity" and his "burning zeal for souls," Pope
John XXIII elevated him to the rank of Cardinal—the second Bostonian to hold that title.

In 1962, Pope John XXIII called for an ecumenical council to
examine relations of the Catholic Church to the modern world.
Although Cushing attended the meetings of the first two sessions
only sporadically, he used the third session of Vatican II as an opportunity to speak out boldly: in September 1964 he urged passage of
the proposed declaration on religious liberty, insisting that the

Church must be "the champion of liberty, of human liberty, and of civil liberty." He also spoke out in support of the declaration denying that Jews were responsible for the death of Christ, and admitting that Christians had not always been faithful to the teachings of Christ in their relations with their Jewish brothers.

By the late 1960s, Cardinal Cushing's health was deteriorating, undoubtedly worsened by the stress of numerous tragic public events. The assassination of President John F. Kennedy hit him hard ("My heart is broken with grief . . ."), and it became increasingly difficult for him to comprehend the changing times. Antiwar protests, student revolts, civil rights marches, and feminist demonstrations rocked the nation, while within the Catholic Church bitter controversies arose over the changes introduced by the Second Vatican Council. The mounting indebtedness resulting from his ambitious building programs created even more worries for the ailing prelate. So serious was his physical condition that he agreed to retire in August 1970, on the occasion of his seventy-fifth birthday. On October 7, 1970, Humberto Medeiros, Bishop of Brownsville, Texas, was officially installed to succeed Cardinal Cushing as Archbishop of Boston. Only a few weeks later, on November 2 (All Souls' Day), Richard Cardinal Cushing passed quietly away. More than half a million people filed past his catafalque in the Cathedral, and mourners stood ten feet deep as the body of their beloved prelate left for its final resting place in Hanover, Mass., at the Portiuncula Chapel of the St. Coletta School he had established for retarded children.

❡ JOHN DEFERRARI

In 1917, after the death of the prosperous attorney and Boston aristocrat Josiah Benton, the Boston Public Library announced that it had received a bequest from his estate of more than a million dollars. Thirty years later, on September 8, 1947, the son of an Italian immigrant, John Deferrari, came to the Trustees Room of the Boston

Public Library, stood beneath the portrait of Colonel Benton, and bestowed on the library an irrevocable trust of more than a million dollars. "At one stride," wrote the *Boston Traveler,* "he has made himself one of the city's foremost citizens and benefactors."

John Deferrari was born June 11, 1863, in Ferry Street in Boston's crowded North End, the eldest son of eight children of Giovanni Baptista Deferrari, an immigrant from a suburb of Genoa. Arriving in the mid-1840s, Giovanni was one of the first Italians to settle in the North End, going into the grocery business and eventually becoming a substantial property owner. Despite his wealth, Giovanni was determined that his son John should learn the family business the hard way. When he left the Eliot School after the eighth grade, therefore, John was given a basket of fruit to sell in the downtown financial district. "I always brought home an empty basket," he later recalled, "and I always gave the money to my father."

While making his rounds selling fruit, the young man got his first vision of the American success story. By the time he was sixteen, he had saved enough money to buy his own horse and wagon, and then he graduated from the wagon to a ground-floor retail shop in Dock Square. He did so well that when the tenants on the top two floors moved out, he took over the entire building for a wholesale business. But his big break came in 1890, when he established a high-quality fruit store specializing in imported delicacies on Boylston Street, only a few doors away from the Boston Public Library, which at that time was located on the site now occupied by the Colonial Theater.

The proximity of the business to the library created a relationship that lasted a lifetime. In the course of his steady and persistent climb up the financial ladder, John Deferrari was just starting to invest in stocks, and was determined to know as much as possible about the companies involved. He went next door to the Boston Public Library to study the volumes on law, particularly real estate law, as well as books on economics and statistics. "I always doped everything out carefully," he explained. "It was all there in the library." One of his first major real estate investments was a building at the corner of Massachusetts Avenue and Boylston Street. And when the Boston Public Library moved to its present location in Copley Square,

Deferrari continued to be a frequent user, intently poring over investment reports and statistical studies.

As he made his rounds through the city, John Deferrari was hardly distinguishable from the thousands of other people who made up Boston's population. A little man, slim and bald, he rarely spoke, did not attend public meetings, and listed "General Delivery, Boston" as his North End address. He maintained his own house, collected his own rents, did his own repairs, and cooked his own single daily meal on an old-fashioned stove. He gave up both wine and tobacco in his youth ("They could not profit me," he said, "so I cut them out") and never married because he never had time to find the right partner. He took great pride in the fact that he became a millionaire without benefit of a banker, a secretary, a bookkeeper, an automobile, or even a telephone.

Over the years, John Deferrari had developed a great respect for the Boston Public Library and the great opportunity it offered young men and women, regardless of race, class, or fortune. As his personal fortune grew, he decided to make a gift to the library that would not only show his own appreciation, but also inspire other young Bostonians to realize the great American dream. It came as quite a shock, therefore, when this eighty-four-year-old, rather nondescript little man let it be known that he was presenting securities worth more than $1,000,000 to the Boston Public Library as an irrevocable trust for the benefit of the library. Milton E. Lord, director of the library, read the announcement of the gift and of the establishment of the John Deferrari Foundation at a press conference on September 5, 1947. Mr. Deferarri was present, beaming happily, dressed in a new gray-blue suit with the flaps of the jacket pockets fastened down securely with safety pins. The following year, a full-length portrait of Deferrari was unveiled in the Central Library at a ceremony attended by Mayor James Michael Curley. A short time later, the financier gave the library an additional grant of half a million dollars in real estate holdings in downtown Boston.

In an ironic twist of fate, on April 29, 1950, John Deferrari was found dead at the age of eighty-seven in an $8.25-a-week room on Beacon Hill, registered under the fictitious name of "Henry Howe" to assure his continued anonymity in a city where he had suddenly become such a well-known public figure.

❦ HARRY ELLIS DICKSON

Harry was a Jewish boy of modest means from Somerville, who played the bass drum in the school band and took up the violin when his sister didn't want to continue her lessons. After graduating from the New England Conservatory of Music, Harry Ellis Dickson ended up spending fifty years as a violinist with the Boston Symphony Orchestra, becoming assistant conductor of the renowned Boston Pops and traveling with both orchestras to all parts of the world. By the time he retired in 1987, he had been showered with honors, given numerous honorary degrees, and named Chevalier dans l'Ordre des Arts et des Lettres by the government of France. It was a great trip for a Boston streetcar conductor's son.

Harry Ellis Dickson (the family name was changed from Duchin) was born on November 13, 1908, in a three-decker on Western Avenue in Cambridge. Harry's father was a tailor from the town of Kozeletz, near Kiev in the Ukraine, who had escaped the Czarist terror and come to America with his young bride. Harry's father first opened a small tailor shop; in 1916 he moved the family to Somerville and gave up the tailoring business to become a streetcar conductor. Harry attended Somerville High School, playing the bass drum in the high school band but concentrating on his study of the violin. He became a member of the Somerville High School orchestra, and was invited to play in the Peabody House Orchestra at the West End settlement house. By the time he was fourteen he was playing at various local social functions, as well as leading a twelve-piece orchestra on the B. F. Keith vaudeville circuit. During his senior year the family moved to Dorchester, but Harry stayed at Somerville High School, from which he graduated in June 1925.

Accepted at the New England Conservatory of Music, Harry had the good fortune to study with Vaughn Hamilton, a violinist with the Boston Symphony Orchestra. All the while, he continued to make money on the side playing at various restaurants and conducting a pit orchestra for silent moves and vaudeville shows at the E. M. Loew's theater in Somerville. At the end of four years Harry received his diploma from the Conservatory, stayed on for another year, and in 1931 traveled to Europe to study with the violinist Max Rostal in Berlin. After associating with numerous artists and musicians, meeting his future wife, Jane Goldberg, and visiting his father's home town of Kozeletz, twenty-six-year-old Harry returned to America in 1934, ready to face the world.

The United States was deep in the Great Depression when Harry Ellis Dickson came home, but under President Roosevelt's WPA program he was able to get an appointment to the Community Recreation Service, heading up an orchestra of unemployed musicians that played in the community center in the West End. In addition to his administrative duties, he also conducted local concerts at the Gardner Museum, as well as teaching one day a week at the Brookline Music School. In 1938 Dickson managed to arrange an audition with the noted conductor Serge Koussevitzky, who signed him up to play with the Boston Symphony Orchestra as well as the Boston Pops, at a salary of $70 a week—the culmination of a young man's dream.

Dickson started out on his half-century as a violinist with the great Boston orchestra, serving his first eleven "golden years" under Koussevitsky. Thirteen years with the "rhapsodic" Charles Munch were followed by the "methodically cool" Erich Leinsdorf, until Seiji Ozawa took over as music director in 1973. During this time Dickson also played with the Boston Pops orchestra, whose leader Arthur Fiedler achieved a success and popularity "never approached by any former conductor." In 1956 Dickson was appointed assistant conductor of the Pops; he hoped to succeed Fiedler after the maestro's death in 1979, but was bypassed in favor of John Williams, a younger and more nationally known composer and conductor. Dickson, however, continued to conduct regular seasonal concerts, as well as directing numerous local orchestras in various parts of the state.

Harry Ellis Dickson also turned his attention to providing special concerts for children and, with the enthusiastic assistance of his wife, Jane, created what became the Boston Symphony Youth Concerts. Dickson also traveled with the BSO on its first tour of Europe in 1952, and on a second tour in 1956 in which the orchestra played 29 concerts in 18 cities in 13 countries. In 1956 the BSO became the first American symphony orchestra to play in the Soviet Union, and in 1979 Dickson accompanied the BSO to China. At the age of seventy-nine, Harry Ellis Dickson finally decided to retire from the Boston Symphony Orchestra, playing his last concert with the BSO in August 1987 at the end of the Tanglewood season. He became music director of the Boston Classical Orchestra in 1983 and continued in that post until 1999, while continuing his association with the Pops as Associate Conductor Laureate. On November 7, 1991, Mayor Raymond Flynn dedicated a small park close to Symphony Hall to honor the many contributions of this celebrated musician to the cultural heritage of Boston.

¶ PATRICK DONAHOE

The Pilot was started in Boston under another name in 1829 by Bishop Benedict Fenwick to combat the hostile attacks of an anti-Catholic press. In 1834 he transferred ownership of the weekly newspaper to one of the employees, an immigrant named Patrick Donahoe, who published *The Pilot* for the remainder of the nineteenth century. Under Donahoe's direction, *The Pilot* became one of the longest-running publications in the United States, providing an invaluable record of Boston's Irish Catholic community.

Patrick Donahoe was born in Munnery, Parish of Kilmore, County Cavan, Ireland, on March 17, 1814. He emigrated to America in 1825 and settled in Boston, where he entered a printing office and learned the skilled trade of typesetting. In 1834, when Bishop Benedict Fenwick, the second Catholic bishop of Boston, decided to sell his newspaper *The Jesuit,* Patrick Donahoe became the proprietor and editor of the weekly, and in 1836 announced that the paper would be called *The Pilot.* In addition to its function as a source of local and national news, *The Pilot* also became such a reliable source on events in Ireland that it became popularly known as "the Irishman's Bible."

At the outbreak of the Civil War, Patrick Donahoe announced the support of Boston's Irish Catholic community for the Lincoln administration and the Union cause, and he took an active role in organizing Irish troops for the defense of the nation. He was treasurer of the funds raised to equip and train the all-Irish 9th Massachusetts Regiment, commanded by Colonel Thomas Cass, and on the day of the regiment's departure from Boston he presented the regiment with ten bags, each containing 100 gold dollars—one for each man. Donahoe later assisted in the formation of the Faugh-a-Ballagh (Clear the Road), the 28th Massachusetts Regiment that went on to become part of New York's Irish Brigade, commanded by Thomas Meagher. Donahoe aided the troops at their training grounds at Camp Cameron in Cambridge during the early part of the war, and *The Pilot* encouraged the federal cause throughout the conflict.

In the course of his career as a publisher, Patrick Donahoe also accumulated a large personal fortune, much of which he gave away to churches, hospitals, schools, and charitable institutions. He served in many positions of trust. He was one of the Board of Directors for Public Institutions for nine years; president of the Emigrant Savings Bank; and president of the Home for Destitute Catholic Children. In addition to publishing *The Pilot,* he also published the popular *Donahoe's Magazine,* which attained a very large Irish Catholic readership, and engaged in a passenger and foreign exchange business, as well as a private banking operation, that greatly increased his income.

The great Boston fire of November 1872 completely destroyed Donahoe's splendid six-story granite block, called "Donahoe's Buildings," on Franklin and Hawley Streets, incinerating his printing equipment and his various publishing enterprises. His financial

losses were so severe that he was forced into bankruptcy. He was rescued by the Catholic archbishop, John Williams, who purchased a
three-quarter interest in *The Pilot* with the intention of using the
profits to pay off Donahoe's debts. Under the editorial direction of
John Boyle O'Reilly, the newspaper expanded its readership, with
the result that the debts were paid by 1883. Patrick Donahoe continued with his numerous financial and publishing enterprises until his
death in 1901.

❡ Mary Dyer

The first Quakers who arrived in Boston, in 1656—Ann Austin of
London and Mary Fisher of Yorkshire—did not receive a hospitable
welcome. Port officials first confined the two women to their ship,
seized their books, burned their papers, and then put them in jail.
The two women were finally deported to Barbados, and on October
14, 1656, the Massachusetts Bay Colony passed the first Anti-Quaker
Act, stating that any shipmaster who brought a Quaker into the colony would be fined one hundred pounds. The law further directs
that any Quaker found in the colony be committed to the house of
correction, "severely whipped," and kept constantly at work. As
Quakers kept arriving, Puritan officials ordered the death penalty for
Quakers who re-entered the colony after having previously been
banished. These were the harsh measures that confronted Mary
Dyer.

Mary Dyer was a resident of colonial Boston, a good friend of
Anne Hutchinson and a sympathetic supporter during her controversy with the Puritan town fathers. After her friend's trial and subsequent exile, in 1639 Mary Dyer and her husband moved south to
Rhode Island. Having become a Quaker, Dyer found herself a member of a religion outlawed in the Massachusetts Bay Colony. Puritans, especially, detested members of the Society of Friends, those
"Children of the Light" who followed the ministry of George Fox in

seventeenth-century England, and who had acquired the name of Quakers. Members of this religious sect declined to pay tithes to the established church, refused to take off their hats, and repudiated the leadership of those they called a "hireling ministry." Puritans, therefore, looked upon Quakers as both religious heretics and political subversives.

Mary Dyer first felt the weight of Puritan oppression when she was arrested while traveling through the town of Boston in 1657. After her release, she returned to Rhode Island, but two years later she was again taken into custody in the Puritan capital when she returned to visit imprisoned Quakers awaiting execution. William Robinson and Marmaduke Stevenson, along with Mary Dyer, were led from their cells with a 200-man guard. Any time one of the Quakers tried to harangue the crowd, the drummers played loudly to drown them out. Following the execution of the two men, Mary Dyer was led to the gallows, blindfolded, and had a noose placed around her neck. Just before the sentence could be carried out, however, her son interceded on her behalf. The authorities relented and ordered the woman transported out of the colony—with a stern warning not to return. Mary Dyer did return, however. And when she came back to Boston the following year to spread the doctrines of Quakerism, she was promptly taken into custody, sentenced to death, and hanged on Boston Common on June 1, 1660.

It was in May 1660 that Charles II was proclaimed King of England after his return from exile in France. While he was not a Quaker, he was a proponent of greater religious toleration. After a number of Quakers called upon him and asked him to intercede on behalf of the Quaker population of New England, Charles issued a mandamus requiring all Quakers condemned to death or imprisonment to be sent to London for trial. Fearing that they would lose a portion of their independence from England if their decisions were overturned by courts in London, Boston authorities ordered imprisoned Quakers to be set free.

In 1959, a seated bronze statue of Mary Dyer was placed in front of the east wing of the Massachusetts State House. The work of sculptor Sylvia Shaw Judson, the statue was erected by the Com-

◀ *Mary Dyer*

◀ *John Bernard Fitzpatrick*

❧ *Doug Flutie*

❧ *Edward Everett*

monwealth of Massachusetts with a legacy from Zenas Ellis of Fair
Haven, Vt. Seated modestly, her eyes lowered and her hands folded
on her lap, Mary Dyer faces the Boston Common, the scene of her
brutal execution some three centuries earlier.

⚶ MARY BAKER EDDY

Religion has always been a significant force in New England, and
the influence of individual women has been an important element
in that history. As early as the 1630s, Anne Hutchinson's controversial teachings led to her imprisonment and exile. During the post-
Revolutionary years, the followers of Mother Ann Lee expanded the
Shaker movement throughout New England. The visionary Ellen
Gould White, of Portland, Me., was crucial to the development of
the Seventh-Day Adventists. And Mary Baker Eddy devised a system
of belief about physical health and spiritual well-being that developed into the religion of Christian Science.

Mary Morse Baker was born on July 16, 1821, on a farm in Bow,
N.H. She spent most of her childhood in poverty, suffering from a
variety of illness and ailments. In June 1844 she married a man
named George Glover, who died a short time after their marriage,
leaving their newborn son to be raised by foster parents. In 1853
Mary Baker was married a second time, to Daniel Patterson, a
twenty-year relationship that ended in divorce in 1873. During these
years, Mary studied with Phineas P. Quimby, a spiritual healer from
Portland, Me., who experimented with natural healing through the
powers of the mind. In January 1866 Quimby died; a month later,
Mary was severely injured in a fall on the sidewalk in Lynn, Mass.,
an important episode in her life.

Using the New Testament as a guide, she recovered from her injuries and began promoting the idea that the Bible contained spiritual
principles essential to health and life. In 1875 Mary published the
first edition of her book *Science and Health with Key to the Scriptures,*

teaching that an understanding of the spiritual ideas contained in the Scriptures combined with disciplined prayer, rather than the conventional techniques of medicine, would lead to improved health. "It is our ignorance of God, the divine Principle," she wrote, "which produces apparent discord, and the right understanding of Him restores harmony." In January 1879 Mary Baker married Asa G. Eddy, her third husband, and in the same year she established in the city of Lynn the Church of Christ, Scientist, for which the teachings contained in her book *Science and Health* became the basis. Two years later, she established the Massachusetts Metaphysical College.

In 1881 Mary Baker Eddy moved her church and her college to headquarters in Boston, and in 1893 had a modest stone church constructed, virtually a chapel with stained-glass windows, that she called "our prayer in stone," and that members refer to as the Mother Church. Eddy's religious ideas spread rapidly, particularly in New England, having a special appeal to Americans of the middle and upper classes as an antidote to the materialism they found in modern industrial society. The First Church of Christ, Scientist, designed by the Boston architect Charles Brigham, was constructed between 1904 and 1905. A grandiose structure whose auditorium was inspired by Hagia Sophia in Istanbul, its central dome incorporates elements of the dome of St. Peter's in Rome and the Duomo in Florence. A long, pillared building next to the Mother Church houses the Christian Science Publishing House, as well as the Mapparium, a 30-foot walk-through globe of the world executed in stained glass. The complex underwent substantial renovation between 1968 and 1973, with the architect I. M. Pei designing an expansive new limestone entrance plaza on Massachusetts Avenue, along with an adjoining world headquarters building and a 700-foot-long reflecting pool along Huntington Avenue.

Mary Baker Eddy was an extraordinarily prolific writer and a dedicated saver of documents. She left a collection of diaries, scrapbooks, poems, sermons, and notes, as well as correspondence with such noted American figures as the suffragist Susan B. Anthony, the publisher William Randolph Hearst, and the First Lady Ida D. McKinley. These valuable papers, described as probably the largest single collection by a leading nineteenth-century woman, are now stored by the church in vaults around Boston. They will soon be available in a new Mary Baker Eddy Library for the Betterment of Humanity, to be constructed on the grounds of the church's international headquarters in Boston.

Mrs. Eddy spent the last three years of her life, from 1907 to 1910, in her home in the Boston suburb of Chestnut Hill. From this home she founded the *Christian Science Monitor*, a newspaper of remarkable objectivity at a time when most publications were engaged in sensational journalism. In the paper's first editorial in 1908, she wrote that the "object of the *Monitor* is to injure no man, but to bless all mankind," an approach to news that has earned the newspaper six Pulitzer Prizes. Mary Baker Eddy was inducted into the National Women's Hall of Fame, cited for making "an indelible mark on society, religion, and journalism."

¶ JOHN ELIOT

The Massachusetts Bay Company prescribed many objectives for its stockholders, including their responsibility to "wynn and incite the natives of the country, to the knowledg and obedience of the onlie true God and Saviour of mankinde." This commitment was integrated into the colony's Great Seal, showing an Indian, holding a bow and arrow, speaking the prayer of the man of Macedonia to St. Paul: "Come over and help us."

One of the major obstacles to Christian conversion, however, was the language barrier. Signs and gestures were satisfactory for the conduct of trade between natives and colonists, but something more substantial was needed for preaching and teaching. Into this vacuum stepped a humble scholar named John Eliot. Born in the village of Widford, Herts., he attended Cambridge University, where he studied the ancient languages and in 1622 received his B.A. from Jesus College. In 1631 Eliot emigrated to New England, first accepting a temporary position at the Boston church, and then moving to Roxbury ("Rocksborough") to become pastor to a group of friends who had arrived from England. A year later he married one of these followers, Anne Mumford, by whom he had six children and with whom he enjoyed a long and happy family life. Although John had not been ordained, he remained in Roxbury as something of a "country parson," delivering simple sermons and taking great pleasure in his pastoral duties.

In the aftermath of the short-lived Pequot War that broke out in 1636, John Eliot became interested in the Indians of the region. Working with recent captives, he used his linguistic training to master the local Algonkian dialect and decipher its grammatical intricacies. In the fall of 1646 he visited a native village called Nonantum, on the Newton side of the Charles River, and preached for an hour and a quarter in the Indian language. Afterward he distributed apples and biscuits to the children and tobacco to the men, giving him a further opportunity to talk with his potential converts. In preaching Christianity, Eliot also emphasized the importance of civilization. Indians, he said, should conduct themselves in an "orderly" manner; they should confine themselves to their own self-governing villages; they should take up more productive forms of agriculture and learn such useful trades as carpentry and blacksmithing. To put these principles into practice, Eliot established a community of "praying Indians," organized along the strict theocratic lines of the Bible. By 1675, according to one contemporary observer, there were seven praying Indian villages in the Bay Colony, with some eleven hundred souls "yielding obedience to the Gospel." The seven towns stretched in an arc from the Merrimack River to the Connecticut border.

Reading the Bible was central to the Puritan faith, so it was essential that the praying Indians learn their letters. There was one problem, however: the Bible had not yet been translated into the Indian tongue, known as Massachusett. This was an oversight that John Eliot was determined to correct; as early as 1650 he began translating the Bible into a language that had never before appeared in written form. Working alone, without assistance, and receiving only occasional financial assistance from the England-based Corporation for the Promoting and Propagating the Gospel of Jesus Christ in New England, he devoted the rest of his life to this missionary labor. In 1658 he reported that he had completed his translation of the Bible, and persuaded the Society to send a man to help the operator print the book on the small hand press at Harvard College. In 1660 the actual printing process began, and within a year the New Testament was done. Forty presentation copies went to the Society in England; two hundred were distributed to Eliot's Indians. By 1663 the entire Bible had been completed—1200 printed pages, dedicated to King Charles II. The decade of the appearance of the Bible was what Samuel Eliot Morison described as "Eliot's harvest." More Indian books came off the Cambridge press, the number of converts increased, and there were signs that a dubious public was becoming reconciled to the parson's optimistic views about the natives. Then came the great tragedy that destroyed everything Eliot had worked for.

In 1675, under the leadership of a Wampanoag chief called King Philip, Indians attacked English settlements in an effort to save their lands. Although the warring Indians did not come from the ranks of converts, the Boston settlers turned against Eliot's praying Indians, whom they regarded as "the enemy in our midst." The peaceful Indians were rounded up, interned on Deer Island in Boston Harbor, and later sold into slavery. The Christian experiment had failed: most of the praying Indians were gone forever, and many original copies of the Indian Bible were destroyed. Even before King Philip's War was over, however, John Eliot, now seventy-five, was back at work, turning out a second edition of the New Testament in 1680, and the whole Bible in 1685. He never gave up his hopes and his visions, and he kept working until 1690 when advanced age and debilitating illness brought him to his bed, surrounded by family members, neighbors, and friends. This "Apostle to the Indians" was certainly an eminent figure in early Boston history, not merely in what he accomplished, but in his implacable determination to accomplish it.

❦ RALPH WALDO EMERSON

Drawing upon the social, intellectual, and theological traditions of the past, Ralph Waldo Emerson became the charismatic leader of a number of young scholars and intellectuals who sought to create a new metaphysics for America. Widely hailed as "the New England Prophet," Emerson developed ideas about God, man, nature, and art that went far toward defining the faith and philosophy of the movement known as Transcendentalism, which promoted American democracy and the distinctiveness of the American mind.

Born in the heart of Boston in 1803, Ralph Waldo Emerson belonged to one of the town's oldest learned families. After graduating from the Boston Latin School and Harvard College (in 1821), he taught school before entering the Harvard Divinity School and being ordained to the ministry. Emerson was named minister of the Second Church of Boston in 1829 and held this position until 1832, when he professed he could no longer find the kind of spiritual and creative vigor in what he referred to as the "corpse-cold Unitarianism of Brattle Street."

After his break with the ministry, Emerson began to devote himself to a life of philosophy, developing a theory of the "oversoul" in a mystical union with God. He embarked on a journey to Italy, Scotland, and England, where he met Coleridge, Wordsworth, Carlyle, Kant, Schiller, Goethe, and other leading European intellectuals. Their idealistic philosophies influenced his first essay, "Nature" (1836), in which he declared that nature was man's greatest teacher. Back in America, Emerson took up a career as a lecturer. Tall, exceedingly thin, with piercing blue eyes and smiling curved lips, he spoke from the podium with a "tranquil authority" that captivated his listeners. In 1837, at Harvard College, he delivered his Phi Beta Kappa address, titled "The American Scholar," urging American scholars to stop imitating the "courtly muses of Europe" and derive their inspiration from those sources of beauty right around them.

Oliver Wendell Holmes called this eloquent address "our intellectual Declaration of Independence."

Meanwhile, Emerson had moved to Concord, where he could write, observe the beauties of nature, and enjoy the company of friends like Theodore Parker, Henry David Thoreau, Bronson Alcott, James Freeman Clarke, and Margaret Fuller. Together they formed the Transcendental Club, an informal group whose main purpose was to discuss German philosophy and current literary trends. In 1840 Emerson became a regular contributor to the well-known Transcendentalist journal *The Dial,* and in 1842 he became its editor. In 1847 he once again journeyed to England on a lecture tour, and now found himself regarded as one of the literary notables of the day. When he returned home, he traveled the lecture circuit, published books of poetry, and formed a monthly discussion group in Boston known as the Saturday Club.

Strongly opposed to slavery, but totally committed to the concept of untrammeled individualism, Emerson at first had difficulty supporting the aggressive methods of the abolitionists. By the 1850s, however, after the Fugitive Slave Act and the violence in Kansas, Emerson joined the ranks of the antislavery forces, and in 1859 declared that John Brown had made the gallows "glorious like the cross." With the coming of the Civil War, Emerson reached what was perhaps his most dramatic moment on New Year's Day, 1863, when a huge crowd gathered in the Boston Music Hall to await word of President Lincoln's signing of the Emancipation Proclamation. When the news finally arrived and the cheering had died down, the sixty-year-old Sage of Concord stepped to the rostrum and delivered the stirring words of "The Boston Hymn," which he had written for the occasion, calling upon trumpets to sound out everywhere to celebrate the freedom of the slaves. Only a few months later, in a moving poem called "Voluntaries," commemorating the young soldiers who had fallen in the war, Emerson especially addressed the unselfish sacrifice of Colonel Robert Gould Shaw, who had died leading his all-black 54th Regiment into battle: "When Duty whispers low, *thou must,* / The youth replies, *I can.*"

Ralph Waldo Emerson lived for twenty more years, dying in his beloved Concord at the age of eighty, but the best of his work was behind him. He remained, however, a truly eminent personage, one everyone seemed to know and many had heard lecture, and who was owed a great debt by most major literary and intellectual figures of the era for the unique inspiration he had provided for their lives and their works.

¶ EDWARD EVERETT

There are very few Bostonians who have held as many prestigious public positions: Congressman, governor, ambassador, college president, Secretary of State, United States Senator. An educator, statesman, and orator, Edward Everett was perhaps the outstanding nineteenth-century example of the ideal scholar-statesman in the best classical tradition.

Born in Dorchester, Mass., in 1794, the son of a minister, Edward Everett attended Harvard College, where he was highly praised for his school orations and was considered the brightest student who had ever passed through that institution. After graduating from Harvard in 1811, he accompanied his friend George Ticknor on their *Wanderjahre* to Germany to meet the Continental scholars of the day. They spent nearly two years at the University of Göttingen, following a demanding schedule of studies that stretched from early morning until well into the evening. Returning to America, Ticknor became the father of modern-language studies at Harvard, while Everett accepted a chair as Professor of Greek, and gave a new impulse to the study of Greek mythology and letters.

The college classroom did not prove large enough to contain Everett's ambitions, however, as the young prodigy looked for a wider audience in the field of American politics. Elected to the U.S. House of Representatives in 1825, he spent the next ten years espousing conservative principles, supporting the commercial interests of his state, and trying to hold back the tide of Jacksonian Democracy.

He was a staunch Unionist, echoing the appeal for the Constitution and the Union enunciated so passionately by Senator Daniel Webster in his Second Reply to Senator Hayne of South Carolina in 1830 at the height of the Nullification conflict.

After President Martin Van Buren took office, Everett returned to Boston, where he was elected to serve as Governor of Massachusetts from 1836 to 1839. During the administration of the Whig president William Henry Harrison, when Daniel Webster was Secretary of State, Everett was appointed Minister to the Court of St. James's, residing in London from 1841 to 1845. Upon his return to America, he was appointed president of Harvard College, where he served from 1846 to 1849, until he was called to Washington to succeed Daniel Webster as Secretary of State in the cabinet of President Millard Fillmore. At the end of his service, he returned to Boston and was elected by the voters of Massachusetts in 1853 to a seat in the United States Senate, but voluntarily resigned his post only one year later, after refusing to take a stand on the controversial Kansas-Nebraska Act.

Still committed to preserving the Union at all costs, Edward Everett remained in the Whig party in the hopes of providing a middle-of-the-road alternative to the Northern Republicans and the Southern Democrats. In 1860, in a vain effort to prevent a Republican victory he feared would precipitate a national crisis, he agreed to run for the office of Vice President on the Constitutional-Union ticket, but went down to defeat. After the Confederate attack on Fort Sumter in April 1861, however, Everett joined with his Whig colleagues in backing the Lincoln administration and giving unqualified support to the war effort. Throughout the four years of the Civil War, he devoted his oratorical skills to the defense of the Union, and on November 19, 1863, he delivered the principal oration at the dedication of the new cemetery at Gettysburg, sharing the platform with President Lincoln, who had been invited to attend and make "a few appropriate remarks." Everett delivered a formal two-hour address in the classical manner, evoking memories of Pericles' famous funeral oration over the ashes of the fallen Athenian warriors. Lincoln followed with a brief, simple, but beautifully crafted address that transformed the tragedy of the moment into a new birth of freedom for America. Everett certainly recognized the power in Lincoln's words, and in a note the next day, told the president that he would have been pleased if he had come as close to the central idea of the day in two hours as Lincoln had in two minutes. A gentleman to the last, Edward Everett died in 1865, at the age of seventy-one, at his home in Boston, satisfied to know that the Union had been preserved.

¶ PETER FANEUIL

Faneuil Hall is acclaimed as a national treasure, and has gone down in history books as the Cradle of Liberty. But the famous structure would never have been built had it not been for the generosity of Peter Faneuil, an early example of the many ways in which immigrants have contributed to the history and culture of Boston.

Benjamin and André Faneuil were brothers, French Protestants known as Huguenots, who emigrated to Boston in 1686 from the French town of La Rochelle by way of Holland. Benjamin moved to New York, while André remained in Boston, joined a group of wealthy merchants, and began the firm of Faneuil and Company. His seven-acre property on Tremont Street was just north of Beacon Street. On it he built a house in 1711 that was said to have cost £4,000, and was described as the "most attractive private mansion then in the Town." Spacious and beautifully decorated, it was constructed from white-painted brick, with a semicircular balcony over the central front door. Since the house was on a hillside, there were steps to the front door and terraced gardens at the rear. Upon André's death in 1738, the large fortune he had amassed passed to his nephew, Peter Faneuil.

Peter was the eldest child of Anne Bureau and Benjamin Faneuil. Born on June 20, 1700, and presented in baptism by his mother and by Claude Baudoin, he grew up in New York. There were eleven children in the family, nine of them girls; after Benjamin's death his brother André adopted his two sons, Peter and young Benjamin, and a daughter. Benjamin fell out of favor with his uncle when he married against his wishes, and Peter became André's favorite nephew and heir.

Peter Faneuil proved to be an enterprising merchant in his own right, and from his estate on Tremont Street operated a business that, according to the maritime historian William M. Fowler, Jr., "spanned the Atlantic world," trading with the West Indies, the Canary Islands, Spain, and England. His warehouses were located at what is now State Street, on the lower end near Merchants Row. By the time he was forty-two, Peter Faneuil was viewed as the "most conspicuous figure in business and the social life of Boston." He was a "high-liver," known for his good kitchen and ample wine cellar. He loved to ride about town in his fine carriage, with the family coat of arms emblazoned on the side, drawn by a pair of matched horses and attended by footmen. He was also an extremely charitable person and lavish in his gifts to the community. John Lovell, the master of the Boston Latin School, observed that Faneuil followed the Biblical injunction to feed the hungry, clothe the naked, and comfort the fatherless and the widows in their affliction.

Like so many of his Huguenot neighbors, Peter Faneuil deeply appreciated the various ways in which Bostonians had extended the hand of friendship and fellowship. "Let us never forget," wrote Andrew Le Mercier, "how we have happily fled from Persecution, found acceptance before the People of this Land; how, when we were strangers, they have taken us in; how several have contributed towards the building of our Place of Worship . . ." In repayment, Faneuil offered to provide Boston with a central marketplace where the residents of the town could buy their produce, instead of having to depend on itinerant peddlers or suburban farmers. If the town would donate a piece of land, he proposed to build, at his own expense, a market building near the town dock.

Not everyone agreed to the need for a central market, however, and to his surprise Faneuil faced considerable resistance to his plan when the issue came up at a special town meeting on July 14, 1740.

When the Town House proved too small to hold everyone who wanted to attend the meeting, it adjourned to the Brattle Street Church, where the debate was fierce and prolonged. Even when Faneuil offered to add a public meeting hall designed to seat a thousand people, the opposition still persisted. Finally a vote was taken, and Faneuil's offer was accepted by a vote of 367 to 360—passed by the slim margin of only seven votes.

Faneuil commissioned his friend John Smibert, a portrait painter, to design the market building. It was a two-story brick structure that took two years to complete. Faneuil Hall opened its doors in September 1742, only six months before Peter Faneuil himself died and was laid to rest in the Old Granary Burying Ground on Tremont Street. His eulogy was delivered by Master John Lovell in the hall he had donated to the town: "Peter Faneuil was the owner of a large and plentiful estate," he said. "No man managed his affairs with greater prudence and industry." The name of this man so prominent in the history of Boston, however, was, and continues to be, misspelled and mispronounced: his monument in the Old Granary Burying Ground had the inscription: "P. Funel, 1742."

❦ FANNIE FARMER

Whether it was Thanksgiving or Christmas, Mother's Day or Father's Day, a birthday, an anniversary, or a date with a new girlfriend, a box of Fanny Farmer Chocolates was sure to be in evidence. The bright yellow box was a staple in the East Coast market from the 1920s, especially since the name had such a familiar ring. Actually, the trade name "Fanny Farmer" was first introduced in 1919 by a Chicago confectioner named Frank O'Connor, who adapted it from the name of Fannie Merritt Farmer, a well-known Boston figure who had been the leading authority on cooking in her day.

Fannie Merritt Farmer, born in 1857, was the eldest daughter of a father who was an editor and printer, and a mother who was described as a "notable housewife." While a junior at Medford High School, near Boston, Fannie suffered the first in a series of medical episodes that left her permanently disabled. Confined to her home, where she helped her mother keep house, Fannie took a special interest in cooking. She soon turned her mother's home into a boarding house that attracted well-paying customers who were impressed by the excellence of the meals that were served. At the age of thirty, Fannie enrolled in the Boston Cooking School; after graduation she was kept on as assistant to the director. When the director died two years later, Fannie Farmer was elected director of the school.

When Fannie was learning to cook, instruction consisted of simple home recipes that called for a "pinch" of this and a "dash" of that. As her interest in the history of cooking grew, Fannie was struck by the fact that there was no scientific approach to the preparation of food, and no adequate textbook to instruct either the novice or the specialist. In 1896, at the age of thirty-nine, Fannie Farmer put together a cookbook of her own, introducing the idea of standard measuring spoons and cups and level measurements, and persuaded a dubious Boston publishing house to print three thousand copies of the book at her own expense. The enterprise proved to be an astounding success, and in future years literally millions of copies of *The Boston Cooking School Cook Book* were sold to a receptive public.

In addition to being a successful author, Fannie Farmer was also a popular public speaker whose lectures on cooking drew audiences of hundreds of cooks, chefs, and housewives. Her lectures were regularly reprinted in the *Boston Evening Transcript* and picked up by other newspapers all over the country, establishing the national reputation of Fannie Farmer as a leading authority in the field. Undoubtedly because of her own disability, Fannie paid particular attention to the preparation of food for sick people, hospitalized patients, and invalids. She often lectured to nurses and dieticians, and one year was invited to give a course on dietary preparations at the Harvard Medical School.

Fannie Farmer spent the last seven years of her life in a wheelchair, continuing to write and to speak about the subject of cooking and giving her last lecture just ten days before she died in 1915 at the age of fifty-eight.

❧ ARTHUR FIEDLER

Many Bostonians can still recall the exciting summer of 1976, when the city celebrated the 200th anniversary of the independence of the United States. The breathtaking arrival of the Tall Ships in full sail was followed by the visit of Queen Elizabeth II of England. Events reached their climax with the Fourth of July concert on the Charles River Esplanade, when Arthur Fiedler conducted a concert at the Hatch Shell for an audience of 400,000, as the bells of the city rang out and fireworks illuminated the summer skies. Almost overnight, the conductor became a national figure.

Arthur Fiedler was born December 17, 1894, in Boston, the son of Austrian parents. As a child he studied music under the tutelage of his father, and then from 1911 to 1915 attended the Royal Academy of Music in London, where he studied violin, piano, and conducting. Upon graduation, he joined the Boston Symphony Orchestra as a violist, although he would also play the violin and piano. Fiedler's primary interest, however, was in the art of conducting, and he soon developed an interest in a musical organization known as the Pops. Back in 1885, a series of "Promenade Concerts" were held in the Boston Music Hall (later Loew's Orpheum Theater) off Washington Street, the original home of the Boston Symphony Orchestra, with Adolph Neuendorff as its first conductor. In 1900, when the orchestra moved to its present location at Symphony Hall on Massachusetts Avenue, the Promenade Concerts became the Symphony Hall Pops, and after that simply the Boston Pops.

In 1926, after he was turned down for the conductorship of the Pops, Fiedler established a chamber orchestra called the Boston Sinfonietta, with members drawn from the Boston Symphony. His eagerness to entertain audiences and bring music to people who might not otherwise be attracted to a classical repertoire led him to organize the Esplanade Concerts in 1929, a series of free outdoor concerts held during the summer months along the east bank of the Charles River. The following year he became the first American conductor of the Boston Pops Orchestra, a position he would hold for fifty seasons. Drawing on the talents of the Pops musicians, mostly members of the Boston Symphony Orchestra, Fiedler was able to present popular music and even jazz in a symphonic orchestral setting, along with the lighter end of the classical repertoire. Fiedler's principal aim was "to give audiences a good time." With the Boston Pops Orchestra, Arthur Fiedler would achieve record album sales of around fifty million copies—becoming the best-selling classical artist of all time. Local radio broadcasts of the Boston Pops concerts began in 1952; the concerts were nationally syndicated each week from 1962 to 1992, and in 1970 the national public television program *Evening at Pops* was officially launched.

Over the years Fiedler became a highly visible and charismatic personality around Boston. To the general public, Fiedler presented an image that was warm and friendly—a kindly Santa Claus with his great shock of white hair, his twinkling eyes, and his expressive face. He was a natural showman who played to his audiences, whether it was on the podium at Symphony Hall or perched atop a fire engine driving through the streets of Boston with his fire-chief's helmet on his head. But the public image of Arthur Fiedler as a lovable and compassionate figure did not always coincide with the reality of his crusty and cantankerous personality. He was "the most insecure, suspicious man I ever knew, as well as the stingiest," recalled Harry Ellis Dickson, who spent many years as Fiedler's assistant. The maestro showed very little personal warmth toward anyone "except his dog," wrote Dickson.

Despite these foibles and eccentricities—or perhaps because of them—Arthur Fiedler remained a favorite with the people of Boston, drawing huge crowds of admirers whenever he appeared at public functions and ceremonies and receiving the city's Medal of Freedom in 1977. After his death on July 19, 1979, at the age of eighty-five, the Pops continued to flourish under the baton of John Williams, a very successful film composer. Keith Lockhart was appointed conductor in 1995, at the age of thirty-five, the same age as Arthur Fiedler when he began his historic tenure with one of Boston's most enduring and beloved musical organizations.

¶ JOHN F. FITZGERALD

When young Jack Kennedy decided to go into politics in the fall of 1945, he found that his long absence from Boston had made him "a stranger in the city of his birth." Indeed, the only person he knew in Boston, he later recalled jokingly, was his eighty-two-year-old grandfather, John F. Fitzgerald, a former mayor of the city. It was old "Honey Fitz" who regaled the young man with stories about the early political history of Boston, and who personally guided his tall grandson through the narrow streets of the North End where, for so long, he had wielded remarkable political power.

John Francis Fitzgerald was born February 12, 1863, in a small wooden tenement in Boston's North End. His father was an immigrant from Ireland who owned a small grocery and package store, where he sold food products by day and operated a popular saloon by night. Young John, who was bright and competitive, graduated from the Boston Latin School and was admitted to Harvard Medical School without examination because of his excellent academic record. The sudden death of his father in 1885 forced the young man to leave school and go to work to help his mother keep the family together.

The North End's ward boss, Matthew Keany, took a liking to young Fitzgerald and trained him in the ways of local politics; when Keany died suddenly in 1892, the twenty-nine-year-old Fitzgerald took over as the new boss of Ward 6. After winning a seat in the state Senate, where he became one of the youngest senators on Beacon Hill, in November 1894 he ran a successful campaign for the U.S.

House of Representatives from the Ninth Congressional District. On September 14, 1905, the popular Irish-born mayor of Boston, Patrick Collins, died suddenly while on vacation, and almost immediately Fitzgerald announced himself a candidate for the vacant position. Despite angry protests from many of the other ward bosses, Fitzgerald barnstormed the city, giving rousing speeches that ended with a mellifluous rendition of "Sweet Adeline," which earned him the sobriquet of "Honey Fitz."

John F. Fitzgerald won the election and was sworn into office on January 1, 1906, promising to create a "bigger, better, busier Boston." Despite his assurances of a "businesslike administration," his City Hall office on School Street was crowded with cronies, lobbyists, contractors, and office-seekers of all kinds, leading Republican critics and Good Government reformers to charge the Fitzgerald administration with graft and corruption. Denouncing the "evils of Fitzgeraldism," in November 1908 the Republicans succeeded in electing George Albee Hubbard as mayor of Boston.

Having removed Fitzgerald from office, the reformers changed the City Charter to make sure that he would not return. They abolished the eight-man Board of Aldermen; they reduced the forty-eight-man Common Council to a nine-member City Council; and they increased the power of the mayor by giving him a four-year term. James Jackson Storrow, a successful Republican banker and impeccable public servant, was put forth as the first in a line of modern executives. Fitzgerald, however, upset all the predictions. Calling for "Manhood against Money," and launching a whirlwind campaign that brought him into every ward in the city, Fitzgerald defeated Storrow in the 1910 campaign and became the first mayor to hold a four-year term.

The only hope the Yankees had left was that when Fitzgerald finished his term in 1914, he would retire to the suburbs and leave the office to some deserving Republican. It came as a complete surprise, therefore, when James Michael Curley, another Boston-born Irish politician, announced his intention to succeed Fitzgerald. When Fitzgerald showed signs of changing his mind and running for another term, Curley cleverly let it be known that he was planning a series of public lectures. One of these, titled "Great Lovers, from Cleopatra to Toodles," was a thinly veiled reference to Fitzgerald's well-known dalliance with a twenty-three-year-old cigarette girl known as "Toodles" Ryan. Deciding that discretion was the better part of valor, Fitzgerald pleaded "ill health" and quietly withdrew from the campaign.

Although John F. Fitzgerald made several attempts at a political comeback during the 1920s and 1930s, he never again won an election. Until his death on October 3, 1950, at the age of 87, however, he continued to be a beloved elder statesman in the Boston political community, and was destined to have an influence on American political history far beyond his own achievements. As the result of the marriage of his daughter, Rose, to Joseph P. Kennedy, the son of Patrick J. Kennedy, his political counterpart in East Boston, "Honey Fitz" became grandfather to a President of the United States (John Fitzgerald Kennedy); an Attorney General and U.S. Senator from New York (Robert F. Kennedy); and a U.S. Senator from Massachusetts (Edward M. Kennedy).

❡ JOHN BERNARD FITZPATRICK

The man who served as Roman Catholic bishop of Boston during the turbulent years between 1846 and 1866 was in a position either to fan the flames of religious hatred or use his considerable influence to calm fears and resolve difficulties. Bishop John Fitzpatrick's role in contributing to a peaceful transition during those trying times was of critical importance both to the history of the city and to the welfare of its citizens.

John Bernard Fitzpatrick was born in Boston on November 15, 1812, one of five children. His Irish immigrant father, Bernard, operated a tailor shop; his mother, Eleanor, had been born in Boston, and her father, James Flinn, had fought in a Massachusetts regiment during the Revolutionary War. John was educated at the Boston

Latin School along with the bright sons of the Brahmin establishment, which allowed him to move easily in their circles and later
serve as a bridge between them and the members of his own Irish
Catholic community. He attended seminary in Montreal and Paris,
and was ordained to the priesthood in June 1840.

The young priest returned to Boston, where only three years later
he was appointed coadjutor bishop with the right of succession.
When Bishop Fenwick died in 1846, the thirty-four-year-old Fitzpatrick became the third bishop of Boston, much to the approval of
native Bostonians, who regarded him as a person of learning and
culture. "Although two-thirds of the city are Protestants," reported a
French priest to his superiors with some apparent surprise, "Bostonians are proud to designate the new Bishop a countryman of their
own."

Fitzpatrick had hardly settled into his new post when the great
potato famine sent thousands of impoverished Irish Catholic immigrants flooding into Boston. Throughout his twenty years as bishop,
Fitzpatrick worked to prevent outbreaks of violence between hostile
nativist groups and resentful Catholic immigrants. Even with the
formation in 1854 of the openly anti-Catholic American Party—
popularly known as the Know-Nothing Party—Fitzpatrick cau-
tioned the members of his flock to obey the laws, express their views
through the ballot box, and avoid physical confrontation, as he resorted to the courts to guarantee the constitutional rights of Catholics as American citizens.

Despite the diocese's limited funds and impoverished population,
Fitzpatrick was eventually responsible for the construction of at least
seventy new churches throughout Boston. He also enlarged the facilities of St. Vincent's Orphan Asylum and created the House of the
Angel Guardian for homeless boys. He helped restore the College of
the Holy Cross in Worcester after a disastrous fire in 1852, and saw
his dream of a "college in the city" for the sons of immigrant families
realized with the opening of Boston College in the city's South End
in 1863.

In 1862, after the outbreak of the Civil War, in spite of deteriorating health, Fitzpatrick traveled to Belgium, where he served in an

unofficial capacity as a spokesman for the Union cause. Returning to Boston in August 1864, he had his friend, Rev. John J. Williams, appointed as his successor, and on February 13, 1866, Bishop John Fitzpatrick quietly passed away. He was originally buried in the small cemetery chapel of St. Augustine in South Boston, but his remains were later moved to the new Cathedral of the Holy Cross in the South End.

Bishop Fitzpatrick had been uniquely qualified to bridge the dangerous gulf that separated the city's two disparate communities. Highly regarded by the Protestant community as a distinguished clergymen and learned scholar, he was a welcome guest at private homes, a member of the Boston Athenaeum, and a charter member of the exclusive Thursday Evening Club. At the same time, he was fondly regarded as "Bishop John" by the members of his Catholic congregation, who looked to him for guidance and direction at a time when they were powerless and rejected. His loss, therefore, was felt throughout the entire Boston community, eliciting sincere tributes from leaders of every denomination in the city—something in which Fitzpatrick would have taken much satisfaction. He was, after all, as one of his curates remarked, "a true patriot of the Yankee sort."

❧ DOUG FLUTIE

In the history of Boston sports, there are certain exciting moments that can never be repeated or forgotten. Celtics fans can still hear the voice of the announcer Johnny Most screaming "He stole the ball! Havlicek stole the ball!" as the Celtic forward stole the ball from Hal Greer in the closing seconds of the seventh game with the Philadelphia 76ers during the 1965 Eastern Conference finals. Bruins fans will never forget Bobby Orr flying through the air after scoring the winning goal in overtime against the St. Louis Blues in the Stanley Cup finals in May 1970. The Red Sox catcher Carlton Fisk's home run off the Cincinnati Red's Pat Darcy in the twelfth inning of the sixth game of the 1975 World Series is still replayed as one of the great moments in baseball. And in college football in the last twenty-five years, nothing has eclipsed the last-minute breathtaking "Hail Mary" pass that Boston College's Doug Flutie threw to Gerald Phelan to defeat the University of Miami in the final game of the 1984 season.

Doug Flutie arrived at Boston College in 1981 after a successful career as a quarterback at Natick High School. Although he had received attractive offers from other colleges who wanted him as a defensive back, he was assured by Coach Jack Bicknell that Boston College would give him a full shot. Not much was expected of the relatively undersized five-foot-ten-inch young quarterback, who sat on the bench until he was sent in as a substitute in a losing effort against Penn State and raked Joe Paterno's defense for 135 passing yards and a touchdown. Flutie quickly became Bicknell's starting quarterback, and with his uncanny accuracy as a passer and great agility as a scrambling runner, he energized the football team, and led Boston College to a 30-11-1 overall record and three post-season bowls—the school's first post-season play in forty years. He was the game MVP of the Tangerine Bowl in his sophomore year against Auburn and in the Liberty Bowl in his junior year against Notre Dame. During his senior year in 1984, with his fabled "Hail Mary" pass against Miami capping a 9-2 season, followed by a 45-28 victory over the University of Houston in the Cotton Bowl, Doug Flutie became the first player in B.C. history to win college football's greatest individual award, the Heisman Trophy. That year he also won the Davey O'Brien National Quarterback Award, as well as the Maxwell Award, given to the nation's outstanding college football player. Doug Flutie's heroics on the gridiron put Boston College football back on the national sports scene for the first time since Frank Leahy led the Eagles to the 1941 Sugar Bowl. The young quarterback's nationally televised success generated million of dollars in income for the Jesuit university as well as promoting applications for admission from one end of the country to the other.

Following his dramatic college career at Boston College, Flutie made headlines with his mega-contract with the New Jersey Generals of the short-lived USFL. Then, after brief stints with the

Chicago Bears and the New England Patriots, in 1990 Flutie moved to the Canadian Football League, where he flourished as no other player had in the history of the league. He captured the league's MVP award six times, led the league in passing five times, and won Gray Cup titles with the Calgary Stampeders in 1992 and the Toronto Argonauts in 1996 and 1997.

In 1998 Flutie returned to the United States and rejoined the NFL as a backup quarterback with the Buffalo Bills. When the first-string quarterback Rob Johnson was injured, Flutie took over five games into the season and directed the Bills to a 7-3 record and a playoff berth in ten starts. His performance that year earned him the NFL Comeback Player of the Year Award and a trip to the Pro Bowl. When the Buffalo Bills decided to bring back Johnson as their first-string quarterback, Flutie signed a contract with the San Diego Chargers, and starting with the 2001 NFL season the "Little General" led that club from last place into bowl contention.

Still playing professional football well into his mid-thirties, at an age when most of his fellow players have gone into retirement, Doug Flutie works out regularly up to four hours a day in order to stay in peak physical condition. He also devotes much of his time to generating donations for the Doug Flutie, Jr. Foundation for Autism he founded to raise awareness and develop support for those affected by the disorder with which his son has been diagnosed. Flutie continues to maintain a residence in his hometown of Natick, which has named a street in his honor, appropriately, "Flutie Pass." His ability and vitality both on the field and off bring back the words of his Natick High School coach when recommending him to Jack Bicknell for a scholarship at Boston College: "He's small, but he's great!"

¶ JOHN MURRAY FORBES

At the height of the terrible potato famine in Ireland, John Murray Forbes, a successful China merchant, suggested that his older brother, Robert, petition Congress for the loan of a warship to take provisions from Boston to the starving people of Ireland. On April 11, 1847, the *Jamestown* put into Cork Harbor, carrying 800 tons of grain, meal, potatoes, and clothing, while throngs on the shore cheered their American benefactors and a band played "Yankee Doodle."

Born in 1813, in Bordeaux, France, John Murray Forbes was the son of a prominent lawyer and diplomat who served as President John Quincy Adams's most trusted agent in South America. Young Forbes began his own financial career in the lucrative China trade, but became increasingly involved in the construction of railroads. Along with other investors, he bought and completed the Michigan Central Railroad, and later financed roads which eventually became the Chicago, Burlington & Quincy, as well as the Hannibal & St. Joseph lines.

After 1854 John Murray Forbes became one of the first conservative Whigs to join the new Republican party in support of its antislavery platform. Forbes did not oppose the expansion of slavery so much on moral grounds as to prevent the slaveholding states from controlling the Congress. During the secession winter of 1860–61, Forbes tried to work out a compromise solution to the national crisis, but once the first shots were fired at Fort Sumter, he became an ardent supporter of President Lincoln and a strong voice for an "overpowering" use of force to end the war. Appointed to Governor John Andrew's war council, Forbes helped to make arrangements for transporting Massachusetts troops to Washington, D.C., by land and by water to protect the nation's capital. Throughout the war's early months, Forbes worked strenuously, buying steamers for transports, securing cannon from the Navy Yard to arm them, and engaging crews to man them.

Forbes continued to be active throughout the war in many different capacities. He took part in the Boston Education Commission, which was charged with educating former slaves on the liberated Sea Islands along the South Carolina coast. He himself went along to observe at firsthand the results of the experiment to instill both the Protestant work ethic and the "Boston style" of education to reform the minds and mold the character of the newly freed slaves so that they would be able to produce cotton under a free-labor system. Forbes also put together his own committee of twenty local business-men, lawyers, ministers, and physicians to form a Boston branch of the U.S. Sanitary Commission, for which he devoted much of his time to raising funds. And in order to protest what he felt was a rather lukewarm support for President Lincoln and the war effort among the members of the local business community, he helped form the Union Club on Park Street as a meeting place for those gentlemen of the city who wanted to demonstrate "unwavering sup-port of the federal government in suppressing the rebellion." He supported Lincoln's Emancipation Proclamation, which went into effect in January 1863, and subsequently became active in helping Governor Andrew create the all-black 54th and 55th infantry regi-ments.

In the spring of 1863 John Murray Forbes traveled to England, ostensibly to work out American loans with British banks, but in re-ality to buy up vessels that were being constructed for the Confeder-ates. Although word got out about the real intention of his visit, Forbes continued to work for the Union cause by meeting with po-litical leaders, writers, and intellectuals, and influencing public opin-ion by writing articles for the British newspapers. The Confederate defeats at the battles of Gettysburg and Vicksburg in July of 1863 greatly reduced the fear of British intervention and allowed Forbes to return to the United States. In September, however, he was back in England, this time using his expertise and personal contacts to purchase heavy coastal guns to improve the defensive fortifications in Boston Harbor and along the Atlantic coast.

Once the war was over, John Murray Forbes returned to his rail-road enterprises, where he brought into the expanding business sound methods of management and finance, as well as an enlight-ened view of the relationship of railroad transportation to the public interest. He also continued his involvement in the Republican party, serving as a member of the Republican national executive committee until his death in 1898 at the age of eighty-five.

↳ John F. Fitzgerald

↳ John
Murray
Forbes

Isabella
Stewart
Gardner

William
Lloyd
Garrison

¶ GEORGE FRAZIER

He was an Irish Catholic kid from South Boston who assumed the image of a Back Bay Brahmin, complete with a pink Brooks Brothers shirt and a carnation in the buttonhole of his custom-made suit. A local Jay Gatsby, a gifted journalist who tilted with all the great arbiters of jazz, sports, fashion, and politics, George Frazier became a modern-day F. Scott Fitzgerald, boozing to the point where he hallucinated little men, and smoking to the day when his lungs couldn't take it any longer. "George was like James Michael Curley or Richard Cardinal Cushing," his brother Andrew once said. "You either loved him or you hated him, but you sure did know all about him, and you always had an opinion about him."

George Frazier was born on June 10, 1911, in the City Point section of South Boston. He went to semipro twilight-league baseball games at M Street Park, played the clarinet in the Gate of Heaven band, and frequented the Boston Public Library to round out his education. At the Boston Latin School he played in the band and practiced his writing skills in the literary magazine. He went on to Harvard in the spring of 1928 and flunked out after his first year, but was readmitted the following year, after spending some time working at a downtown brokerage company. This time, Frazier was determined to succeed. He moved on campus, developed a circle of friends, and applied himself to his studies. Although he failed to get honors, his undergraduate paper was awarded the prestigious James Bowdoin Prize.

After graduating in spring 1933, Frazier did a brief stint with a small journal called *Playhouse,* while sending pieces to such popular magazines as *Vanity Fair, Collier's,* and *Mademoiselle.* But his most important forum was *Downbeat,* in which he reported on the jazz bands that played in the Boston clubs. In 1941 he married Marion Madden, a librarian from West Roxbury, and in the fall of 1942 went to New York to write for *Life* magazine. Once World War II was over, however, Frazier left *Life,* tried his hand at an unsuccessful play, and continued to write occasional magazine articles. His work habits became erratic, his drinking increased, he and "Mimsi" were divorced, and by 1955 he was heavily in debt.

In 1961 the publisher George Minot hired George Frazier to bring some excitement into the rather staid *Boston Herald.* Within months he was the most talked-about journalist in town. In his column, "Another Man's Poison," he launched irreverent attacks on local social and political figures, as well as taking on such national personalities as Frank Sinatra, Benny Goodman, and Norman Mailer. In 1963 he really came into his own when he discovered the use of the word *duende* to describe that indefinable quality that separates the truly outstanding from the merely acceptable. Robert Frost, for example, had *duende,* but not Carl Sandburg; Babe Ruth, but not Lou Gehrig; Fred Astaire, but not Gene Kelly. The flood of mail that arrived in response to these opinions convinced Frazier that he had discovered what he was looking for—a device that got everybody in the street talking about his column.

In 1963 George Frazier resigned from the *Herald,* worked briefly for the *Record American,* and then went off to New York for several years where he wrote pieces on men's fashion for *Esquire* and *Holiday* magazines. Frazier got a new lease on life in June 1969 when Tom Winship of the *Boston Globe* hired him to write a column for the "Living" page. The journalist came to life again, sharpening his *duende* pieces and taking on all kinds of sacred cows, flailing out at Johnny Carson, Milton Berle, Gloria Steinem, Spiro Agnew, and Richard Nixon, and crowing with delight in June 1973 when his name appeared on Nixon's famous "enemy list." George Frazier was once more the most controversial journalist in Boston, and Tom Winship got his boost in circulation—but at a price. Frazier was once again drinking heavily, and soon began missing his deadlines and neglecting his mail, to the point where, in September 1971, an exasperated Winship finally severed his relations with the newspaper.

Frazier returned to the *Globe* in January, apologetic and contrite, and once more assumed his onslaught against all those who did not conform to his high standards of *duende.* He was not only once again the most widely read journalist in town, but he also developed into a celebrity in his own right, appearing on a WNAC television program in Boston, becoming a media critic on the *CBS Morning News* from New York, and making appearances on the Dick Cavett and Merv Griffin shows. He was riding high when the years of constant drinking and heavy smoking caught up with him. Early in 1974 he was diagnosed with lung cancer. He was hospitalized for a short time and died on June 13, 1974, at the age of sixty-three. Even at the end, however, he could not refrain from his cutting edge of patrician wit. When he complained at one point about having to take another blood test, the nurse inquired: "Well, aren't we here because we're sick?" "No," replied George in his most precise manner, "I'm just here for the Yale game." It was that kind of remark that always had Boston readers asking one another, "Did you read Frazier's column today?"

❡ MARGARET FULLER

She was a woman in a man's world who refused to accept the inferior position assigned to females in the early nineteenth century. Intellectually brilliant, Margaret Fuller always resented the prevailing opinion that a woman's mind was either different from or inferior to that of a man. She made no attempt to disguise her conviction that she was much smarter than anyone else. "I know all the people worth knowing in America," she once told a friend, "and I find no intellect comparable to my own."

Sarah Margaret Fuller was born in Cambridgeport in 1810, the first of nine children of a schoolteacher mother and a father who was a lawyer and prominent political figure. Timothy Fuller determined to educate Margaret as a son would have been educated in those days, instructing her in the finer points of Latin and English grammar when she was as young as six. By the age of ten she was reading Virgil and Horace in the original and following a rigorous program of academic studies that denied her the opportunity to play with other children. When she went away to a girls' school, her advanced learning and precocious eccentricities set her apart from the other students.

In 1836–37 she taught in Bronson Alcott's Temple School and began lifelong friendships with the prominent literary and intellectual leaders of the period from whom she derived much of her inspiration, acknowledging a special debt to Ralph Waldo Emerson for his constant friendship and advice: "His influence," she wrote, "has been more beneficial to me than that of any American." The distinctive power of her mind was recognized by the Transcendentalists, who admired her talents as a critic and a poet, although several of them regretted the emotional insecurity that left her restless and unfulfilled. With Emerson and George Ripley, Fuller served as editor of *The Dial,* the Transcendentalist journal, and in 1839 started her famous "Conversations" with a group of women from cultivated Boston society who met regularly at Elizabeth Peabody's home. These meetings continued through the winter months, until she went to New York at the invitation of Horace Greeley to write literary criticism for the New York *Tribune,* where she won a reputation as one of the best American critics.

An outspoken feminist, in 1845 Margaret Fuller produced a significant and influential piece of scholarship called *Woman in the Nineteenth Century* that touched upon all the major issues of the woman's movement in the United States. She condemned the prevailing laws that gave men rights over their wives and their children, and called for the opening of every occupation and profession to women. Minds and souls, she said, are neither masculine nor feminine; genius, she insisted, has no sex. She demanded that women should be accepted intellectually and be allowed to advance professionally without discrimination because of their sex.

Fuller traveled to Europe in 1846, and while in England visited with Thomas Carlyle, William Wordsworth, and other notable intellectual figures. Moving on to Italy, she became passionately involved in the political struggle and met and married Giovanni Angelo, the Marchese d'Ossoli, who fought with the Republican forces. She assisted in the organization of hospital facilities and sent occasional dispatches to the *Tribune* describing the 1849 siege of Rome. When French troops marched into Rome and finally suppressed the Roman Republic in July 1849, Margaret Fuller fled to Florence with Ossoli and their year-old son, spending the winter writing a history of the Roman revolution. In May 1850 the family sailed from Leghorn for America, but all drowned when the vessel went down off Fire Island, New York.

Although Margaret Fuller passed from the American scene at the early age of forty, her influence continued to live on in the people she influenced and in the causes she supported. Her irrepressible spirit, her wide range of interests, and her energetic enthusiasm were characteristic of the age and the group with which she was identified, observes historian Alice Felt Tyler, and her "capacity for friendship is evidenced in every contemporary account of her life and work."

℣ ISABELLA STEWART GARDNER

Often referred to as "Mrs. Jack"—but never to her face—Isabella Stewart Gardner became one of Boston's most unpredictable and flamboyant citizens, whose enduring legacy to the city is a museum that displays both her refined tastes and her idiosyncratic notions. The daughter of a prosperous New York dry-goods merchant named David Stewart, in 1860 she married John Lowell Gardner, son of the last of the East India merchants, and moved to the Gardner family home in Boston, at 152 Beacon Street. With all the money she needed, Mrs. Gardner could do whatever she pleased and, indeed, she was often heard to remark, with a wave of her hand, "C'est mon plaisir," a phrase she later had engraved over the main entrance to the residence she constructed at Fenway Court.

Isabella Stewart Gardner made her mark on late nineteenth-century Boston society in three ways: as a colorful and capricious woman who bedazzled staid Boston society with her eccentricities; as a patron of the arts who discovered unusual talent; and as a connoisseur of fine art who left to Boston the results of her extraordinary good taste. At a time when most Proper Bostonians were either Unitarians or Episcopalians, Mrs. Gardner became a Buddhist for a while, before becoming a devoted High Church Episcopalian. She rode around the city in an elaborate carriage, was reported to drink beer (a scandalous accusation for a society woman), and on one occasion strolled down Tremont Street with a lion named Rex on a leash. Although she was said to be "plain of face," she was proud of her attractive figure, and in 1888 chose John Singer Sargent to paint her portrait in a black low-cut gown with a rope of pearls around her waist. This particular painting was considered to be in such questionable taste that it was withdrawn from public view until after her death.

When her two-year-old son died in 1865, Mrs. Gardner fell into a deep depression. As a cure, her husband took her on an extended visit to foreign countries. Her exposure to so many different cultural experiences stimulated her interest in the fine arts, and when she returned to Boston she made friends with members of Boston's artistic and cultural community. She patronized painters like John Singer Sargent and James McNeil Whistler, as well as writers like Henry James and Henry Adams. Mrs. Gardner also demonstrated an active interest in music. William Gericke, conductor of the Boston Symphony Orchestra, was a constant visitor, as was Tymoteusz Adamowski, first violinist of the symphony, and his colleague Charles Martin Loeffler, co-first violinist and a distinguished composer in his own right. Mrs. Gardner, however, was perhaps most conspicuous as a patron of women artists and musicians. She encouraged the work of Ruth St. Denis, a major influence in modern American dance; she supported the Australian soprano Nellie Melba; and she was influential in helping Margaret Ruthven Lang become the first woman musician to have her compositions performed by the Boston Symphony Orchestra.

When her husband Jack died in 1898, Mrs. Gardner suffered another depression, and was advised by her physician to take up a hobby. With typical enthusiasm, she threw herself into the acquisition of great works of art. With the assistance of the young art critic Bernard Berenson she acquired, among other important works, several Rembrandts, two Botticellis, two Raphaels, a Rubens, a Degas, and a Titian. While on a visit to Italy, Mrs. Gardner purchased a complete Venetian palazzo, much of which she had dismantled and shipped back to Boston. Subsequently, the sixty-year-old woman worked closely with the architect Willard T. Sears to reconstruct the palazzo, showing up daily to supervise the project. Each of the priceless works she had acquired, including Titian's *Rape of Europa*, Vermeer's *The Concert*, and Sargent's *El Jaleo*, was assigned a permanent location within the palace.

Work on the palazzo was completed in 1901, and for the next two years Mrs. Gardner arranged her collections on three floors surrounding a courtyard filled with flowering plants and trees. She opened Fenway Court on New Year's night 1903, supplying her guests with champagne and doughnuts. Thereafter, Mrs. Gardner used Fenway Court as her home, inviting the public into the galleries two weeks a year. After her death in 1924, Fenway Court (or "Mrs. Jack's Palace," as some called it) was opened as a public museum. It became a permanent tribute to "the greatest of grandes dames," as Cleveland Amory described her in his *Proper Bostonians,* a woman who "persisted in regarding herself as a sort of dedicated spirit to wake up Boston."

A sad footnote to the story of Mrs. Jack's Palace took place on March 18, 1990, when thieves made their way into Fenway Court and walked off with thirteen major works of art, valued at an estimated $200 million, including Vermeer's *The Concert,* two major Rembrandts, a beautiful work by Degas, and an oil painting by Manet. Since Mrs. Gardner's will expressly forbade any changes in the permanent location of her art pieces, only empty spaces denote the absence of these priceless works of art.

¶ WILLIAM LLOYD GARRISON

Along Boston's Commonwealth Avenue Mall, just off Dartmouth Street, there is a statue of William Lloyd Garrison. Sculpted by Olin Levi Warren and unveiled in 1886, the seated figure's relaxed pose and placid features give little indication of the violent passions this man unleashed in the heart of nineteenth-century Boston as the leader of the new and radical abolition movement.

William Lloyd Garrison was born in 1805 in the North Shore seaport town of Newburyport, Mass. Deserted by his father and abandoned by his mother by the time he was twelve years old, young Garrison worked at various jobs before becoming an apprentice in the printing trade. In 1829 he was editing a small newspaper in Vermont when he was visited by an antislavery editor from Baltimore named Benjamin Lundy, who asked the young man to become co-editor of his *Genius of Universal Emancipation*. Garrison later moved to Boston, where he became active in working for the antislavery cause, denouncing the American Colonization Society for "White-Manism" because it proposed to send slaves back to Africa.

On January 1, 1831, from a small building on Washington Street in downtown Boston, William Lloyd Garrison published the first issue of his own newspaper, *The Liberator*, which denounced slavery as a moral evil and demanded the total and immediate emancipation of slaves. The stirring words he used to describe the determination in this effort are inscribed on the base of his Commonwealth Avenue statue: "I am in earnest. I will not equivocate. I will not excuse. I will not retreat a single inch. And I will be heard." A short time later, in the basement of the African Meeting House on Beacon Hill, Garrison helped found the New England Anti-Slavery Society as the vehicle by which his goal of immediate emancipation could be achieved.

From the very start, Garrison and his followers were regarded by most Bostonians as members of a small lunatic fringe, who were perverting the natural law, defying Biblical tradition, and endangering good financial relations between the New England mill owners and the slaveholders of the South. Members of the abolition movement were subject to personal ridicule, social ostracism, and occasional violence. In 1835, Garrison himself was attacked and almost lynched when an angry mob burst into a meeting of the Boston Female Anti-Slavery Society and dragged him off to Boston Common at the end of a rope. Only the fortuitous appearance of city constables saved him from further harm.

Garrison, however, was never deterred from his moral purpose by threats or by force. Even when some of his friends and supporters suggested he adopt more moderate tactics or make political adjustments, he would never agree to the slightest compromise. He steadfastly refused to cooperate with political parties as long as they continued to function under a Constitution that sanctioned slavery. "The Constitution," as he viewed it, was "a covenant with death and an agreement with hell."

Despite his strict insistence on pacifism and nonviolence, after the 1861 attack on Fort Sumter, Garrison came out in support of President Lincoln's carefully worded call for troops—to suppress a rebellion, not to fight a war. Seeing the Civil War as a heaven-sent opportunity that would inevitably lead to the emancipation of the slaves, Garrison continued to support Lincoln patiently and loyally, even when some of his more radical colleagues, like Wendell Phillips, became critical of the President's methodical approach and deliberate pace.

With the military defeat of the Confederacy in 1865 and the subsequent passage of the Thirteenth Amendment, the freedom of the slaves finally became the law of the land. Now that his goal had at last been achieved, in May 1865 William Lloyd Garrison formally resigned as president of the American Anti-Slavery Society, and in December 1865 he published the last issue of *The Liberator*. In spite of declining health, Garrison continued to work until his death in 1879 at the age of seventy-four, laboring on behalf of the newly freed African Americans while fighting for greater equality between the races in the new nation that emerged from the Civil War.

❧ PATRICK SARSFIELD GILMORE

Thanks to Arthur Fiedler, the Pops Concerts and the annual Fourth of July concerts on the Charles River Esplanade have become a favorite part of the Boston musical scene. It was over a century ago, however, that an Irish immigrant named Patrick Gilmore first conceived of outdoor Fourth of July concerts to celebrate the nation's birthday, and designed the type of popular "promenade" concerts that would eventually become known as the Pops.

Patrick Sarsfield Gilmore was born in Ballygar, County Galway, Ireland, on December 5, 1829. He received a common education from a local schoolmaster, and was sent out to work at an early age. He served as an apprentice for seven years with a wholesale grocer, but spent every moment after his working hours developing his skills with a variety of musical instruments. By the time he was sixteen, he was a member of the Athlone Amateur Band and was already composing military marches.

In 1848, at the age of nineteen, Gilmore sailed for America, landed in Boston, and within a few weeks had become a cornet player with the Charlestown Band. A short time later he was engaged as leader of the Suffolk Band, but left to take a position as trumpeter with the Brigade Band. By the time he left Boston for three years to take a position with the Salem Band, he had made a reputation as the finest E-flat cornet player in the country. While in Salem, Gilmore conceived the idea of putting on gala Fourth of July concerts on the Boston Common, as well as a series of promenade concerts that would later be given at the Boston Music Hall. In 1858 Gilmore returned to Boston, where his projects were put into effect.

With the outbreak of the Civil War, Patrick Gilmore enlisted in the 24th Massachusetts Regiment Band and saw service in North Carolina. After the band was mustered out of service, he returned to Boston and assisted in organizing regimental bands at the direction of the War Department. Governor John A. Andrew commissioned Gilmore as Bandmaster General and Chief Musician of Massachusetts. In that capacity he recruited bands for the Department of the Gulf, a region of the occupied South that was under the command of Major-General Nathaniel Banks, a Massachusetts native; Gilmore traveled to New Orleans to direct musical organizations in the occupied city. He later returned to Boston, where he inaugurated a series of public concerts featuring prominent musical artists from both America and Europe. He was not only the first American bandmaster to conduct band arrangements of such classical composers as Mozart, Liszt, and Rossini, but he was also a composer himself. He wrote such popular works as "When Johnny Comes Marching Home," the music to "John Brown's Body," and "Seeing Nellie Home," a melody inspired by his wife, Ellen O'Neil, organist and choir director at St. Patrick's Parish in Lowell.

In 1869 Patrick Gilmore successfully produced the great National Peace Jubilee in Boston, supported by such prominent Boston financial figures as Eben Jordan, and featuring a chorus of 10,000 voices and 1,000 musical instruments, an extravaganza that attracted some 60,000 spectators daily. Three years later, he engineered the even more gigantic Music Jubilee of All Nations, staged in Copley Square, featuring a chorus of 20,000 voices, 2,000 musical instruments, and 100 Boston firemen pounding anvils during Verdi's "Anvil Chorus." Gilmore's guest during this musical extravaganza was Johann Strauss, the famous Waltz King, who composed the "Jubilee Waltz" and "Boston Dreams" for the occasion. For his creative efforts, at the end of the Jubilee the executive committee gave Gilmore a present of $50,000. In 1873 Gilmore left Boston to organize the 22nd Regiment Band, which he made the best in the country. He took the band on tour and gave highly publicized concerts before huge audiences in all the principal cities of the United States and Europe.

Gilmore's monuments are many: New York's Madison Square Garden was first called Gilmore's Garden; Gilmore Street in Quincy, Mass., is named for the "Father of the American Concert Band," as is the Patrick Sarsfield Gilmore Society. Patrick Gilmore died in St. Louis, Missouri, at the age of sixty-two in 1892, the same year a group similar to Gilmore's Band was formed by a young admirer named John Philip Sousa.

❡ EDWARD EVERETT HALE

As visitors to Boston walk from the Boston Common across Charles Street and enter the Public Garden, they are greeted by a slightly oversized statue of an elderly Boston gentleman, out for his after-noon stroll. Hat in hand, leaning heavily on his cane, Edward Everett Hale looks out onto the passing scene of his familiar city with the knowing eyes of a wise and compassionate man. He extends a rather warm and friendly welcome to the beauties of one of the city's attractive public parks.

Born in Boston in 1822, Edward Everett Hale was the son of Na-than Hale, editor of the *Daily Advertiser,* the oldest of New England daily newspapers, and the nephew of Edward Everett, perhaps the most distinguished public figure in Boston at that time. His great-uncle was the American patriot and martyr Nathan Hale, who uttered the words "I regret that I have but one life to give to my country" before he was executed by the British as a spy during the Revolutionary War.

Like many boys of his age, young Hale attended the dancing school of Lorenzo Papani, a veritable Boston institution, before going off to Harvard College, where he graduated second in his class in 1839—despite, as he mentions in his diary, being summoned be-fore the Faculty for wearing a coat of "illegal color" on a Sunday. He went on to study for the ministry and became minister to the South Congregational Church in Boston, where he served conscientiously for forty-three years, from 1856 to 1899. In 1887 the South Church united with the Hollis Street Church and built the structure at the corner of Exeter and Newbury Streets that was later occupied by the Copley Methodist Church. Hale became so identified with so many good causes that he was described by Edwin D. Mead, editor of the *New England Magazine,* as "the incarnation of the Boston spirit."

In addition to his duties as a clergyman, Edward Everett Hale also found time to turn his hand to publishing, displaying a mind that the historian Van Wyck Brooks has described as "ingenious and alert, breezy and even salty." Perhaps because his father was a news-paper publisher, as an author Hale was influenced more by the down-to-earth prose of journalists, essayists, and evangelical writers than the more cerebral musings of the literati. His later works such as *A New England Boyhood* (1893), *James Russell Lowell and His Friends* (1899), and *Memories of a Hundred Years* (1902) are fairly unimaginative but engaging observations of the society in which he lived and the many well-known personalities with whom he associated.

There were occasions, however, when Edward Everett Hale embarked on something more creative and original. One such work was "My Double, and How He Undid Me," published in the 1859 issue of the *Atlantic Monthly;* but clearly the most dramatic example of Hale's imaginative talents is "The Man without a Country," which was instantly recognized as one of the best short stories by an American author. This story tells of Philip Nolan, a U.S. Navy officer who disowned his country and expressed the hope that he would never have to see or hear about the United States again. He was punished by banishment, and as he sailed the seven seas, he was never allowed to hear the name of or read anything concerning his native country for the rest of his life, a separation he came to regret bitterly. That it was published in the 1863 issue of the *Atlantic Monthly,* at the height of the Civil War when patriotic feeling was at a pitch, undoubtedly contributed to the great emotional appeal of the story—even when the reader discovers on the last page that it is all fiction. So great did Hale's fame become throughout the nation that he was invited to serve as chaplain of the U.S. Senate from 1903 to 1909.

The statue of Edward Everett Hale at the gates of the Public Garden was unveiled in 1912, four years after his death, by his grandson, also named Edward Everett Hale, as his widow watched the ceremony from a carriage on Charles Street. "If you seek his real monument," said Mayor John F. Fitzgerald, who formally received the statue in the name of the City of Boston, "you will find it in the hearts of the poor and the oppressed." Former President William Howard Taft described Dr. Hale as a man of "irresistible personality": "His culture, his nobility, his oratory, and his disposition," said the President, "all helped to gain him a just reputation which has made every individual in this country, whether of New England or not, proud that Edward Everett Hale was an American."

❡ SARAH HALE

Current publications such as *Vogue, Harper's Bazaar,* and *Good Housekeeping,* magazines written by women for women, can trace their origins back to early nineteenth-century Boston, and to a woman named Sarah Hale. A young widow with five children and no income to speak of, Sarah Hale turned what began as a temporary job into a lifelong career as one of the most influential writers and publishers of her age, and a powerful influence in determining the role of women in American society.

Born in 1788, Sarah Buell grew up on a New Hampshire farm and in 1811 married a promising young lawyer named David Hale. Between 1815 and 1822 the couple had five children, but just a few days after the birth of the last child, David Hale died. For the next few years, the young widow eked out an existence making women's hats and doing millinery work, while developing her skills at writing. She sent articles to magazines, mailed poems to journals, entered literary contests, and in 1827 published a novel called *Northwood.* On the strength of this book, a Boston minister invited her to become the editor of a monthly magazine for women called the *Ladies' Magazine.* Hale readily accepted, and threw herself into the enterprise with such enthusiasm that within a year the publication was a success.

A magazine for women was not a new idea—there were several published in Boston during the 1820s. Most, however, were edited and published by men. They were filled with fashion plates, sentimental stories, and news items clipped from other publications. *Ladies' Magazine* was the first of its kind to be edited by a woman; it was also the first to publish its own original material. Moreover, Sarah Hale had no intention of fostering either fashion or frivolity. She was about the more serious business of "female improvement," encouraging women to develop their powers and abilities so that they would become moral and spiritual exemplars within that "woman's sphere" that was uniquely their own. Hale reassured any male readers that if women read her magazine they would become better wives, mothers, daughters, and housekeepers, thus promoting a high degree of "domestic felicity" in their homes.

As the editor of such a well-known journal, Sarah Hale went far beyond her own "sphere" to become a notable public figure. Whether in articles extolling motherhood, essays denouncing violence, poems lamenting the loss of a loved one, editorials promoting patriotism, or tracts decrying materialism, Sarah Hale continually emphasized the importance of women's education. She came out in support of public schools, academies, and seminaries for women; she saw the educated woman working from her home as a subtle force for culture and progress, having an effect not by engaging in political action or public demonstrations, but by the power of female "influence." What becomes of the world, and what becomes of mankind, Hale told her readers in 1832, depends on "the secret, silent, influence of women."

Hard hit by the effects of a financial depression, by 1836 the *Ladies' Magazine* was in such serious financial trouble that Sarah Hale consolidated it with a Philadelphia rival, *Godey's Lady's Book*. Hale remained in Boston for a few years after the merger, but in 1841 she moved to Philadelphia. *Godey's* continued to be an influential fashion magazine, expanding its illustrations of bonnets, crinolines, bustles, and hoops by using colored plates, woodcuts, and copper plates. But largely through Sarah Hale's influence, it also began to assume the characteristics of a literary periodical, with original essays, poems, and stories that attracted a large national audience. In addition to her work on the magazine during the 1840s and 1850s, Hale also wrote and edited a number of popular books for women on such subjects as etiquette, child-rearing, and housekeeping, becoming a nationally known figure to an expanding market of American female readers.

¶ JOHN HANCOCK

The Hancock family set an early example of Yankee thrift and business enterprise. During the eighteenth century Thomas Hancock was one of the richest men in Boston, although his grandfather, Nathaniel, had started out in the colony as a simple shoemaker with a family of thirteen children to support. Young Thomas began his own career as a bookbinder's apprentice, but scraped together enough money to go into his own bookselling business, which he soon expanded into a substantial trade with England. By the early 1700s he had branched out into a variety of import-export enterprises with Nova Scotia, the West Indies, England, Holland, and Spain. After building himself a handsome mansion on the southern slope of Beacon Hill, he was able to bequeath to his nephew and adopted son, John Hancock, the modern equivalent of a million dollars, as well as a successful mercantile business.

John Hancock was born in Braintree, Mass., in 1736, and at the age of seven was adopted by his uncle, Thomas, who had no children of his own, and went to live in the elegant mansion on Beacon Hill. He was sent to the Public Latin School, and then went on to Harvard College. After graduating from Harvard in 1754, John entered his uncle's mercantile firm, became a partner in 1763, and quickly rose to become the head of the firm. In 1768, after the passage of the Townshend duties, many of the local merchants resorted to smuggling to obtain the goods that were proscribed by the British regulations. At one point a riot ensued when Hancock's sloop *Liberty* was seized for smuggling wine, an event that caused Governor Bernard to call for the additional troops who subsequently were involved in the Boston Massacre. Hancock now became a popular figure among the townspeople. He had already been elected to the Massachusetts General Court in 1768, and after 1770 grew to be an influential figure among the Boston committee of patriots.

Once Hancock was involved in politics, Samuel Adams soon

became a formative influence in his life. When he became president of the Massachusetts Provisional Congress during 1774–1775, he was the richest New Englander on the patriot side; the following year he was elected president of the Second Continental Congress and in that position was the first member of the Congress to sign the Declaration of Independence. As he added the final flourishes to his distinctive, copperplate signature, he is reported to have said: "There! King George can read my name without spectacles." Obviously conscious of his influential position in the body, Hancock expressed a desire to be made commander-in-chief of the new Continental Army, but the Congress thwarted his military ambitions by appointing George Washington of Virginia to the post—a slight that Hancock never forgot or forgave. In 1777 Hancock resigned his post as president of the Congress and, although he continued to remain a member of that body, he spent most of his time in Boston, concentrating more on local politics than on national issues.

As the fighting drew to a close and independence became assured, Massachusetts drew up its new constitution, and in 1780 John Hancock was elected the first governor of the Commonwealth of Massachusetts. He served in that capacity until 1785 when, in the face of the troubles and uprisings that culminated in Shays's Rebellion, he had an attack of gout and resigned his office. After the rebellion was over, however, he was once again elected governor.

In 1788 a special convention was held in Boston to decide whether to ratify the new Federal Constitution. The delegates were sharply divided over the issue: those from urban areas wanted a stronger national government to promote trade and commerce; those from rural areas feared the effect of centralization on the liberties of the people. Throughout the proceedings, John Hancock kept to his bed with another attack of gout, but at a critical moment allowed himself to be carried into the chamber to assume the chair as presiding officer. He broke the deadlock, and with the support of Samuel Adams worked out a compromise that allowed the Constitution to be ratified by Massachusetts by a vote of 187 to 168—a margin of only 19 votes. Hancock was again elected governor under the new constitutional government, and was in the process of serving his ninth term as chief executive of the state when he died in 1793, at the age of fifty-seven.

❧ LEWIS HAYDEN

Boston has always had a significant African American population, stretching back to the early 1600s. Free people and slaves made their homes in the extreme tip of the North End until, in the early 1800s, they moved inland and settled on the north slope of Beacon Hill. The African Meeting House on Beacon Hill, founded in 1809, not only served as a gathering place for religious observances but also, under the direction of such influential citizens as Lewis Hayden, became a center for the exchange of ideas and information for the benefit of the community.

Lewis Hayden was born about 1815, as the slave of a Presbyterian minister in Lexington, Ky.. In 1848, at the age of thirty-three, he escaped with his wife and ten-year-old son to Canada on the Underground Railroad. He later came back across the border to Detroit, where he worked with a group of black citizens to construct a building to house the Colored Methodist Society. About 1850 Hayden moved to Boston and settled on the north slope of Beacon Hill, where the Boston City Directory listed his occupation as "lecturer." In Boston, Hayden established a clothing store that became the second-largest African American–owned business in the city. Out of the profits of the store he provided money for many community programs, and later contributed a significant amount to support John Brown's raid at Harpers Ferry.

Once established in Boston, Lewis Hayden turned his great energy and vision toward the cause of ending slavery and became one of the leading black abolitionists in town. Recognizing that unity and organization were vital to ending racial prejudice, he displayed a willingness to collaborate with committed white reformers like William Lloyd Garrison in agitating for emancipation in the South, as well as in working to integrate Boston's segregated public school system, a goal that was finally achieved in 1855. At his home at 66 Phillips Street, Hayden held meetings with many persons who were involved in a variety of reform and protest movements, and also directed the operations of a well-known "station" on the Underground Railroad. It is estimated that about seventy-five escaped slaves were sheltered in his house, probably one-fourth of all the fugitives who passed through Boston on their way to sanctuary in Canada. Hayden himself kept vigil in his living room, heavily armed, prepared to give his life in defense of the runaways hidden in his house. At one point he boasted that he had a barrel of gunpowder rigged to blow up if the authorities invaded his home.

After the passage of the Fugitive Slave Act of 1850, Hayden became one of the five African American members of the Boston Vigilance Committee that warned local black people of the presence of "slavecatchers" in the city. In 1851 he was a member of a group of local African Americans who rescued a runaway slave known as Shadrach from the clutches of the U.S. Marshals and spirited him away to safety. That same year, along with other local black leaders such as William C. Nell, Charles Remond, and Joshua B. Smith, Hayden petitioned the state legislature for the erection of a monument in honor of Crispus Attucks, the first African American patriot to die in the 1770 Boston Massacre. Thirty-seven years later, in 1888, the request was finally honored when a monument to the victims of the Boston Massacre was erected on Boston Common.

When the Civil War was over and the Thirteenth Amendment had guaranteed the end of slavery, Lewis Hayden was elected to the Massachusetts General Court in 1873, thus becoming one of the first African American legislators in Massachusetts history. After Hayden died in 1889, he and his wife Harriet left an estate of $5,000 for a scholarship fund to assist African American medical students at Harvard University. His home at 66 Phillips Street on Beacon Hill is at present a site on the Black Heritage Trail.

❧ Henry Lee Higginson

On October 15, 1900, the new hall on Massachusetts Avenue, designed to house the Boston Symphony Orchestra, was officially opened. The inaugural gala concluded with a performance of Beethoven's *Missa Solemnis* under the direction of the symphony's music director Wilhelm Gericke. For the hall, as well as for the orchestra that performed there, the city of Boston owed eternal gratitude to their creative founder and generous supporter, Major Henry Lee Higginson.

Henry Lee Higginson was born in New York City. He always insisted that the idea of creating a symphony orchestra came to him in 1854, when, at the age of twenty, he had traveled to Vienna to see if he had enough talent to become a professional musician. Although his European tour convinced him that he was not cut out to be a performer ("I had no talent for music," he said), the conviction that America should have "a fine orchestra" remained with him for the rest of his life.

Young Higginson returned to the United States in 1860, just in time to enlist in the Union army during the Civil War. After his military service was over, he settled down in Boston and went into banking. As a stockholder, he was made a partner in Lee, Higginson & Company, and eventually became a generous benefactor of numerous schools and colleges. But the idea of a symphony orchestra would not go away, and with the development of the fashionable Back Bay during the 1870s, the construction of the new Boston Public Library, and the founding of a Museum of Fine Arts, Higginson decided that the time had come for Boston to have a symphony orchestra.

Higginson laid out a plan to form, in his own words, "an orchestra of excellent musicians under one head and devoted to a single purpose." The first conductor was Georg Henschel, whom Higginson heard conduct at a Harvard Musical Association concert in

March 1881. The Boston Symphony Orchestra gave its inaugural concert on October 22, 1881, in downtown Boston at the old Music Hall in Hamilton Place, where it remained until the city announced plans to construct a street through the location. At that point, Higginson and his friends commissioned the well-known architect Charles Follen McKim to design a new Symphony Hall. The hall's original oak floors, the leather covers on the seats, and its plaster walls, carefully designed and engineered by the Harvard physicist Wallace Clement Sabine, contribute to the superior acoustics of the building, which recently celebrated its hundredth birthday and is widely acknowledged as one of the top three symphony halls in the world. Until 1918 Henry Lee Higginson remained the sole under-writer of the Boston Symphony Orchestra, declaring himself emi-nently satisfied with the work that he had accomplished. "The pub-lic enthusiasm for the symphony," he wrote in 1900, "showed how completely the cause of music had won its way in Boston."

Eventually Major Higginson was persuaded to share the financial responsibility of supporting the Symphony with other Boston fami-lies, who were expected not only to contribute to the annual deficit, but also to personally attend concerts on a regular basis. In this re-spect, the women of the city proved some of the most loyal and dedi-cated supporters of this civic commitment. Every Friday afternoon during the winter months, the Boston woman would arrive promptly at Symphony Hall for the 1:30 P.M. concert and be es-corted to the seat her family had held for generations. The commen-tator Lucius Beebe has described the craning of the necks at the last moment to make sure that "the Hallowells and the Forbeses are in their accustomed stalls."

With that kind of earnest support and encouragement, Henry Lee Higginson saw his lifelong dream come true. The Boston Symphony Orchestra has gone on to become one of the finest in the world, boasting a series of internationally acclaimed conductors, as well as numerous composers who have written works especially for that orchestra to play in one of the best concert halls to be found any-where.

¶ OLIVER WENDELL HOLMES

The Holmeses were related to a number of distinguished Boston families—the Olivers, the Bradstreets, the Wendells, the Quincys, the Cabots, the Jacksons, the Lees—all of whom had prospered since the days of the Puritans. Oliver Wendell Holmes regarded himself as a Boston Brahmin, a term he coined himself in one of his novels, and took great pride in belonging to a city he regarded as "the Hub of the solar system"—another phrase he originated.

Born in Cambridge in 1809, the son of Abiel Holmes, Oliver Wendell Holmes graduated from Harvard in 1829 and achieved early popularity as a writer. His poem "Old Ironsides," protesting the breakup of the USS *Constitution,* was published in the *Boston Daily Advertiser* in 1830, and helped save the famous old vessel from destruction. Holmes decided on a career in medicine, however; he studied at Paris, and received an M.D. from Harvard in 1836. He joined the faculty of the Harvard Medical School, where he eventually served as dean, preferring teaching and lecturing to medical practice. In 1843 he published a paper on the causes of puerperal (childbed) fever that turned out to be a landmark work in the germ theory of disease and established his reputation in the medical profession. Named Parkman Professor in 1847, he became famous for his lectures on anatomy and other medical subjects not only at Harvard but also on the public lecture circuit, where he was in great demand.

Despite his medical fame, Oliver Wendell Holmes was much better known to the general public as a writer who produced appealing verse and literary prose, and who concluded each of his twelve Lowell Institute lectures on the English poets (1853) with an original poem. He wrote hundreds of verses and three novels, and by the latter part of the nineteenth century many successive editions of his poetry, travel notes, biographies, and numerous memorial addresses had appeared in print, establishing his reputation as one of Boston's most prominent and productive literary figures. He was also described by his contemporaries as "a great talker," and was fondly remembered by such contemporaries as Ralph Waldo Emerson, Henry Wadsworth Longfellow, Nathaniel Hawthorne, Richard Henry Dana, and James Russell Lowell as an indefatigable conversationalist at the regular meetings of the Saturday Club. Holmes was a founder of the *Atlantic Monthly* (a title he invented), in whose pages he published a popular column of witty and sophisticated observations on contemporary society. The series called "The Autocrat of the Breakfast Table" was followed by "The Professor at the Breakfast Table," and later by "The Poet at the Breakfast Table," as Holmes recorded in his inimitable style the changes taking place on the Boston scene. Boston was always the center of his world and the object of his affection—he called it "the thinking centre of the continent, and therefore of the planet."

While Oliver Wendell Holmes was a confirmed rationalist, utterly opposed to the theocracy of old Calvinist theology, he saw no reason to reject the essentially elitist social principles of the Puritan tradition that encouraged good breeding and proper behavior. He was a staunch supporter of the Union, a great admirer of Daniel Webster, and an early critic of the abolitionists, whose extremist views he felt would disrupt orderly society and endanger the peace of the nation. As the slavery issue grew more critical, however, and as the factions moved closer to violence, Holmes became a member of the Republican party, and when the Civil War broke out he supported the Lincoln administration and the national war effort. Indeed, his son, Oliver Wendell Holmes, Jr., left Harvard College to join the 20th Massachusetts Regiment, in which he served with great distinction.

Oliver Wendell Holmes died in Boston in 1894, at the age of eighty-five, but not before he had seen his son called to Harvard Law School in 1882 as Weld Professor of Law, and then appointed to a seat on the Massachusetts Supreme Judicial Court. Young Holmes served on the state bench for twenty years, rising to the position of chief justice. In 1902 President Theodore Roosevelt appointed him an Associate Justice of the United States Supreme Court in 1902, where he remained a commanding legal figure for thirty years, retiring just two years before his own death in 1935 at the age of ninety-four.

¶ JULIA WARD HOWE

For many Americans, Julia Ward Howe will forever be associated with her authorship of "Battle-Hymn of the Republic," the stirring anthem that helped transform the Civil War from a political conflict into a crusade for human freedom. The influence of Julia Ward Howe continued long after the Civil War, however. Throughout the remainder of the nineteenth century, and even into the twentieth, she served as a powerful and pivotal force in women's politics as well as a recognized leader of suffrage societies and women's clubs in the United States.

Born in 1818 to a banker's family in New York City, after the death of her mother Julia Ward was raised by her father. He provided her with formal schooling until she was sixteen, after which she had tutors in German, Greek, French, and other academic subjects. While visiting a friend in Boston, the twenty-one-year-old Julia met the forty-year-old Dr. Samuel Gridley Howe, who at the time was director of the Perkins Institution for the Blind. The two were married in 1843, and Julia moved into an old colonial house in South Boston, not far from the Perkins Institution. Named Green Peace, it was a happy home in a bucolic location, staffed by a cook, a gardener, a governess, a nurse, and several servants. Julia played the piano, taught songs to her five children, supervised family plays, and greeted the procession of important visitors from all over the world who came to visit Dr. Howe's institution.

Julia Ward Howe also wrote stories and children's plays, despite her husband's disapproval, and in 1854 published an anonymous book of poems with Ticknor and Fields. When the Civil War broke out Dr. Howe was named to the United States Sanitary Commission, and in November 1861 Julia accompanied her husband to

Washington, D.C. While sitting in a carriage with a friend, Julia heard a unit of Union soldiers marching along singing a lusty but rowdy version of "John Brown's Body," and her companion suggested that she should write "some good words" for that stirring tune. Later that night, according to her own account, Julia awoke from sleep and "the long lines of the desired poem began to twine themselves in my mind." She submitted her poem, "Battle-Hymn of the Republic," to the *Atlantic Monthly,* which published it in its February 1862 issue. The stirring verse, with its strong Biblical allusions following the opening words "Mine eyes have seen the glory of the coming of the Lord," was taken up all over the North. Mrs. Howe's inspirational vision had captured the most sublime ideals for which the Civil War was being fought.

Julia Ward Howe continued her literary career, but after the war she became increasingly active in the movement for women's suffrage. She was elected president of the New England Women's Club, a position she held for forty years, and in 1868 she became president of the New England Woman Suffrage Association. When her husband died in 1876, however, Julia was faced with serious financial worries, and to raise enough money to support herself, she set off on a series of lecture tours that took her not only across the United States, but also to England, Europe, and the Middle East. Howe was a strong advocate of all sorts of female reform groups, which she imbued with her idealistic vision of universal sisterhood, seeing women as members of a distinctive sex-class whose "sacred claims" bound them to one another.

Although Julia Ward Howe had become a much more prominent national and international figure as a lecturer than as a writer, she was content to spend her later years quietly ensconced in her home on Beacon Hill, reading and writing. Julia Ward Howe died on October 5, 1910, at the age of ninety-one, and was buried at Mount Auburn Cemetery in Cambridge. As a moving tribute to her and to her husband, a group of blind children from the Perkins Institution attended the burial services and sang a final tribute to her memory.

❡ SAMUEL GRIDLEY HOWE

If there were such a creature as a professional reformer, Samuel Gridley Howe would certainly fit into that category. Whenever there was a struggle for freedom, a fight against oppression, or a movement to alleviate suffering—wherever it might be—Dr. Howe was ready and eager to enlist in the cause.

Samuel Gridley Howe was born in Boston in 1801, graduated from the Boston Latin School and Brown University, and in 1824 graduated from Harvard Medical School. After fighting in the Greek war for independence, he returned to Boston in 1831 and looked for some good work to which he could apply his reformist energies. When he was approached by some local philanthropists and asked to assume the directorship of a proposed new asylum for the blind, he immediately accepted, and spent several months in Europe observing the latest innovations in education of the blind.

After his return, Dr. Howe set up his first school for the blind in his own home, where he worked with six pupils. His experiments aroused the interest of Colonel Thomas Handasyd Perkins, a wealthy merchant, who offered his spacious house in downtown Boston to the school if the city would match his gift with fifty thousand dollars. The women of Boston held one of the first great municipal fairs in Faneuil Hall and, within six weeks, raised the entire amount to found the Perkins Institution for the Blind. Early in 1839 the Mount Washington Hotel, constructed only a few years earlier on the corner of Broadway and H Street in South Boston, was offered to the trustees of the Perkins Institution in exchange for the Boston property. The trade was agreed upon, and during May 1839 the clients were transferred to the new site, with the moving expenses paid by the private contributions of Samuel Appleton and several other prominent Boston gentlemen.

From that time on, the Perkins Institution for the Blind became a well-known feature of the South Boston landscape, attracting visitors from other parts of the country as well as from many parts of Europe. They came to observe the mechanical devices and experimental techniques Dr. Howe used to educate and rehabilitate blind persons. With the aid of the American Bible Society, he produced a vast amount of printing in raised type in order to bring the Bible within the reach of the blind. Visitors especially marveled at the progress Howe made with Laura Bridgman, a young woman born without sight or hearing. In 1849 a large three-story workshop was erected adjacent to the main building, where clients were provided with occupational training in such manual skills as furniture upholstery, mattress stuffing, and the manufacture of fiber mats. Dr. Howe established this workshop with some reluctance, because he had observed in Europe that most blind adults spent their entire lives in sheltered workshops. It was his hope that his workshop would prepare his students to go out into the world and "earn a livelihood by honest work."

Dr. Howe was also named superintendent of what was called the Massachusetts School for Idiots, a residential facility located in the City Point section of South Boston that accommodated some fifty retarded and emotionally disturbed young people, ranging from seven to fifteen years of age. Under Dr. Howe's direction, the clients followed a carefully regimented program of meals and activities, with a period set aside every day for exercises in a gymnasium located in a separate building. The clients attended school classes for a total of six hours a day. Those who were educable were taught the basics of reading, writing, and speech; those with more limited abilities were instructed in "form, color, and size." The girls were also given needlework lessons.

Samuel Gridley Howe made his home for many years in South Boston, not far from the Perkins Institution, with his five children and his wife, Julia Ward Howe, who was to gain fame as the author of the "Battle-Hymn of the Republic." As a man committed to freedom, Howe soon became caught up in the abolition movement and committed to its goal of total and immediate emancipation. When runaway slaves began to be apprehended by federal marshals and returned to their Southern owners under the new Fugitive Slave Act of 1850, Howe joined with other Bostonians to form the Boston Vigilance Committee. This was a volunteer group that warned local blacks of the presence of "slavecatchers" in the city and provided funds for the legal defense of any who were taken into custody.

After the passage of the Kansas-Nebraska Act in 1854, Dr. Howe became active in supporting the movement of Free-Soilers into Kansas Territory, and in 1859 he was one of a group of New Englanders who secretly provided funds to support John Brown in his attack on Harpers Ferry. In 1863 Howe was made a member of the Massachusetts Board of State Charities, a post he held until his death in 1876.

¶ WILLIAM DEAN HOWELLS

When *The Rise of Silas Lapham* was published in 1885, it became one of the most controversial novels of its time—one of the earliest fictional treatments of the modern American businessman, and a generally sympathetic one at that. Writing in the realistic style of late nineteenth-century literature, William Dean Howells depicted the class conflicts and social differences between the established elite of Boston and the newly rich family of a hard-working and upwardly mobile paint manufacturer. That the author was not a native of Boston made his perceptive insights into the life of the city and the unique character of its society all the more remarkable.

William Dean Howells was born in 1837 in Martin's Ferry, Ohio, where his father once published an antislavery newspaper. William read diligently and attended the local common school whenever he could, but was largely self-educated. He learned the printer's trade at his father's country newspaper, and later recalled his early years in *A Boy's Town* (1890) and *My Literary Passions* (1895). From 1856 to 1861 he was a reporter and editorial writer on the *Ohio State Journal*, and during that period of his life he collaborated with John J. Piatt to produce *Poems by Two Friends* (1860). His successful campaign biography of the Republican candidate Abraham Lincoln in 1860 earned him an appointment as U.S. Consul to Venice, Italy, from 1861 to 1865.

On his return to the United States after the Civil War, William Dean Howells moved to Boston, becoming sub-editor of the *Atlantic Monthly* and in 1871 editor-in-chief. In addition to his editorial responsibilities, he produced two urbane comedies of manners, *A Chance Acquaintance* (1873) and *The Lady of the Aroostooks* (1879). In 1881 he left the *Atlantic Monthly,* put off the "Bostonian quiet," and applied himself to a wider range of more aggressive and challenging social themes, turning out *A Modern Instance* (1882), *A Woman's Reason* (1883), and then perhaps his greatest masterpiece, *The Rise of Silas Lapham* (1885).

A quiet, congenial, unassuming, "decent" sort of man, Howells displayed a catholicity of literary taste that many people found surprising in someone who seemed so ordinary. As a prolific essayist for most of the influential American journals of his day and the author of numerous other publications, he tried to make American literature more cosmopolitan. In addition to promoting the work of his good friends Henry James and Mark Twain, he also helped popularize the writings of such Russian writers as Turgenev and Tolstoy, as well as a number of contemporary French, Italian, German, and Scandinavian literary figures.

In 1891, Howells moved to New York City, where he further explored economic issues and class problems in modern American society in such works as *The Quality of Mercy* (1892) and *The Story of a Play* (1898). In *A Traveler from Altruria* (1894) he displayed his socialist tendencies, which were also apparent in *The Landlord at Lion's Head* (1897) and *The Son of Royal Langbrith* (1904). Honored by many colleges and universities, Howells was the first president of the American Academy of Arts and Letters.

Howells was not particularly impressed by New York, however, either by the city itself or by the celebrated "four hundred" that made up its social elite. He much preferred the understated cultural life of Boston, where he had become more Brahmin than most of the native breed. "The Bostonian who leaves Boston," he once remarked, "ought to be condemned to perpetual exile." When in Boston he made his home on Beacon Hill, in fashionable Louisburg Square, along with such other literary notables as the writer Louisa May Alcott; her father, the educator Bronson Alcott; the historian John Gorham Palfrey; and the novelist Henry James. Howells also served as the first president of Boston's exclusive Tavern Club, which was formed to provide young writers, scholars, and artists a comfortable place for good conversation and inexpensive dinners. In time, Howells also purchased a house at Kittery Point, Me., overlooking Portsmouth Harbor, where he worked in an old attached barn that he remodeled into a studio—a house that his family later donated to Harvard University as a literary retreat. Although after his death in 1920 William Dean Howells's work went into something of an eclipse, he was an important influence on American letters during the late nineteenth and early twentieth centuries.

¶ ANNE HUTCHINSON

"Puritan authorities believed that women were innately weaker of brain and easily seduced by bad influences," writes the historian Nancy Woloch, "especially if they strained their minds beyond reasonable limits and crossed the line between piety and critical thought." Anne Hutchinson was an intelligent, pious, and determined woman who crossed that dangerous line while living in the heart of the Puritan commonwealth. For that transgression she suffered the dreadful consequences of what the Reverend Increase Mather later described as the "observable work of Providence."

Daughter of a prominent clergyman, Francis Marbury of Lincolnshire, England, Anne Hutchinson was soon recognized for her intellectual brilliance, spiritual knowledge, and religious devotion. In September 1634, Hutchinson arrived in Boston with her husband and children, following her favorite preacher, John Cotton, to his new post in the Massachusetts Bay Colony. The Hutchinsons and their fifteen children lived on a piece of land that would eventually become the site of Boston's Old Corner Bookstore. Anne became well known in her community for her skills as a midwife, but she attracted ever greater attention for her outspoken views on biblical and theological matters expressed during popular weekly meetings at her home. At these meetings, she and other women of the town would discuss the sermons of the previous Sunday, analyzing them for errors, omissions, and examples of hypocrisy. By 1636 her meetings had expanded to include both men and women. Hutchinson and her followers declared that many of the local clergymen were unfit to preach, and on one occasion walked out of a service en masse when a particular clergyman rose to give a sermon. Hutchinson herself argued a doctrine called Antinomianism, which held that the Holy Spirit dwells in every person and that there is no need to provide evidence of good works or sanctification in order to achieve salvation, other than the realization of Christ in one's self.

Hutchinson's outspoken religious ideas were regarded as a dangerous assault on the authority of the Puritan congregation as well as the Puritan magistrates. Governor John Winthrop finally made up his mind to put an end to her influence, and in November 1636 had her brought before the magistrates, charged with the civil offense of acting in disruptive ways inappropriate for a woman. Winthrop had no doubt that this woman of "haughty and fierce carriage, of nimble wit, and active spirit, and a very voluble tongue" was the ringleader of all "these distempers" he felt were disturbing the peace of the colony. But thanks to the Lord, he concluded, the snare had been broken, and the woman who was the "root of all these troubles" now stood before the seat of justice.

Questions and accusations were flung angrily by the magistrates against Anne Hutchinson, who defended herself with rhetorical skill and biblical knowledge until, in the midst of a heated exchange, she blurted out that God would punish her accusers. Asked how she knew this, she snapped: "My own immediate revelation." Declaring that this statement alone constituted heresy, the magistrates ordered her banished from the colony. A few months later, this civil punishment was followed by formal excommunication from the church.

Hutchinson and her family left Boston and, with a few others, founded a settlement in what is now Newport, R.I., where she once again was involved in political squabbles and ended up questioning the authority of the local magistrates. She moved with her family to a small settlement near Long Island Sound, where she and all her younger children but one were killed by Indians in 1643. Back in Boston, Puritan leaders inevitably viewed the massacre as divine retribution for her errors, and rejoiced that the "American Jezebel" had finally been struck down by the hand of the Almighty.

A figure of Anne Hutchinson, her face uplifted to heaven, her small daughter by her right side, with her left arm clasping a Bible to her breast, now stands outside the west wing of the Massachusetts State House on Beacon Hill. The work of the well-known sculptor Cyrus Dallin, the bronze statue was donated in 1922 to the Commonwealth of Massachusetts by the Anne Hutchinson Memorial Association and by the State Federation of Women's Clubs.

❧ THOMAS HUTCHINSON

There are figures in history who personify the tragic fates of characters in the dramas of William Shakespeare. Certainly Thomas Hutchinson has all the characteristics of such a figure. The eminent historian Bernard Bailyn recognized this when he titled his biography of the last royal governor of Massachusetts *The Ordeal of Thomas Hutchinson*. It was the classic ordeal of a man torn in two by love of his native land and loyalty to his king.

Thomas Hutchinson was born in Boston in 1711 to a family of successful merchants which had been in Boston since its founding. His most prominent ancestor was Anne Hutchinson, the seventeenth-century religious dissenter who refused to bow to the will of the Puritan community and who was subsequently banished from the Massachusetts Bay Colony. Hutchinson entered Harvard College before he had turned twelve, and earned a small fortune on investments in the fish trade even before he graduated. He entered politics while still a young man and proceeded to forge a remarkable career as he moved steadily up the political ladder from provincial assemblyman to speaker of the Massachusetts House of Representatives, to councillor, to lieutenant governor, to chief justice, and finally to the exalted position of Governor of the Massachusetts Bay Colony. In addition to his political achievements, Hutchinson was America's most accomplished historian, turning out a three-volume history of Massachusetts.

Throughout his public career, Thomas Hutchinson showed himself to be a man of firm principles who was opposed to abuses of imperial power, but who also could not be persuaded to go beyond traditional colonial limits in defending American rights. Basically autocratic, with a strong respect for authority, he showed both intellectual and physical courage in arguing against prevailing ideas or standing up to angry mobs. He clearly loved his native Massachusetts, but he hated the mob actions of people he viewed as ignorant and unstable. Because of his insistence on authoritarian rule and his opposition to revolutionary action, he was considered by many Bostonians as a traitor to his own people.

Hutchinson's character and principles led to open conflict with local patriotic groups in at least three critical incidents leading up to the American Revolution: In supporting the prerogatives of Parliament with the passage of the Stamp Act in 1765, he was accused by many Bostonians of violating the rights of true-born Englishmen, and denounced by John Adams for his "very ambitious and avaricious disposition." In supporting the Townshend Duties of 1767, he was held responsible for the increase of tensions in the town between British soldiers and local civilians that led to the Boston Massacre in 1770. And in refusing to use his authority as governor to prevent the British tea from being landed in December 1773, he was held responsible for causing the Boston Tea Party and precipitating the final crisis with Great Britain. Many Bostonians believed that Hutchinson's policies were dictated by his personal ambitions, and Mercy Otis Warren referred to him as "dark, intriguing, insinuating, haughty, and ambitious," an expert on "the intricacies of Machiavellian policy."

The passage by Parliament of the punitive Coercive Acts in the spring of 1774 made Thomas Hutchinson the last royal governor of Massachusetts. He was succeeded by General Thomas Gage as military governor of the Massachusetts Bay Colony. Hutchinson left America and sailed to England, where he died in 1780. On July 4, 1776, the very day that his fellow Americans were proclaiming their independence from England, Thomas Hutchinson was awarded an honorary doctorate of civil laws at Oxford University. Ironically, he was being honored as an American, and the most distinguished and loyal colonial-born official of his day.

¶ WILLIAM JAMES

William James simply could not make up his mind, whether it was about volunteering to serve in the Civil War in 1861 when he was nineteen, or retiring from his teaching position at Harvard University in 1903 when he was sixty-one. It comes as no surprise, therefore, that he became a leading American philosopher by examining the nature of truth and the process of decision-making, founding a system called pragmatism.

William James, the older brother of the novelist Henry James, was born January 11, 1842, the descendant of an Irish Protestant grandfather who had settled in Albany, N.Y., where he became extremely wealthy in the dry-goods business. William's father, Henry James, Sr., had started out as a young wastrel but in the burst of Christian revivalism that swept through western New York State during the 1830s he became intensely religious, although decidedly opposed to most traditional denominations. He chose, instead, to experiment with an eclectic and sometimes bizarre mixture of prevailing spiritual movements; his influence can be seen in his son's later work, *The Varieties of Religious Experience* (1902), which assembled accounts of spirituality from all over the world.

Growing up as part of a remarkably talented family that was intimate with Emerson and the Transcendentalist writers, as well as

Garrison and the abolitionist reformers, William and his siblings received a cosmopolitan but unorthodox education. Making repeated trips from New York to Geneva, to London, to Paris, to Boulogne, and to Bonn, the young man received both private tutoring as well as formal training at a variety of schools and academies. In 1860 he returned to the United States, settling in Newport, R.I., to take up a career in painting. He promptly discarded painting, however, and entered the Lawrence Scientific School at Harvard to pursue a career in science. William moved from one field of specialization to another, switching from chemistry to anatomy and then to natural history, until he finally settled on medicine, in which he received his M.D. degree in 1868. Instead of establishing a medical practice, however, he began teaching physiology at Harvard in 1872; once again he switched fields, this time to experimental psychology, and in 1890 published a two-volume work called *Principles of Psychology* that brought him worldwide fame. He turned next to philosophy, and in 1897 produced *The Will to Believe and Other Essays of Popular Philosophy*, which introduced the idea that a person must take immediate action in certain situations, even when there was no rational basis for deciding which course to take.

As a philosopher, William James is perhaps best known for developing the ideas that came to be known as pragmatism. James held that fulfillment and salvation are neither necessary nor impossible, and that our own actions make a vital difference in what happens. He maintained that human existence is conditioned by freedom, and that hope—something that is at the heart of all human life—finds its natural expression in various forms of religious faith. What we ordinarily call "truth," he wrote, should be attributed not to reality but to our own beliefs about it. A particular truth must be "about" something, a certain particular object; and it must "work, that is, it must satisfy the purpose or interest for which it was adopted."

The final years of William James were spent traveling, lecturing, writing, and recovering from bouts of bad health and periods of depression. During the early part of the twentieth century he came out in opposition to the growth of American imperialism, and was especially critical of America's involvement in the Philippines following the Spanish-American War. In 1906 he traveled to California to visit Stanford University as a guest lecturer, and upon his return to Boston he delivered at the Lowell Institute a series of lectures published in 1907 under the title *Pragmatism: A New Name for Some Old Ways of Thinking,* the definitive statement of the philosophical system that has come to be associated with his name. In 1909 he visited England and gave a series of lectures at Oxford that later appeared as *A Pluralistic Universe.* One year later, on August 26, 1910, his weakened heart gave out and he died in Chocorua, N.H. The legacy of his restless and brilliant mind included foundational works with a distinctly American approach to religion, psychology, and philosophy that are still influential today.

❧ EBEN JORDAN, JR.

In 1841, an enterprising nineteen-year-old named Eben Dyer Jordan opened a small dry-goods store at 168 Hanover Street in Boston's North End. Ten years later, Jordan went into partnership with Benjamin L. Marsh, launching a retail enterprise that would make Jordan Marsh a household name in Boston. As business expanded and new properties were acquired to accommodate merchandise imported from around the world, Jordan Marsh changed locations several times before it finally settled on 450 Washington Street as its permanent location in the heart of the city.

When Jordan died in 1895, his son Eben Jordan, Jr., together with Edward J. Mitton, took over direction of the company and led it in more efficient and profitable directions. They modernized ways of doing business, installing telephones, electric lights, and elevators in their store, and made the bold move of selling to customers on credit. Conscious of the role his business played in the economic life of Boston, Jordan wanted to enhance its social and cultural life as well. Just as Henry Lee Higginson had wished to provide Boston

with its own fine orchestra, so Eben Jordan desired to found an opera company for the city. Up to this point, Boston had never had its
own opera company, and visiting companies from other parts of the
country or from foreign lands had to perform at general-purpose
theaters like the Howard Athenaeum (later the "Old Howard") and
the Boston Theater. Eben Jordan erected a beautiful opera house at
his own expense on Huntington Avenue, not far from the new Museum of Fine Arts, and formed the Boston Opera Company. Some
seven hundred stockholders were enlisted, forty-six boxes were sold
with a guarantee for three years, and a managing directorship of
fifteen members was created, including Jordan, who guaranteed all
expenses for three years. In a further display of his interest in fine
music, Eben Jordan gave a large auditorium, Jordan Hall, to the
New England Conservatory of Music, also located nearby on Huntington Avenue.

The new Opera House, designed by Parkman B. Haven, was
dedicated on November 8, 1909, with a brilliant performance of
Ponchielli's *La Giaconda,* followed by presentations of Delibes'
Lakmé, Verdi's *Aida,* and other operas that were quite popular. After
a successful first season, however, public enthusiasm began to die
down, stockholders lost interest, subscriptions fell off, and debts began to increase substantially. At the end of the third season, with the
threatened outbreak of war in Europe, the experiment came to an
end, and the Boston Opera Company was disbanded. Although
Bostonians enjoyed fine opera, noted one disappointed observer,
they were reluctant to pay for the very best and equally reluctant to
hear anything else. After Eben Jordan's death in 1916, the Opera
House was sold, along with all the scenery, costumes, properties, and
orchestral scores. In succeeding years the Opera House was used by
touring opera companies such as the Chicago Opera and the New
York Metropolitan Opera; the Russian Ballet performed there in
1916, and it was home to productions of Shakespearean plays as well.

Eben Jordan's legacy, the Boston Opera House, managed to maintain itself through the Great Depression and the war years that followed, but its cramped quarters and the changes in its surrounding
neighborhood led to poor attendance at events. The building was

demolished in 1958, to make way for the expansion of Northeastern University along Huntington Avenue. Some forty years later the family name of the long-established retail business called Jordan Marsh gave way to the demographic changes of sprawling suburban shopping malls and corporate mergers. In 1996 Jordan Marsh changed its name to Macy's, and thereafter operated as a division of Federated Department Stores, Inc., signaling the loss of another uniquely Boston identity. But Jordan's interest in the arts lives on in Jordan Hall, still one of the city's prime concert venues, and in the many attempts over the years to establish a permanent opera company in Boston.

❧ ROSE FITZGERALD KENNEDY

Raised amid the sights and sounds of grass-roots politics in old Boston, Rose Fitzgerald Kennedy lived long enough to witness more than a century of United States history. A writer, campaigner, humanitarian, fund-raiser, and matriarch of a family that would dominate American politics for a generation, she saw three of her sons gain election to high public office—and two of them die at the hands of assassins. Her story is one of high achievement and unthinkable tragedy.

Rose Fitzgerald was born in the North End section of Boston on July 22, 1890, the eldest child of John "Honey Fitz" Fitzgerald, a prominent figure in Boston politics. Boss of the North End, one of the youngest ward bosses in the city, Fitzgerald served three terms in the U.S. Congress before becoming mayor of Boston. His daughter Rose grew up in the political spotlight, accompanying her father to all kinds of civic functions, ceremonial occasions, and political gatherings. After graduating from high school at the age of sixteen, Rose wanted to attend the prestigious Wellesley College but, at the urgings of Cardinal O'Connell, went instead to the Convent of the Sacred Heart, and later studied in Europe.

Upon her return to the United States, Rose fell in love with Joseph P. Kennedy, the son of Patrick Kennedy, ward boss of East Boston. Although Honey Fitz respected the young man's ambitions (Joe Kennedy would become the youngest bank president in United States history), he never really liked the young businessman, and discouraged the relationship. Rose continued to keep company with Kennedy, however, and in 1914 the couple was married. The Kennedys had nine children during their fifty-five-year marriage. Joe subsequently became a multimillionaire, attracting considerable attention at times for questionable business dealings—he was rumored to have been involved with bootlegging during Prohibition—as well as for his liaisons with other women. In public Rose Kennedy seemed completely oblivious of these stories and rumors, immersing herself in the business of raising her family. She schooled her children in the history of the Democratic Party tradition, and nurtured the political ambitions of her sons by emphasizing their responsibility to public duty.

In 1937 Joseph P. Kennedy was named ambassador to Great Britain, and for about three years the family lived abroad. Despite the glamour, these years were marked by the beginning of a series of sorrowful events in the family's life. In 1941, their third daughter, Rosemary, who had been born mentally handicapped, had to be placed in an institution after an attempt at surgery only worsened her condition. Three years later, the family suffered a second blow when the oldest son, Joseph Jr., a Navy pilot, was killed when his plane exploded while on a secret mission. In 1948 a third calamity occurred when another daughter, Kathleen, was killed in a plane crash in Europe. Rose Kennedy survived these family tragedies with an astonishing composure and unshakable religious faith. To many of her admirers, her stately courage and her abiding belief in the will of God made her the very embodiment of the best of the Irish Catholic tradition in America.

After the death of Joe Jr., the family turned to his younger brother John to carry the political banner, and the Kennedy women turned out to write a new chapter in political campaigning when he ran for

Congress from Massachusetts. Jack's sisters, Eunice and Pat, proved to be resourceful campaigners at VFW posts, Legion halls, church receptions, and house parties, but it was his mother Rose who was always in greatest demand. "Rose was so important to Jack in 1946," recalled Dave Powers, "because she was better known than anyone else in that district." And when she was not involved in political campaigns for her son, Rose was on the lecture circuit speaking out on behalf of the mentally handicapped and raising funds for programs to benefit their cause.

In 1961 Rose's husband suffered a debilitating stroke, less than a year after his son, John F. Kennedy, was inaugurated as the 35th President of the United States. Joseph lingered on in an invalid state for more than half a dozen years before dying in 1969, leaving Rose to confront the most trying times of her life, including the assassination of John in 1963 and the murder of her son Robert in 1968, without the support of her husband. But once again, as the nation mourned these new tragedies, Rose Kennedy found her greatest solace in religion as she faced the public with poise, dignity, and restraint. Her only surviving son, Ted, went on to have a long and distinguished career in the U.S. Senate, although one not without its measure of scandal and controversy.

Weakened by a stroke in 1984, Rose Kennedy spent the last decade of her life at the family home at Hyannis Port on Cape Cod. She died of the complications of pneumonia on January 22, 1995, at the age of one hundred and four, leaving behind five children, twenty-eight grandchildren, and forty-one great-grandchildren. Her funeral, attended by celebrities from all over the nation, took place at the historic St. Stephen's Church in the heart of Boston's North End, where Rose had been born and where she grew up. Some day, when the Big Dig is completed and the Central Artery torn down, a section of the open space created will be known as the Rose Fitzgerald Kennedy Greenway, in honor of a woman whose character—as her son, Ted Kennedy, remarked in his funeral eulogy—combined "the sweetest gentleness" with "the most tempered steel."

❧ *Lewis Hayden*

❧ *Julia Ward Howe*

❧ James
Russell
Lowell

❧ Henry
Wadsworth
Longfellow

☝ Amos A. Lawrence

"We went to bed one night, old-fashioned, conservative, compromise, Union Whigs, and waked up stark mad Abolitionists." With these words, Amos A. Lawrence reflected the sense of shock and alarm with which much of Boston's financial community reacted to the passage of the Kansas-Nebraska Act in 1854. In leading the fight to prevent slavery from spreading into the free territories of the West, Lawrence became a dramatic symbol of changing attitudes among Northern conservatives before the Civil War.

Amos Adams Lawrence was born in Boston in 1811, into a family that had become prominent in the textile business. His father, Amos Lawrence, together with his brothers Abbott and William, had originally been importers before experimenting with cotton textile manufacturing during the War of 1812. With the expansion of the textile industry after the war, the Lawrence brothers became prosperous manufacturers, founded the mill town of Lawrence, invested in railroads, and bought into the Suffolk Bank.

With the success of his father and uncles, young Amos A. Lawrence could look forward to becoming a rich man after he graduated from Harvard in 1835. But he was determined not to become one of those "plodding, narrow-minded" merchants cooped up in the noisy city. No. He would be a man of the world, a literary man "in some measure," and a farmer, too, with a happy cottage in the countryside. Young Lawrence got his wish. He learned the business from the ground up, traveling through the Southern states, meeting with cotton planters and merchants and developing close relations with his "Southern Brethren." Within ten years of his graduation from Harvard, Lawrence was president of the Cocheco Company and treasurer of the Salmon Falls Mills, and held directorates in such important corporations as the Suffolk Bank and the Middlesex Canal.

The growth of the abolition movement and the agitation over slavery, however, disturbed the amicable relations between what Charles Sumner called the "Lords of the Lash" and the "Lords of the

Loom"—Southern slave owners who produced cotton and Northern industrialists who processed it into cloth. Most conservative Northern businessmen disliked slavery, but had no intention of tampering with it in those states which had chosen to maintain it. The industrialists were willing to live with slavery as long as it remained confined to its present limits, and for this reason during the 1840s they opposed both the war with Mexico and the eventual annexation of Texas.

The passage of the Kansas-Nebraska Act in 1854 disrupted this policy of coexistence by allowing slavery to expand northward into Kansas and Nebraska—and presumably into the whole Northwest. Northern business interests who expected the West to be reserved for "free soil, free labor, and free men" found this unacceptable. Amos A. Lawrence became a vigorous supporter of the New England Emigrant Aid Society, which furnished free transportation for free-soilers to settle in Kansas and save the territory for freedom, founding the city of Lawrence, named for Amos. They later provided modern repeating rifles for the free-soil settlers to protect themselves from attacks by proslavery settlers from Missouri.

Despite his active involvement in Kansas, Lawrence refused to become an abolitionist, remaining a "Cotton Whig" in contrast to younger "Conscience Whigs" who joined the new Republican party. He supported the middle-of-the-road Constitutional Union party in the election of 1860, and engaged in last-minute efforts to find a compromise solution to the national crisis. When the Civil War broke out in April 1861, however, Lawrence became a loyal supporter of the Lincoln administration and the Union cause, and became a charter member of the Union Club, which established its headquarters at Abbott Lawrence's old home on Park Street.

After the war, Lawrence lived a quiet and comfortable family life with his wife and seven children, horseback riding around his estate in Chestnut Hill, skating on Jamaica Pond in the winter months, and spending his summers at Nahant. He was chairman of the finance committee that raised funds for Memorial Hall to honor the Harvard men who fell in the war; some years later he funded Lawrence Hall as a dormitory for theology students at Harvard. He also founded Lawrence University in Appleton, Wisconsin, and the college in Lawrence that became the University of Kansas. In June 1885, he met with the "old boys" at Harvard for the fiftieth anniversary of the Class of 1835, sadly reflecting that this would be "the last meeting on earth for most of us." And he was right. Just a little over a year later, on August 22, 1886, Amos A. Lawrence died at the age of seventy-two, and was buried in Mount Auburn Cemetery.

❧ ELMA LEWIS

An article in the *New York Times* once suggested that Boston's Elma Lewis "could be Black America's version of Sol Hurok, Tyrone Guthrie, and P. T. Barnum—all fused into one generous package." This tribute to the remarkable talents of Elma Lewis may seem somewhat irreverent, but it certainly recognizes the range of her many skills. Consummate artist, ingenious impresario, flamboyant publicist, and energetic fund-raiser, Lewis carried out her dream of bringing the fine arts to the young people of Boston's African American community.

Elma Ina Lewis was born in Boston, the only daughter of Edwardine and Clairmont Lewis, both of whom had emigrated from Barbados. Her parents were ardent followers of Marcus Garvey and his Universal Negro Improvement Association and regularly attended the Sunday meetings in Boston. Elma herself belonged to the Girl Guides, and later expressed her belief that participating in the movement gave her a "sense of self." Elma attended the Boston public schools, and during her early years took classes in dance, voice, and piano, received elocution lessons, and earned small sums of money giving dance and dramatic performances. After graduating from high school in 1939, she taught dancing at a local dance studio and worked as a student speech therapist at the Massachusetts Mental Health Habit Clinic in Boston. With the money she earned she was able to pay her way through Emerson College, from which she graduated in 1943. She wanted to become an actress, but at that time there were few parts for African Americans. Instead she enrolled in the Boston University School of Education, receiving a master's degree in 1944 in the education of exceptional children.

In 1945 Lewis taught in the Boston public schools, and then became a speech therapist again at the Massachusetts Mental Health Clinic. From 1945 to 1949, she was a fine arts instructor at the Harriet Tubman House in the South End, and from 1946 to 1948 worked at the Robert Gould Shaw House as director and choreographer for a series of operas and operettas put on by the Robert Gould Shaw Chorus. But it was in 1950 that Elma Lewis found her true niche, when she established the Elma Lewis School of Fine Arts, designed to offer "quality education in the arts to children in the neighborhood." With $300 from her father, some folding chairs and tables, and a second-hand piano, she started out with four instructors teaching dance and drama to twenty-five students in a six-room apartment in Roxbury.

The school led a nomadic existence, supported by private donations and neighborhood bake sales, until 1968, when Lewis arranged the purchase of a former Jewish synagogue building for the price of one dollar, in the Mattapan area of Boston where a Jewish neighborhood had been transformed into an African American community. With the new site, additional faculty, and an enrollment of 250 students, a much higher level of funding was necessary to keep the new school going. Local businesses and public utilities provided financial assistance until Lewis could attract the attention of larger philanthropic institutions. In 1969, and again in 1974, the Rockefeller Foundation provided substantial grants of money, and during the same period the Ford Foundation also offered generous challenge grants.

Elma Lewis was able to spread knowledge of her programs and her school by serving on a number of influential boards and committees. She was a consultant to the Office of Program Development for the Boston public schools, as well as to the National Education Association and the National Endowment for the Arts. She was an overseer of the Museum of Fine Arts, a trustee of the Massachusetts College of Arts, and a member of the American Academy of Arts and Sciences. She was named a fellow of the Black Academy of Arts and Letters, and in 1977 served on the board for the second World Festival of Black Arts in Nigeria. In 1968 Lewis became founder and director of the National Center of Afro-American Artists.

Perhaps one of Lewis's most enduring legacies has been the production of "Black Nativity," a folksong rendering of Langston Hughes's story-play about Mary and Joseph. First performed in Boston at the Elma Lewis School of Fine Arts in 1969, it has expanded into a pageant with a cast that includes many members drawn from the local community and more than a hundred gospel singers of all ages. "Black Nativity" has become an annual tradition in the Boston Christmas season thanks to the vision and determination of Elma Lewis. At the conclusion of the Gospel Jubilee in Boston's Jordan Hall in February 2002, hosted by the New England Conservatory of Music, Elma Lewis was presented with a lifetime achievement award. From her wheelchair, she reminisced about her years of service to the African American arts community, and then closed with one word as her legacy: "Teach."

❡ MARY RICE LIVERMORE

"During the [Civil] war," Mary Rice Livermore recalled, "I became aware that a large portion of the nation's work was badly done, or not done at all, because woman was not recognized as a factor in the political world." Livermore was one of a number of Boston women for whom the Civil War was a turning point in their lives. Moving out of the purely domestic sphere that had constituted the acceptable boundary of their lives, they found the national conflict provided them with new skills and proficiencies that dramatically changed the way they saw themselves and the way they viewed their purpose in the world.

Born in Boston on December 19, 1820, the fourth of six children, Mary Rice grew up in a strongly religious household. Her father, Timothy Rice, a laborer, was a Baptist of strict Calvinist faith; her mother, Zebiah Vose Glover, was more lenient, but also joined in family religious services every morning and evening. Mary attended Miss Hall's primary school in Boston, and continued her schooling at the nearby Hancock Grammar School. After a brief period in western New York, the family returned to Boston, and Mary attended a female seminary in Charlestown where, after graduation, she remained as a teacher of French, Latin, and Italian.

In 1839 Mary became a tutor for a family on a plantation in southern Virginia, where she witnessed the brutality of slavery at firsthand. Returning north in 1842, she subscribed to the *Liberator* and became a strong supporter of emancipation. Taking a teaching position at a coeducational school in Duxbury, Mass., she met and married, over her father's objections, a young Universalist minister, Daniel Parker Livermore, in May 1845. Performing the usual tasks expected of the wife of an itinerant pastor, Mary also found time to become active in the temperance movement as well as to write stories and poems for various religious periodicals. In 1857 Daniel Livermore's family joined the antislavery emigration to Kansas, but a daughter's illness en route forced the family to halt in Chicago, where they eventually settled after Daniel found a suitable pastorate. Mary continued her writing and engaged in charitable activities caring for elderly women and destitute children.

The Civil War provided a wider field for Mary Livermore's activities, as she threw herself into the work of the Chicago chapter of the U.S. Sanitary Commission. Under the direction of Mrs. Livermore and her friend, Jane C. Hoge, the Chicago branch became extremely effective, especially in furnishing food for General Grant and his Army of the West; according to the historian John Newberry, "a line of vegetables connected Chicago and Vicksburg." Perhaps her greatest wartime achievement was planning and directing the great women's Sanitary Fair in October 1863, which raised more than $70,000 for the Sanitary Commission.

The Civil War experience convinced Mrs. Livermore that the only way women could fight evils like drunkenness, poverty, and prostitution was to become active in politics. She became president of the Illinois Woman Suffrage Association and a founding member of the American Woman Suffrage Association. She returned to the Boston area and found a home in Melrose, while her husband accepted the Universalist pastorate in the South Shore town of Hingham. Mary continued her activities in the suffrage movement, in 1893 taking over Lucy Stone's position as president of the Massachusetts Woman Suffrage Association.

During this same period, Mary Livermore began acquiring a national reputation as a public speaker. She made her first major lecture tour in 1870, and for the next twenty-three years was a regular feature of the lecture circuit from coast to coast, delivering an average of 150 lectures a year. Tall and matronly, with auburn hair, she spoke without notes about a wide range of topics—"biographical, historical, political, religious, reformatory, and sociological"—in a rich and authoritative voice. Aided and encouraged by her husband, she conducted a successful European tour in 1878, while continuing with her writing. In 1887 she published *My Story of the War*, which became a national bestseller, and ten years later she turned out an equally successful work called *The Story of My Life*. In addition to her commitment to suffrage, Livermore continued her activities in the temperance movement, serving as president of the Massachusetts Woman's Christian Temperance Union from 1875 to 1885. She was largely responsible in June 1877 for pressuring the mayor and city council of Boston to banish "strong drink" from a banquet honoring President Rutherford B. Hayes.

After 1895, now in her seventies, Mary Livermore's boundless stamina began to wane, and she was forced to cut back on her public appearances, especially after suffering serious eye problems. The death of her husband in July 1899 was another blow; she herself died in May 1905, at the age of eighty-five, after a long, fulfilling, and productive career.

❡ HENRY CABOT LODGE

"From the Rio Grande to the Arctic Ocean there should be but one flag and one country," wrote Senator Henry Cabot Lodge at the turn of the century in a popular magazine called *Our Blundering Generation*. This enthusiastic support for a vigorous America that would assume the responsibility of world leadership was one of the notable characteristics of a Boston statesman who served for nearly thirty years as a leading member of the U.S. Senate.

Great-grandson of George Cabot, a wealthy Federalist merchant, Henry Cabot Lodge was born in Boston in 1850. After graduating from Harvard College in 1871, and from Harvard Law School in 1874, he served as assistant editor on the *North American Review* from 1873 to 1876, the year he received the first Ph.D. degree offered by Harvard in the field of political science. For a number of years he continued to pursue the career of an academic and biographer, publishing *The Life and Letters of George Cabot* (1877), *Alexander Hamilton* (1882), *Daniel Webster* (1882), and *George Washington* (1888).

The increasing partisanship in Lodge's journalistic writings reflected his growing interest in an active political career, and after serving in the Massachusetts legislature, in 1883 he managed the state's Republican gubernatorial campaign. In 1886 he was elected to Congress, where he became a well-known figure on the floor of the House before the end of his first term. Chosen U.S. Senator in January 1893 by the Republican-dominated Massachusetts legislature, he was regularly sent back to his seat in Washington until his death in 1924.

A thoroughgoing protectionist and an opponent of free silver, Lodge helped draft the Sherman Anti-Trust Law, the Pure Food and Drugs Law, and several tariff measures. As a staunch conservative, he opposed the direct election of senators and women's suffrage, and voted against the adoption of the Eighteenth Amendment. Lodge's acceptance of the principles of Social Darwinism only served to confirm his belief in the superiority of the white Teutonic and Anglo-Saxon nations as the "most fit" races. While serving in the

House, he had already spoken in favor of establishing more effective barriers against the increasing influx of immigrants from southern and eastern Europe. He introduced a bill calling for a literacy test designed to exclude members of those nationalities he considered "most alien to the body of the American people." There was a limit, he said, to the capacity of any race to assimilate an "inferior race"; and when you begin admitting people of "alien or lower races of less social efficiency and less moral force," then you are running a frightful risk: "The lowering of a great race means not only its decline, but that of civilization."

When he moved to the Senate, Henry Cabot Lodge applied similar theories to the role of the United States in international affairs. He steadfastly opposed any proposal for compulsory international arbitration or disarmament, supported the annexation of the Philippines as a means of expanding American influence into the Pacific, and assisted Theodore Roosevelt's machinations in Panama in order to advance the construction of the Panama Canal. The militant theories of Captain Alfred Thayer Mahan informed Lodge's views on the importance of sea power as a determining factor in American foreign policy. The judgment of Henry Cabot Lodge on international affairs was highly valued by Theodore Roosevelt and his advisors.

Although Lodge served for many years on the Senate Foreign Relations Committee, he did not become chairman until late in his career, when his leadership against President Woodrow Wilson in the fight over the ratification of the Treaty of Versailles in 1919 made him a powerful national figure. As one of the "reservationists," Lodge adamantly opposed any departure from America's traditional policy of isolation. He was convinced that he was representing majority American opinion in his opposition to the coupling of the peace treaty with a guarantee of U.S. participation in the League of Nations, and was equally convinced that Wilson was wrong in opposing the popular will. Lodge's role in effecting the eventual defeat of the Treaty of Versailles, and the rejection of the League of Nations, gained for him at the time both fervent admiration as well as bitter resentment.

After this battle, Henry Cabot Lodge continued as an influential member of the Senate until his death in 1924, and was among those responsible for the nomination of Warren G. Harding as the Republican candidate for President of the United States. His grandson and namesake Henry Cabot Lodge, Jr., also served as a Senator from Massachusetts and ran for Vice President in 1960 on the ticket with Richard Nixon.

¶ MARTIN LOMASNEY

On October 27, 1945, Archbishop Richard J. Cushing announced that $100,000 for the establishment of the new Catholic Boys Guidance Center in Boston's Fenway district had come from the estate of the late Martin M. Lomasney. This was an appropriate bequest from a Boston political leader who had been himself an orphan and who had spent most of his life working for the benefit of the poor and the disadvantaged of his district in the West End.

Born in Boston on December 3, 1859, of immigrant parents from County Cork, Martin Lomasney was forced to leave grammar school at the age of eleven when both his father and his mother died within the same year. He earned money by selling newspapers and shining shoes, until a local politician provided him with a series of city jobs as a laborer, a lamplighter, and a health inspector. Lomasney grew up to be a thickset man, with a "massive dome," gold-rimmed spectacles, a small moustache, and a jaw that "jutted forth at a pugnacious angle." He could be easily identified at a distance by the battered old straw hat he wore rain or shine throughout the year. A perennial bachelor, he lived a single life in a modest rooming house, attended church regularly, neither drank nor smoked, and avoided public functions whenever possible.

In 1885 Martin Lomasney, his brother Joseph, and a group of friends founded the Hendricks Club, named after Grover Cleveland's first Vice President, who was regarded as a friend of the Irish.

The Hendricks Club was a gathering place where men of the West End's Ward 8 could meet, gossip, exchange information, play cards (dice and drinking were strictly forbidden), and engage in political discussions. Lomasney kept a permanent office in the second floor of the club, which was originally located near North Station, but was later moved to Bowdoin Square. From this office, the "Mahatma," as he came to be known because of his exalted rank in the community, worked day and night to provide for the needs of his people and to protect them from what he called the "inquisitorial terrors of organized charity." Lomasney was well aware that the humiliating experience of poor Irish immigrants being rudely interrogated by insensitive and often hostile city welfare officials brought back painful memories of the treatment of the Irish by their English overlords.

Lomasney and his associates' headquarters served not only as an employment agency and a charitable bureau, but also as a center for political planning and strategy, turning the Hendricks Club into what he called "a machine for getting votes." The basic needs of the poor were largely unattainable at a time when social security and unemployment compensation did not exist. Poor people needed food and clothing, dentures and eyeglasses, jobs and pardons, medical care and legal advice, and political support for a boss depended on his assurance that he would supply these basic needs. As Lomasney once philosophized: "The great mass of people are interested in only three things—food, clothing, and shelter. A politician in a district like mine sees to it that his people get these things. If he does, then he doesn't have to worry about their loyalty and support." It was as simple as that. Power and patronage went hand in hand in the Irish neighborhood.

"The Lomasney methods were not always above reproach," admitted his biographer, Leslie Ainley. "He practiced his politics realistically, ruthlessly, and with an eye to ultimate success rather than to ideals and ethics." But he always stayed on the right side of the law, constantly warning his lieutenants to "keep it legal." In addition to establishing himself as the undisputed boss of the West End's Ward 8, Martin Lomasney also decided who would, and who would not, receive the backing of his powerful political organization when running for city office. Lomasney himself also participated in public affairs of both the city and the state. Starting in 1896, he ran success-fully for two terms in the state Senate; served another year in the House of Representatives; then held a seat on the Board of Alder-men, where he wielded a significant influence on citywide affairs. Lomasney later returned to Beacon Hill to resume his House seat in the state legislature, where, known as the legendary "Sphinx of Boston," he would remain for the greater part of the next twenty years, until his death in August 1933.

Today, a small street called Lomasney Way runs beside the Fleet Center that replaced the old Boston Garden. Ironically, that street looks out onto the fashionable townhouses of the Charles River Park project, constructed during the 1960s on the rubble of the old West End where Martin Lomasney once exercised his influence as one of the city's most powerful ward bosses.

❧ HENRY WADSWORTH LONGFELLOW

One by one the members of America's Revolutionary generation had passed away, and by the early part of the nineteenth century most of the Founding Fathers had also gone to their rest. The United States had finally achieved a recognizable history, and during the 1840s and 1850s a number of Harvard historians emerged to chronicle the events of that history. Bancroft, Sparks, Hildreth, Prescott, Motley, and Parkman were among the scholars who carefully pieced together the historical tapestry. But it was a poet, Henry Wadsworth Long-fellow, who used the rhythms of his verse to capture the sweeping panorama of American history, not only for his own generation, but also for future generations of schoolchildren who would find the colorful excitement of their country's beginnings in the epic style of Longfellow's poetry.

Henry Wadsworth Longfellow was born in 1807 in Portland, Me., the son of Stephen Longfellow, a lawyer and a member of the Massachusetts legislature at a time when Maine was still part of the Bay State. Henry showed signs of exceptional literary talent at an early age, and was already publishing verses when he was thirteen years old. When he graduated from Bowdoin College in 1825, he was offered a professorship there on condition that he continue his studies abroad first. He spent the next three years, from 1826 to 1829, in France, Spain, Italy, and Germany, before returning to America and taking up his academic duties at Bowdoin. He remained there for the next six years teaching, writing texts and primers, and contributing essays and sketches to various magazines.

In 1835 Longfellow accepted a professorship of modern languages at Harvard, once again prefaced by travels in Europe to increase his knowledge of German literature. Goethe and the German romantic lyricists, and especially their use of hexameters in narrative poems, are said to have influenced the young American's own poetic style. Upon his return, he took up residence at Craigie House in Cambridge, settled into teaching, and became a well-known and highly popular addition to the social scene. He often walked across the old West Boston Bridge (in 1927 renamed the Longfellow Bridge) into Boston to court Frances Elizabeth Appleton, daughter of the prosperous Boston merchant Nathan Appleton. They married in 1839, lived a long and happy married life, and filled Craigie House with the happy laughter of their six children.

Longfellow worked steadily at his poetry. In 1839 he produced *Voices of the Night,* a volume that included such favorites as "Hymn to the Night" ("I heard the trailing garments of the Night . . .") and "A Psalm of Life" ("Tell me not, in mournful numbers . . ."). In 1842 he turned out *Ballads and Other Poems,* containing such well-known poems as "The Skeleton in Armor," "The Wreck of the *Hesperus,*" "The Village Blacksmith" ("Under the spreading chestnut tree . . ."), and "Excelsior," which seemed to capture the optimistic spirit of the age. Longfellow showed a decided skill at managing his business affairs, and learned that he could make more money by publishing his individual poems in small volumes as they were written and then offering several volumes together in collected editions. He would repeat the cycle, adding more poems and enlarging the collections.

In 1845 Longfellow decided to resign his professorship at Harvard and devote himself entirely to his studies and his poetry. The first result of his new freedom was a series of epic poems, telling of the early history of the New World and drawing upon his own boyhood in rural Maine with its ancient forests, flickering campfires, Indian summers, wayside taverns, and village blacksmiths. *Evangeline* (1847) was the first poem to draw upon the tragic experience of French-Canadian peasant people, but it was the appearance of *Hiawatha* in 1855 that increased his already substantial popularity as America's leading poet, selling more than five thousand copies in its first run. Antonín Dvořák, the noted Czech composer who visited America and incorporated American Indian motifs into his music, recalled reading *Hiawatha* in his own native language as a young man. *The Courtship of Miles Standish* (1858), re-creating the society of the first Pilgrim settlers at Plymouth, also proved to be a great success; it was reported that ten thousand copies of the poem were sold in London on the first day it appeared.

A distinguished figure with large expressive eyes, a strong Roman nose, a full white beard, and hair worn long in the back, Longfellow represented everything a great poet should be. Although the death of his beloved wife in July 1861 left him with a profound grief that lasted many years, and entrusted him with the care and upbringing of their six children, he worked steadily at his poetry until his death in 1882 at the age of seventy-five. Longfellow was honored as the first American poet to be commemorated in Westminster Abbey. The Vassall-Craigie-Longfellow House still presides over Brattle Street in Cambridge, preserved as a National Historic Site that serves as both a museum and a venue for literary and cultural events.

❧ JAMES RUSSELL LOWELL

Poet, critic, editor, educator, and diplomat, James Russell Lowell was the foremost American man of letters in his time. Grandson of John

Lowell, a legislator and jurist, and brother of Robert T. S. Lowell, an
Episcopal clergyman and headmaster of St. Mark's School, James
was born in Cambridge in 1819, graduated from Harvard in 1838,
and completed Harvard Law School in 1840. In 1844 he married
Maria White, whose loving inspiration for her husband's poetry can
be seen in such early works as *A Year's Life* (1841) and *Poems* (1844).
His first book of literary criticism, *Conversations on Some of the Old
Poets,* was published in 1845.

In the year 1848, Lowell published *Poems: Second Series;* the rol-
licking critical satire *A Fable for Critics;* the first volume of *The
Biglow Papers;* and *The Vision of Sir Launfal,* a Christian parable. It
was during this period that Lowell visited the grave of three British
soldiers who had been killed at the North Bridge in Concord on
April 19, 1775, and was moved to write a reflection that included the
lines now inscribed on the marker:

> They came three thousand miles and died
> To keep the past upon its throne:
> Unheard, beyond the ocean tide
> Their English mother made her moan.

All of Lowell's work was highly competent, some of it was even brilliant, and yet there was truth to Margaret Fuller's criticism that "his
great facility at versification has enabled him to fill the ear with a co-
pious stream of pleasant sound. But his verse is stereotyped; his
thought sounds no depth." In *The Biglow Papers,* Lowell reproduced
Yankee dialect with extreme exactness, and his satiric criticism of the
national government in its conduct of the Mexican War was remarkably telling. Nearly twenty years later, the second series of *The
Biglow Papers,* which appeared in 1867, dealt with equal skill with the
Civil War. These satires may be regarded as his most distinctive contribution to the literature of his time.

Desolate after the death of his wife in 1853, Lowell busied himself
writing magazine articles and taking part in the local social whirl. In
1855 he succeeded Longfellow as Smith Professor of French and
Spanish and professor of belles lettres at Harvard, and held that chair
until 1886, when he assumed emeritus status. In 1855 he became edi-

tor of the *Atlantic Monthly,* resigning in 1861, and three years later became an associate editor of the *North American Review.* He was also influenced by his wife to become involved in the antislavery movement, although his naturally conservative nature kept him from agreeing with the extreme radicalism of abolitionists like William Lloyd Garrison. During the 1850s he became a strong supporter of the new Republican party, and often extolled its principles in the pages of the *Atlantic Monthly.* During the Civil War, he expressed his moderate and essentially gradualist views of slavery and emancipation in his second series of *Biglow Papers,* which began appearing in serial form in the *Atlantic* in late 1861. He feared that those abolitionist leaders who were pressuring President Lincoln for immediate emancipation would cause the Republican party to lose sight of its main goals of establishing order and preserving the Union. In January 1864 he published in the *North American Review* an eloquent defense of Lincoln's Emancipation Proclamation as a sensible and practical solution to the slavery problem that kept alive the moral idealism of the Republican party.

Although Lowell had been spending more of his professional time as a literary critic, his poem written at the end of the Civil War, "Ode Recited at the Harvard Commemoration, July 21, 1865," remains a moving testament to his poetic skill. Echoing Emerson's Phi Beta Kappa address, Lowell rejoices that young American scholars had been drawn from their vain search for truth "amid the dust of books" to learn about truth by fighting for it. The martial valor of these young Harvard men demonstrated once again that "the best blood" is that which "hath the most iron in it."

In 1877 Lowell's career took a rather surprising turn when, at the age of fifty-eight, he accepted an appointment as minister to Spain, where he served with skill and enthusiasm for three years; he then moved on to England, where he served as minister to the Court of St. James's until 1885. As a well-known literary figure, an excellent public speaker, and a charming dinner companion, the American writer did much to establish good relations between the two countries. Shortly after the death of his second wife, James Russell Lowell returned to the United States and at the age of seventy-two died in Boston.

❡ Ralph Lowell

With his distinctive Brahmin pedigree, his Harvard background, his downtown Yankee bank, his hand-tailored tweed suit, and his clipped military moustache, he looked as though he had just stepped out of the pages of John P. Marquand's classic novel, *The Late George Apley.* Indeed, Ralph Lowell so thoroughly personified the spirit of the Beacon Hill Brahmin that in his later years he was almost universally known as "Mister Boston."

Born in July 1890, Ralph Lowell was a member of a distinguished Boston family that included two notable poets, four federal judges, a famous college president, a pioneering industrialist, and an eminent astronomer. Ralph (named after Ralph Waldo Emerson) graduated from Harvard in 1912, and after the obligatory world tour took a position at the First National Bank of Boston. After service in the United States Army during World War I, Lowell began working for the investment banking house of Lee, Higginson & Company, where he was made partner in 1929. At that point he began assuming the kind of social responsibilities he felt commensurate with his family's name and his own good fortune—for instance, he joined the boards of the Massachusetts Society for the Prevention of Cruelty to Children and the North Bennet Street Industrial School, which taught manual skills to immigrant youths in the North End.

After suffering personal losses during the Depression, when Lee, Higginson was forced to liquidate in 1929, he persuaded the New York firm of Clark, Dodge & Company to take over Lee, Higginson's stock department and put him in charge of the Boston office, where he became a partner in 1937. He survived the Depression, continuing to admire Herbert Hoover and professing to despise Franklin Delano Roosevelt and his "crackpot schemes." In 1942, the chairman of the Boston Safe Deposit & Trust Company died, and Ralph Lowell was invited to become chairman of the company, which specialized in administering trusts. At about the same time, he became Trustee of the Lowell Institute, and began looking for new ways to expand his family's commitment to adult education. In 1947 he persuaded several neighboring colleges and universities to join Harvard University in forming the Lowell Institute Broadcasting Council for the promotion of educational radio. In 1951 he formed the WGBH Educational Foundation, Inc., in order to secure a television license, which the FCC granted in 1953. By 1960 Ralph Lowell had become popularly known as "Mister Boston"—one of the city's busiest corporate executives and most prominent civic leaders. Bank president, Trustee of the Lowell Institute, member of Harvard's Board of Overseers, President of the Museum of Fine Arts, life member of the MIT Corporation, he was also a member of the boards of sixty-five other organizations, including six hospitals and twelve welfare associations.

Although he remained thoroughly committed to old Boston ways and old Harvard traditions, Ralph Lowell also saw that Boston was changing, and made an effort to change with it. While he highly respected Boston's dignified Catholic archbishop, William Henry Cardinal O'Connell, he later came to enjoy a warm personal relationship with the prelate's more informal successor, Richard Cardinal Cushing. In 1960 Lowell agreed to serve on Boston College's Board of Regents, and two years later he accepted an honorary degree from that Jesuit institution. At the same time, he expanded his associations with members of Boston's Jewish community, attending the seventieth anniversary dinner of the Combined Jewish Philanthropies, and joined the executive board of the Massachusetts Committee of Catholics, Protestants, and Jews.

In December 1959 Ralph Lowell agreed to accept the chairmanship of a coordinating committee of leading Boston businessmen to work with the newly elected mayor of Boston, John F. Collins, in planning the future of the "New Boston." Because the group held most of its meetings in a basement conference room adjacent to the Boston Safe Deposit & Trust's giant vault, the group was quickly dubbed "The Vault," and under Lowell's seven-year chairmanship it became a critical force in changing the face of an old city.

In 1973, on the occasion of the 150th anniversary of Boston's city charter, the eighty-three-year-old Ralph Lowell was among seven persons awarded the title of "Grand Bostonian," an appropriate tribute to the lifelong service and dedication he had provided to the city. On May 15, 1979, Ralph Lowell died. His funeral service was held at a crowded Memorial Church in Harvard Yard—something the Late George Apley would have warmly approved.

❡ Horace Mann

Boston has always prided itself on the quality of its education. As early as 1635 the Boston Latin School was founded; in 1636 Harvard College was established; in 1647 the General Court ordered all townships with more than a hundred families to establish a grammar school. Over the next two hundred years, however, education remained haphazard and largely undemocratic. There were some excellent private schools for those who could afford the tuition, but the "free schools" were usually unheated one-room schoolhouses, where ungraded classes were taught by untrained and poorly paid schoolmasters who ruled with the paddle and the switch. It became the mission of Horace Mann to reform this decrepit system and establish a system of public education that would be professional, efficient, and democratic.

Horace Mann was born in the town of Franklin, Mass., in 1796, and lived through an unhappy childhood marked by poverty at home and repression in school. He eventually graduated from Brown University in 1819, studied law and, after being admitted to the bar in 1823, began a successful law practice in Dedham and in Boston. During this same period he served in the Massachusetts State Legislature as a member of the House from 1827 to 1833, and then as a member of the Senate from 1833 to 1837.

As President of the Senate during his final year in the legislature, he signed a significant education bill, which became law on April 20, 1837. This bill provided for the establishment of a state board of education, which was empowered to appoint a secretary. Through the influence of Edmund Dwight, a prominent textile manufacturer and noted philanthropist from Springfield who was also concerned with education, Horace Mann was appointed to the new post of secretary. During his years of service, between 1839 and 1848, Mann almost completely transformed the moribund school system in Massachusetts.

. His first task was to arouse awareness of the purpose, value, and needs of public education. He organized a series of annual educational conventions in every county throughout the Commonwealth, which were attended not only by teachers and school officials but also by members of the general public, and which were addressed by civic leaders and persons of intellectual distinction. Mann also edited and published a semimonthly magazine called *The Common School Journal,* as well as preparing a series of annual reports that persuaded his fellow citizens to recognize public education as the best hope of preserving democratic institutions in the United States.

In his post as secretary of the Massachusetts Board of Education, Horace Mann conducted a campaign for better school buildings, textbooks, libraries, and equipment. He established a six-months' minimum school year, insisted on dividing pupils into grades, and succeeded in getting the legislature to double educational appropriations. Fifty new schools were founded, curricula and teaching methods were revamped, and teachers' salaries were substantially increased. To improve the teaching profession itself, he brought about the establishment of teachers' institutes and created the first three state "normal schools" in the United States. Mann was generally opposed to flogging and other forms of corporal punishment, encouraging teachers to rely upon what he called moral suasion in disciplining students. Despite some bitter opposition by critics who objected to the higher taxes required by his program, his use of German and Swiss educational techniques, and his advocacy of a nonsectarian Christian ideology, Mann's efforts at educational reform were remarkably successful in a short period of time.

In 1848 Horace Mann resigned his post as secretary of the Massachusetts Board of Education and returned to political life, serving as an antislavery Whig in the U.S. Congress from 1848 to 1853. After that he accepted a post as a professor at Antioch College in Ohio and took office as the college's first president. After the college was forced to shut down temporarily in 1859 for lack of funds, Mann retired from teaching and died later that year at the age of sixty-three. Throughout his life and career, he never relented in his conviction that education was essential to democracy. "In a republic, ignorance is a crime," he once wrote. "If we do not prepare children to become good citizens—if we do not develop their capacities, if we do not enrich their minds with knowledge—then our republic must go down to destruction."

❡ COTTON MATHER

In 1691 William and Mary issued a new charter for the Massachusetts Bay Colony, abolishing the traditional religious requirements for officeholding and thereby expanding participation in the political affairs of the Puritan colony. This set the stage for the gradual decline of Boston's "aristocracy of saints," and paved the way for the emergence of the town's mercantile aristocracy. In many ways, the Reverend Cotton Mather personified the strains and tensions in late seventeenth-century Boston, as the religious orthodoxy of the Puritan commonwealth gave way to the enlightened rationalism of a trade center.

Cotton Mather was born in Boston in 1662, the son of Increase Mather, a distinguished Puritan pastor who served the town's Second Church for many years. Cotton graduated from Harvard College in 1678, took his M.A. degree in 1681, and after his ordination in 1685 served with his father at the Second Church for the rest of his life. Elected a Fellow of Harvard in 1690, he was recognized early on as one of the most eminent divines in New England. Young Mather fought against the witchcraft hysteria that broke out in Salem, and in June 1692 he and eleven other ministers from the Boston area drew up a statement cautioning the court to pay greater attention to the objective facts of the cases than to reports of demons and witches. Four months later, at a conference of ministers in Cambridge, he delivered a paper in which he stated flatly that "It were better that ten suspected witches should escape than that one innocent person should be condemned." There were critics, however, who argued that Mather's book, *Wonders of the Invisible World* (1693), did much to excite the general public imagination about such phenomena as devils, imps, and witches.

Mather gained popularity with his efforts to create societies for such causes as the assistance of the poor and the relief of the needy. In a work called *The Negro Christianized,* he claimed that slaves had souls "as white and pure as those of other Nations"; he admitted them to his church and established a school for their education. In political circles, however, there were many townspeople who objected to the way he joined with his father in accepting the new royal charter in 1691 and in defending the views of Sir William Phips, the new royal governor.

Along with many members of the town's conservative Puritan ministry, Mather was very much disturbed by the people's growing preoccupation with the material concerns of business and trade, as well as with the new secular philosophies that were beginning to come in from England during the early part of the eighteenth century. In 1796 he published *The Good Old Way,* decrying the lessening of old-time Puritan influences in the American colonies and bemoaning the younger generation's lack of respect and reverence for the clergy. At the same time, Mather found himself torn between the inherited values and traditional orthodoxy of the seventeenth century and the new scientific ideas and rational concepts of the eighteenth century, which he often saw as an additional way of comprehending the greatness of God. When a smallpox epidemic broke out in Boston in 1721, for example, he convinced Dr. Zabdiel Boylston to inoculate large numbers of the Boston population, and later defended in print what he regarded as a beneficial medical procedure. Although he continued to hold on to the basic principles of Calvinism, in 1721 he expounded in his book *The Christian Philosopher* doctrines which represented what many readers felt were steps toward a form of deism.

Constantly overworking himself, and beset by domestic tragedies,

Cotton Mather was often unstable and contradictory, overwhelmed by the prospect of death and eternal damnation. At times he could be thoughtful and compassionate; at other times so argumentative and contentious that Samuel Sewall found him "profoundly disturbing." His contributions as a writer, however, won him significant recognition both at home and abroad. His numerous books and essays reveal a remarkable range of knowledge, but it was his *Magnalia Christi Americana,* published in London in 1702, that won him praise as the most impressive American literary figure up to that time. A curious mixture of biographies of lay and religious leaders, an account of church history, and a series of what he called "remarkable providences," this work was designed to convince his Boston readers that unless they mended their ways and returned to the teachings of their forefathers, they were doomed to perdition. A foundational text of New England theology and literature, it remained a work to be reckoned with long after the Puritan commonwealth was overtaken by secular society.

❡ ABIGAIL WILLIAMS MAY

The abolition movement and the Civil War forced many American women out of their traditional "domestic sphere" and involved them in activities that greatly expanded their horizons. Abby May of Boston was typical of a number of middle-class women who gained managerial skills and political experience far beyond what was considered "women's work" and went on to apply these techniques to achieve their cherished goal of women's suffrage.

Born in Boston on April 21, 1829, Abigail Williams May (usually known as Abby) was the third daughter and youngest of seven children of Samuel and Mary May, descendants of old Boston families. Both parents had become Unitarians and had risked the displeasure of many of their friends and neighbors by supporting William Lloyd Garrison and his abolitionist ideas. Abby's first cousin, Samuel

Joseph May, was a well-known Unitarian minister with strong abolitionist tendencies, and her older brother, the Rev. Samuel May, Jr., was similarly outspoken in his antislavery views.

Growing up in a family with such strong reformist notions, Abby was attracted to progressive philosophy on her own. After attending various private schools in Boston, she became an enthusiastic follower of the liberal Transcendental clergyman Theodore Parker, who began preaching in Boston in 1845. Following his concept of an active social Christianity, Abby did charitable work for many years among the poor children of the city. With the outbreak of the Civil War, she served from 1861 to 1866 as a member of the New England Women's Auxiliary Association of the U.S. Sanitary Commission, first as secretary, but eventually as chairman of the executive committee. In this responsible position, she received and disbursed millions of dollars in money and supplies for Union troops, and in June 1862 traveled aboard a hospital transport vessel in Virginia to get firsthand knowledge of the distribution of supplies.

After the war, Abby May involved herself in aiding the cause of the freed slave, but gradually turned her time and attention to movements to improve the condition of American women. With her friends Julia Ward Howe and Ednah Dow Cheney, she helped found the New England Women's Club in 1868, and during the temporary absence of Mrs. Howe she served as president of the club. She worked with prominent women from many states as a member of the Association for the Advancement of Women, becoming a vice-president for the organization as well as serving as a representative from Massachusetts. Like her mother, Abby was an ardent suffragist, and in 1874 became a member of the executive committee of both the New England and Massachusetts Woman Suffrage Association. In 1880 she joined the Massachusetts Society for the University Education of Women, and in that same year served as president of the Massachusetts School Suffrage Association. For several years Abby had been working to persuade women throughout the state to take part in local school elections, and one of the specific reforms launched by the Women's Club was to win representation for women on the Boston School Committee. Abby herself, along with three other members of the club, was elected to the Boston School Committee in 1873, but the committee refused to seat them because they were women. The following year, after a special act of the state legislature permitted women to serve, Abby May and five other women were duly elected to the school committee. May was re-elected for a three-year term in 1875, but was defeated in 1878. Although she refused to run again for a seat on the Boston School Committee, Abby won an appointment to the State Board of Education, where she served from 1879 until her resignation in 1888.

As she grew older, Abby May suffered from severe bouts of ill health, and during her last two years she gradually withdrew from most public activities. She died at the age of fifty-nine at Boston Homeopathic Hospital and was buried at Forest Hills Cemetery in Boston, near other members of her family. Throughout her life she was sustained by the conviction that it was within the power of the individual to improve social conditions, and that her particular role in life was to help increase opportunities for women in all fields where they could lead socially useful lives.

¶ John W. McCormack

One of the great misfortunes suffered by Irish immigrant families who fled the Great Famine of the late 1840s was the loss of so many of their children. Children in the Irish district of Boston, wrote Lemuel Shattuck in his 1845 census report, seemed "literally born to die." The grandparents of John W. McCormack were among those who had fled the Great Hunger. Joseph H. McCormack married Mary Ellen O'Brien and settled in the Andrew Square section of South Boston to raise their family. Of their twelve children, only three—John and his two brothers, Daniel and Edward (later known as "Knocko")—survived to adulthood. From an early age, therefore, John McCormack was only too conscious of how susceptible poor people were to the insecurities of life, the inadequacies of housing, and the ravages of disease.

After completing eighth grade at the John Andrew Grammar School, John was sent into the working world at the age of thirteen by the death of his father. He sold newspapers, worked as an errand boy, and then took a job as an office boy in the law office of William T. Way, Esq., who made his law books available to the young man. After a full day's work, McCormack "read for the law" at night, and in 1913 passed the Massachusetts bar examination at the age of twenty-one—just a few months before the death of his mother. His devotion to his mother was one reason he supported the movement for women's suffrage. "Who dares tell me," he once said after returning from a political rally, "that my mother cannot vote as well as any man, and better than most?"

After a period of service in the U.S. Army during World War I McCormack returned to his law practice and decided to try a political career. He served two years as a state representative from 1920 to 1922, and then moved on to four years in the Massachusetts senate. In 1926, he made a run for the U.S. Congress, hoping to unseat the popular James A. Gallivan from the Twelfth Congressional District. The newcomer was handily defeated, however, and returned to his law practice until the unexpected death of Gallivan in 1928. This time McCormack was elected to the House of Representatives—a position to which he would be reelected twenty times, serving forty-two years as a member of the House.

When John W. McCormack arrived in Washington, he came under the tutelage of two able Texas politicians: John Nance Garner, soon to be Franklin D. Roosevelt's first Vice President, and Sam Rayburn, who would serve as Speaker of the House almost continuously from 1940 until McCormack succeeded him in 1962. The older men took a liking to the tall, feisty, congenial Irishman from Boston, whom they regularly included in their after-hours poker games. After only two terms, he was appointed to the powerful Ways and Means Committee, a clear indication that rural Southerners wanted to draw this Northeast Democrat into the New Deal coalition.

During the Depression years and the World War II era, John McCormack fashioned a reputation as a tenacious debater and a skillful parliamentarian who helped move the New Deal legislative program through the Congress. Social security, unemployment compensation, the minimum wage, and low-cost housing were meaningful issues for McCormack. Whenever he spoke before Irish Catholic audiences in Boston he often compared the ideals of the New Deal with the principles he found in Pope Leo XIII's encyclical *Rerum Novarum,* emphasizing the dignity of the working man and the necessity of a living wage.

Before Pearl Harbor, he fought to keep the Selective Service Act alive. During the war, he helped conceal millions of dollars of appropriations for the highly secret Manhattan Project, which produced the atomic bomb. After the war, as the first chairman of the House Science and Aeronautics Committee, he promoted advances in science and research to keep ahead of the Soviet Union. After the death of Sam Rayburn in January 1962, John W. McCormack was elected Speaker of the House of Representatives, the first Roman Catholic to hold that office—coincidentally, during the term of the first Catholic president, John F. Kennedy.

With the assassination of President Kennedy on November 22, 1963, and the elevation of Vice President Lyndon B. Johnson, Speaker McCormack became next in the line of presidential succession until the 1964 election. Serving President Johnson loyally, McCormack used all his powers as Speaker to help carry through the civil rights and social programs of the Great Society. In 1970, at the age of seventy-eight, John McCormack retired from the House and from the Speaker's chair, returning to his Boston home and to his beloved wife, Harriet, who passed away the following year. It became part of the lore of Massachusetts politics that in the half-century of their married life, the McCormacks never failed to have dinner together. John remained active in his retirement years, keeping an office in the John W. McCormack Federal Post Office Building in Boston, where the door was always open. He died quietly on Saturday afternoon, November 22, 1980—seventeen years to the day after the death of John F. Kennedy. "Speaker McCormack was the

Horatio Alger of politics," said Congressman Joseph Moakley. "He made a great, great mark not only on Massachusetts but on the entire country."

❡ DONALD MCKAY

Castle Island is a small knob of land in Boston Harbor, just off the shoreline of the South Boston peninsula. In colonial times, the English constructed Castle William there as a defense against the French warships; after the Revolution, the U.S. government erected Fort Independence to protect Boston Harbor. Today, it is a delightful recreation area, a place of promenades and picnics for Bostonians of all ages and incomes. Along the north side of Castle Island, facing seaward, is a 52-foot-high granite shaft commemorating the master shipbuilder Donald McKay, a tribute to the man and his famous clipper ships.

Donald McKay was born September 4, 1819, on a farm in Shelburne County, Nova Scotia. At the age of 16 he went to New York and became an apprentice to Isaac Webb, one of the city's outstanding shipbuilders, who agreed to take him on if he promised not to marry, play at cards or dice, nor "haunt ale-houses or dance halls." Pleased with the young man's work, Webb terminated the apprenticeship early so that McKay could marry Albenia Boole, the daughter of a fellow shipbuilder. She was a great help to her husband, who had little formal schooling. When Albenia died in 1848, McKay married Mary Litchfield, who often sailed with him and was reputed to have good business sense.

McKay started out in New York shipyards, worked in Wiscasset, Me., and then moved to Newburyport, Mass., where his work attracted the attention of the ship owner Enoch Train, who persuaded him to come to Boston. McKay set up shop in East Boston, on Border Street, near Chelsea Creek, at the foot of Eutaw Street, where he built traders and packets for the West Indies trade, and where he launched his first large ship, the *Washington Irving,* in 1845. The lucrative profits from the China trade had created a demand for fast ships that led to the creation of the revolutionary clipper ships. These ships first had to be "sharp," that is, long and narrow; second, they were heavily sparred, which meant taller masts and longer yards to carry an extensive area of sail; and third, they had to have a "driver" for a captain, a man who never seemed to sleep and was always on deck driving the crew to trim the sails for maximum speed. Donald McKay did not invent the clipper ship, but he perfected the slender, concave hull shape, and made the clipper ship famous for its speed and beauty.

It was the discovery of gold in California in 1848, however, that provided McKay with the opportunity to use his talents as a builder and designer to the fullest. Fast ships were in great demand to take the "forty-niners" and supplies around Cape Horn, and to return with gold and other cargoes. In his shipyard in East Boston, McKay set about building the fastest ship possible. His first great clipper ship was the *Flying Cloud* of 1851, which won a race to San Francisco by a full 19 days. Although the crew was mutinous, and parts of her rigging were torn away in storms, the *Flying Cloud* reached the Golden Gate in 89 days and 21 hours, a record that was never broken by a sailing ship. The *Lightning,* built in 1854 for the Australian trade, made some phenomenal passages, and was faster than the steamships of the day in a good wind. She set a speed record with a run of 436 miles in 24 hours, an average of over 18 miles an hour.

But the day of the clippers was short—the beautiful vessels carried too little cargo and required too large a crew to be economical after the first rush to California and later to the gold fields in Australia. Unlike some of his contemporaries, McKay foresaw the change to iron and steam, went to England to learn the new techniques, and returned to build some of the new ironclads for the Union Navy. His last clipper, *Glory of the Seas,* was launched in 1869, and set a record of 39 days from San Francisco to Australia. Bowing to the inevitable, McKay sold his shipyard in 1869, worked for other builders for a time, and then returned to Hamilton, Mass., to become a scientific farmer. Donald McKay died at the age of seventy on September 20, 1880.

In his day, Donald McKay's reputation as a shipbuilder was known and honored all over the world. To insure that this reputation be preserved, and his contribution to the city of Boston be recognized, a group of Bostonians in later years formed the Committee for a Memorial to Donald McKay. Money was raised from private sources, William T. Aldrich was selected as architect, and the granite shaft was erected on Castle Island, facing the harbor. The monument, with a medallion of Donald McKay superimposed on a billowing square sail below a half-hull of the *Flying Cloud,* was completed and turned over to the United States government in 1933.

❡ HENRY MORGAN

There is hardly a highway parking area, a church parking lot, or a major industrial outlet that does not have a large white metal box soliciting donations of used clothing for the Goodwill Industries. Goodwill is the modern by-product of a movement started in Boston during the early nineteenth century by a man named Henry Morgan.

Henry Morgan was born in Newtown, Conn., on March 7, 1825. Four years later his father died, and for the next twelve years he and his mother lived in poverty. When he was sixteen years old, Henry left home to get a formal education, after which he got a job teaching school in rural areas of Connecticut. During this period he became a Methodist and, after seven years of teaching, he left that occupation to travel throughout the eastern part of the country as an itinerant preacher. Resolved to make preaching his life's work, he tried to get a license from the local Methodist church, but was refused. Thereupon Morgan dubbed himself the "Poor Man's Preacher" and formed an independent church of his own near

Bridgeport, Conn. After he was ousted by a licensed competitor, he moved to Boston, where he would spend the rest of his life.

Because the lack of a license was a serious impediment to preaching in most Methodist churches, Morgan rented the Boston Music Hall, off Washington Street in the downtown part of Boston, and there on February 27, 1859, delivered his first sermon. He told his audience that he was going to present the Gospel to the "working classes" and that he planned to open a "mission for the poor" in a hall where no admission fee would be required and where all people would be "on a common level." Morgan's Music Hall sermons drew large and enthusiastic crowds, and Morgan himself soon became a well-known personality in the city. A short time later, an interdenominational group formed the Union Mission Society and offered Morgan the position of pastor. Under his leadership the Union Mission Society soon developed into a vital institution ministering to the poor. The members of the Society established a new denomination, the First Independent Methodist Church, that granted Morgan the ordination that the Methodist Episcopal Church had denied him.

In addition to daily prayer meetings and Sunday services, the Union Mission also addressed the temporal needs of the poor parishioners, emphasizing the importance of voluntary efforts of the community rather than institutional actions. Under Morgan's direction, the Mission set up a regular employment agency, found homes for the poor, solicited donations of new and used clothing, and established a sewing school for young girls. Morgan was particularly concerned with aiding poor children, many of whom could not attend public school because they had to work all day. For such children, many of them newspaper boys, the Mission established a night school that educated hundreds of children with the help of volunteer teachers. The success of this school influenced the Boston School Committee to establish a public night school system that gradually incorporated Morgan's school.

Formal recognition of Morgan's accomplishments came in January 1868, when he was elected chaplain of the Massachusetts Senate. As a result of this position, Morgan became acquainted with Wil-

liam Claflin, a future governor of Massachusetts, who was impressed
by Morgan's work and eventually provided him with financial backing to secure an old church that was remodeled into what became
known as Morgan Chapel. While Morgan centered most of his
activities around the church and its neighborhood, he continued to
make guest appearances as the "Poor Man's Preacher" before audiences throughout New England, New York, and Pennsylvania.

Morgan was a vigorous supporter of women's rights, and regularly invited women to give Sunday lectures in Morgan Chapel. He
was also an outspoken defender of the rights of workers, taking the
side of striking railroad workers in 1877 against their employers.
Convinced that "whole communities aroused to philanthropic action" could accomplish more to prevent crime and reform the fallen
than "a few paid officials in costly institutions," Morgan spent the
remainder of his life trying to alert the citizens of Boston to the social problems around them and arouse them to take appropriate
action.

In March 1884 Henry Morgan died at the age of fifty-nine, apparently from pneumonia, and was buried at Mount Auburn Cemetery
in Cambridge. His tombstone reads: "An earnest Preacher and a Beloved Pastor of the Poor." In 1895 Dr. Edgar J. Helms was installed as
pastor of the church which had been renamed Morgan Memorial.
Building upon the work of Morgan, Dr. Helms turned the Morgan
Memorial into a true institutional church, and paved the way for
what is known today as Goodwill Industries, at present the country's
seventh-largest nonprofit organization and one of the world's leading
nonprofit providers of employment services for the disabled and dis-
advantaged.

❧ SAMUEL ELIOT MORISON

His lookout perch is on the Commonwealth Avenue Mall, just off
Exeter Street. Dressed in simple weather gear, a tall, lean figure sits in

a contemplative pose on a pyramid of jagged granite, binoculars in hand, his mouth tight and decisive, the long beak of his captain's sailing cap shading his hawklike nose as he peers out toward the city whose remarkable origins he did so much to preserve in his momentous works of history. He is "the Admiral"—Samuel Eliot Morison.

Samuel Eliot Morison was born July 9, 1887, the son of John Holmes Morison, known as "the Maryland Squire," and Emily Eliot of the renowned Boston Eliots. Morison's maternal grandmother, Emily Marshall Otis, was the granddaughter of Harrison Gray Otis (1765–1848), the urbane Federalist who would later become the subject of Morison's historical efforts, first in a doctoral dissertation at Harvard and later in a two-volume biography. Through these familial connections, Samuel inherited a legacy of Boston traditions going back some five or six generations.

Morison grew up at 44 Brimmer Street, at the foot of Beacon Hill, in a house built by his maternal grandfather in 1869, and later featured in his delightful boyhood memoir called *One Boy's Boston*. He graduated from Harvard in 1908, received an M.A. in 1909, and was awarded the Ph.D. in 1912, appropriately enough during the administration of President Charles W. Eliot, his third cousin. He assumed his first lectureship in 1915 at the age of twenty-eight, and the following year took over Professor Channing's famous course on American colonial history. After serving in the U.S. Army during World War I, he returned to his teaching duties at Harvard, and in 1922 was offered the first appointment to the Harmsworth Chair of American History at Oxford, where he remained for the next three years. While busy with his lectures, Morison also found time to write the widely acclaimed *Oxford History of the United States*.

Returning to Cambridge, Morison resumed his career at Harvard, where he enhanced his reputation as an exciting, stimulating, and demanding teacher. In 1926 President A. Lawrence Lowell appointed the young scholar to be the official historian of the 300th anniversary of Harvard College. After ten years of research and study, Samuel Eliot Morison produced the incomparable four-volume *Tercenten-*

nial History of Harvard College and University, as well as the popular *Three Centuries of Harvard,* for which he received the Jusserand Medal and the Loubat Prize.

While Morison's wide-ranging interests and extraordinary breadth of knowledge led him to write about many different aspects of New England history, he was an inveterate sailor who loved the sea. "My profession is history, my avocation is sailing. I combined them," he once explained. After a five-month expedition to sail Columbus's route and check what he experienced against contemporary accounts of America's discovery, his two-volume life of Columbus, *Admiral of the Ocean Sea,* made Morison famous. It paved the way for other maritime histories including *The Maritime History of Massachusetts* and *"Old Bruin,"* a biography of Commodore Matthew C. Perry. Never confined solely to the study or the stall, Morison enjoyed the camaraderie of his clubs—the St. Botolph Club (where his portrait now hangs), the Somerset Club, and especially the Cruising Club of America. He was active as well in political affairs and liberal causes, and surprised many of his more conservative colleagues by always voting Democrat. This "proper Bostonian" campaigned for Al Smith in 1928, became a fervent admirer of Franklin D. Roosevelt, belonged to the Charitable Irish Society, spoke out on behalf of Sacco and Vanzetti, and voiced his opposition to the Teacher's Oath Bill in Massachusetts.

During World War II, Samuel Eliot Morison was asked by President Roosevelt to supervise the writing of the official naval history of that conflict. He went to sea at the age of fifty-five, served on twelve different vessels during the war, saw action in several theaters of operation, earned seven battle stars, and retired from the Navy in 1951 with the rank of rear admiral. The fifteen volumes of *The History of United States Operations in World War II* remain a tribute to his zeal and dedication. Morison officially retired from teaching at Harvard in 1955 at the age of sixty-eight, at which point he was named the Jonathan Trumbull Professor of American History, Emeritus. With remarkable vigor and determination he continued his active historical pursuits; when he was well into his eighties he produced two more volumes of research under the general heading of *European Discovery,* dealing with the voyages of discovery that opened up the New World.

Samuel Eliot Morison died in May 1976, at the age of eighty-nine, but he continues to keep a weather eye on the changing history of Boston from his perch along the Commonwealth Avenue Mall.

❧ ROBERT MORRIS

In pre–Civil War Boston, Irish immigrants and African Americans occupied the lowest rungs of the economic ladder and lived separate lives in their own segregated areas. Despite similar experiences, however, there were surprisingly few attempts by members of either group to develop a community of interests. An exception to this pattern was Robert Morris. A black attorney admired and respected in his own African American community, he also gained the trust and confidence of the local Irish Americans.

Robert Morris was born on June 8, 1828, in the seaport town of Salem, Mass., which had an African American community of almost two hundred persons. As a youth, he worked after school as a table boy for his father, York Morris, a highly regarded waiter employed by the wealthy King family. In November 1836 Ellis Gray Loring, a prominent Boston attorney and a strong antislavery advocate, came to Salem to have Thanksgiving dinner with the Kings. Impressed with young Robert Morris, and in need of a household servant, Loring hired the young man and took him back to his home in Brookline. In addition to Robert's household duties, Loring began sending Robert to his law office to copy legal briefs. Pleased with the lad's fine penmanship, as well as his hard work, Loring gradually entrusted Morris with additional clerical work and finally took him on as his full-time law clerk.

On February 2, 1847, after completing his apprenticeship with Judge Loring, the twenty-three-year-old Robert Morris was admitted to the Suffolk Bar. Acutely aware that as a black attorney his work and demeanor would be scrutinized and evaluated in terms of his race, he was determined to prove himself "a man and a gentleman." He would either succeed in the practice of law, he wrote, or die. After he won his first case, he said he "felt like a giant," and went on to win others, mostly small-claims cases. As a new attorney who charged modest fees, Morris attracted so many Irish clients that he became known in some quarters as the "Irish lawyer." He established good relations with the Boston Irish, who eventually made up three-quarters of what became a prosperous law practice.

Robert Morris was acutely conscious of racial discrimination in Boston, and on several occasions publicly criticized local theater owners and lecture-hall managers for not allowing African Americans to use their facilities. In 1849 his reputation was enlarged when he was asked to serve as the legal aide for Charles Sumner, a gifted lawyer soon to be elected Senator from Massachusetts, in the famous Sarah Roberts case. This was a suit brought against the Boston School Committee for denying the right of a five-year-old black girl to be admitted to an all-white school. Although the court ruled unanimously against the plaintiffs, Morris continued to fight for an end to segregated schools in Boston.

In October 1850 Morris became an active member of the Committee of Vigilance and Safety to safeguard African American residents against seizure under the terms of the new Fugitive Slave Act. In February 1851 he volunteered to defend an accused runaway slave called Shadrach, and was later arrested, along with several other antislavery advocates, for participating in the rescue and abduction of the fugitive. When the Civil War broke out, Morris worked with other local African American residents to persuade state authorities to raise a regiment of black volunteers. This attempt was unsuccessful until 1863, when the Emancipation Proclamation gave Governor John A. Andrew the authority to recruit the all-black 54th Massachusetts Infantry Regiment. Although Morris was disappointed that it was led by white officers, he supported efforts to recruit the soldiers who formed this gallant unit. Morris was among those black leaders who continued to fight for equal pay and equal facilities for

❧ Elma Lewis

❧ Cotton Mather

❧ *Samuel Eliot Morison*

❧ *John Boyle O'Reilly*

the black troops who now formed an integral part of the Union army.

After the Civil War, Morris and his family moved into a spacious house at 78 West Newton Street in an affluent section of the city. His son, Robert Jr., who had been educated in France because he would not have been allowed to enroll in any of Boston's all-white schools, returned to enter Harvard Law School and in 1874 was admitted to the Suffolk Bar. Morris spent his later years working at his law office and sometimes serving as a judge in a magistrate court in Boston. In 1881 he suffered a serious illness, and on December 11, 1882, he died quietly at home. Mourners from all parts of the city filled the Church of the Immaculate Conception in the South End, where Morris had been a regular communicant and where he had taught Sunday School. Many of his friends and acquaintances followed the cortege to the Catholic cemetery in Brookline. As Boston's first black attorney, Robert Morris spent his life trying to change the racial inequities he found in Boston, and to build bridges between its segregated communities.

❡ ELLIOT NORTON

Boston could boast of its art museum and symphony orchestra, but as far as the legitimate theater was concerned, Boston was always a tryout town. During the nineteenth century the city had a mix of local acting companies and touring groups, but by the early 1900s it was clear that New York had become the center of the acting world. Seaboard cities like Philadelphia, New Haven, and Boston had become places where shows were tried out before they went on to Broadway. While the plays were in Boston, however, the New Yorkers awaited the reviews of Elliot Norton, the one Boston theater critic who, for nearly half a century, set the standards by which all major productions were to be judged.

William Elliot Norton was born May 17, 1903, in Boston, the son of William Laurence and Mary Elizabeth Norton. He attended the Mather Grammar School in Dorchester, went on to the Boston Latin School, and enrolled at Harvard College. After graduating from Harvard in 1926, Elliot became a newspaper reporter; in 1934 he married Florence Stelmach, with whom he had three children, and began specializing in covering theatrical productions. From 1934 to 1956, he was a drama critic for the *Boston Post;* from 1956 to 1962 he wrote for the *Boston Daily Record* and the *Boston Sunday Advertiser;* from 1962 to 1973 he joined the staff of the *Boston Record American* and the *Sunday Advertiser;* from 1973 to 1982 he was with the *Boston Herald American.* During a period in American theatrical history that saw such memorable productions as *Oklahoma!, South Pacific,* and *The King and I* on their way from New Haven to Broadway, Norton's reviews were the ones most eagerly awaited by producers and directors. A close personal relationship developed between Norton and the playwrights Richard Rodgers and Oscar Hammerstein ("They were my pals," Norton often said), and when Rodgers died of cancer, it was Elliot Norton who was asked to give the eulogy at the Players Club. "We generally disliked critics," Hammerstein once said, "but our friendship with Elliot Norton endured forever."

By the time he retired in 1982, Elliot Norton had covered more than six thousand productions in and out of Boston, and in 1971 became the only American theater critic to receive a special Antoinette Perry (Tony) Award. Along the way he also received the Rodgers and Hammerstein College Presidents' Award to the person who has done the most for theater in Boston (1962); the George Jean Nathan Award for the best dramatic criticism of the 1963–64 season; and the New England Theater Conference Award in 1974. He was designated by the city as a "Grand Bostonian" in 1978. In addition to writing critical reviews for Boston newspapers, Norton also found time to teach courses in dramatic literature at Emerson College, Boston College, and Boston University. Tall, slender, and articulate, with a shock of white hair, Norton was an obvious choice for the new medium of television, and in 1958 he made his television debut on WGBH, the public broadcasting station in Boston, with a series of presentations called *Elliot Norton Reviews,* which were popularly received and for which he was awarded in 1962 a George Foster Peabody Broadcasting Award.

In light of such an outstanding career, William Morris Hunt II, a Boston impresario and theater historian, solicited funds to support an annual Elliot Norton Medal, bestowed on an individual who made a distinguished contribution to the Boston theater. The award, a silver medallion bearing Norton's likeness, along with a cash award, was first sponsored by the Boston Theatre District Association and then by the League of Boston Theatres. Starting in 1983, the Norton Medal has been presented to directors, playwrights, producers, and performers. In 1990, the medal was supplemented by prize awards to an outstanding Boston actor and actress, keeping alive the distinctive commitment of Elliot Norton to the Boston theater. In 1993, a gala ceremony and banquet accompanied the annual presentation of the awards as a celebration of Elliot Norton's ninetieth birthday.

Living in quiet retirement, Norton listens intently to the baseball game on the radio ("I'm a Red Sox nut, you know"), looks forward to his ninety-ninth birthday, and rejoices in the fact that he still has "all his marbles." "That's pretty good at my age, isn't it?" he asks, with a hint of pride.

❧ Hugh O'Brien

Although Irish immigrants in Boston enjoyed politics, went to the polls regularly, and supported Democratic candidates loyally, nativist hostility prevented Irish Americans from holding positions of significance in any political party until well after the Civil War. Only with the appearance of Hugh O'Brien did the city finally find a mayoral candidate impressive enough to persuade both Irish and Yankee voters that an Irish-born Roman Catholic could become mayor of Boston.

Born July 13, 1827, in Howth, County Dublin, Ireland, Hugh O'Brien came to America with his parents when he was five years old, and attended public school in the Fort Hill section of Boston until he was twelve. He worked for a time as a printer's apprentice on the *Boston Courier,* and then took a job with the printing firm of Tuttle, Dennet & Chisholm on School Street, where he rose to foreman at the age of fifteen. Later he published his own *Shipping and Commercial List,* a complete annual report of Boston's trade and commerce that quickly became indispensable to the city's business community and was adopted as the authority at the Merchants Exchange. By 1874 it was reported in the *Daily Advertiser* that Hugh O'Brien "is well known in the community, and has the respect and confidence of everyone."

In addition to his position in the business community, Hugh O'Brien was also involved in numerous social and civic activities. He was one of the earliest members of the Franklin Typographical Society, and for a long time served as its treasurer. He was also prominent in the Union Institution for Savings since its beginnings, and its president for many years. For over thirty years he was the director of the St. Vincent's Orphan Asylum for Girls in the South End, and also served as president of the Charitable Irish Society. He was instrumental in helping Fr. John McElroy secure loans for the construction of the Church of the Immaculate Conception and for the start of Boston College.

In 1875 O'Brien decided to enter Boston politics, and as a Democratic candidate won a seat on the Board of Aldermen, where he took up the cause of the working man. He consistently opposed the Republican majority, who wanted to reduce city expenditures by cutting the wages of city workers. In later years he would fight for a minimum wage of $2.00 a day for city workers and for the elimination of the poll tax as a prerequisite for voting. On May 21, 1887, speaking before the Joint Special Committee on Parks, O'Brien delivered a powerful speech favoring a park system, not only to beautify the city but also to provide places where workingmen and their families could enjoy the pleasures of an outdoor environment. "Bostonians owe to him, more than any other man," wrote the *Boston Globe,* "the parks that soon will be opened for their use."

When Mayor Palmer announced that he would not run for reelection in 1883, the Democratic Ward Committee chose Hugh O'Brien as best qualified to run against the Republican candidate Augustus Martin. Although O'Brien lost on his first try, he ran again in 1884, voicing opposition to Martin's high-tax fiscal policies and inefficient management. Supported by Patrick J. Maguire's newspaper, *The Republican,* and benefiting from the temporary alliance between Democrats and Reform Republicans ("Mugwumps"), O'Brien won the election. Forty-eight years old, a stocky 200 pounds, with a florid complexion, moustache and beard, and keen blue eyes, the new mayor was true to his campaign promises. He cut the tax rate 24 percent and maintained it below $15 for the next four years. His preoccupation with holding down the tax rate and widening the city streets made him almost indistinguishable from previous Yankee mayors, although he did order the Boston Public Library closed on St. Patrick's Day. After completing his first one-year term, he was reelected to a second term with the enthusiastic support of many prominent Bostonians. In 1886 O'Brien was reelected to a third term; and in 1887 he again defeated his Republican opponent and went on to a fourth consecutive term. Despite his fiscal conservatism, O'Brien urged greater speed in the construction of the new Boston Public Library in Copley Square, which he said should be "the most attractive building in Boston." He was pleased to preside at the laying of the cornerstone on November 28, 1888.

By the end of the 1880s, a renewed emphasis on temperance and a vigorous attack on parochial schools produced a distinctly anti-Catholic atmosphere in Boston, and Hugh O'Brien was defeated by Thomas Norton Hart in the 1888 election. O'Brien returned to his business activities and also served as chairman of the city's Board of Survey, which planned new streets for the city. He died suddenly, at the age of sixty-eight, on August 1, 1895, in the rectory of St. Catherine's Church, Somerville, while visiting with his son, the Rev. James J. O'Brien, the first pastor of that church. A conciliator, a dedicated civil servant, and a conservative with high standards of conduct, Hugh O'Brien, as the first Irish Catholic mayor, did much to bridge the chasm between the Yankee and the Celt in late nineteenth-century Boston. He was, in the words of the *Boston Globe*'s

General Charles Taylor, "an honored and respected member of his craft and society."

¶ WILLIAM HENRY O'CONNELL

Throughout the nineteenth century, mindful of the social and economic disadvantages of their immigrant parishioners, most Catholic Church leaders in Boston had adopted a generally accommodationist relationship with the city's Protestant establishment. In 1907 William Henry O'Connell was named Archbishop of Boston and ushered in the twentieth century with a much more militant and confrontationist approach: "The Puritan has passed; the Catholic remains," he proclaimed. "It is time for Catholic manhood to stand erect, square its shoulders, look the world in the eye and say, 'I am a Roman Catholic citizen; What about it?'"

Born December 5, 1859, of working-class parents in the mill town of Lowell, Mass., young O'Connell graduated from Boston College, entered the priesthood, and studied at the North American College in Rome, where he excelled academically and met prominent Church officials. After his ordination in June 1884, O'Connell served as a curate in Medford, and later spent nine years at St. Joseph's Church in Boston's congested West End. In 1895 he was brought to Rome to become the rector of the North American College, and in 1901 he was named Bishop of Portland, Me. He remained in that capacity until 1907, when he assumed office as Archbishop of Boston after the death of Archbishop John Williams.

Taking office with vigor and determination, the forty-eight-year-old O'Connell set his sights on several objectives. The first was to transform a rather loose confederation of independent parishes into a highly centralized administration, with all institutional plans and financial decisions ratified by the archbishop personally. Needless to say, this approach did not win the new archbishop many friends among those who had been accustomed to drawing up their own

budgets, making their own decisions, and running their own do-
mains. O'Connell was adamant, however, and a new administrative
system went into operation for the archdiocese.

The second area of concern for the new prelate was to forge a
highly unified Catholic community by encouraging men, women,
and children to participate in religious organizations and associations. With an abundant supply of priests and nuns, Cardinal
O'Connell (he was elevated to the rank of Cardinal in 1911) presided
over an era of almost unparalleled zeal and devotion involving
masses, rosaries, stations of the cross, novenas, missions, retreats, de-
votional ceremonies, and public gatherings that impressively displayed the collective strength and unity of the Catholic Church.

In attempting to build a more powerful and responsible church,
O'Connell wanted his parishioners to discover their own Catholic
and Celtic roots, rather than continuing to rely upon Anglo-Saxon
values. For this reason, he established a sharp distinction between
the members of the Catholic community and their non-Catholic
neighbors. Catholics were not to enter a Protestant church or attend
non-Catholic ceremonies; young Catholics were encouraged to join
the Catholic Youth Organization (CYO) instead of involving themselves in such nonsectarian organizations as the Boy Scouts and Girl
Scouts, or the YMCA and YWCA. Catholics were to attend Catholic schools and colleges whenever possible, and the Cardinal persuaded Mayor John F. Fitzgerald of Boston to have his daughter
Rose give up plans to attend Wellesley College in favor of instruction at the Academy of the Sacred Heart.

During the first half of the twentieth century, "the Cardinal"
meant only one person in Boston. Members of the state legislature
spoke respectfully of "Number One"; city councilors waited to hear
about the position of "Lake Street" on public issues; newspaper reporters referred to "Number Eight" in reference to His Eminence's
single-digit license plate. Until his death in 1944 at the age of eighty-
five, William Henry O'Connell was one of the most powerful figures
in Boston, a portly and lordly prelate who lived in princely style in
his Florentine residence near Chestnut Hill. There were those who
strongly opposed the Cardinal's personal style as autocratic, and who

saw his ecclesiastical politics as divisive. Others, however, staunchly supported his determined and successful efforts to transform what had long been an insecure and deferential Catholic population into a strong, unified, and self-assured community. Some felt that this accomplishment was particularly relevant in a city whose strong Puritan traditions had once held immigrant Catholics in such low esteem that the infamous phrase found in want ads, "No Irish Need Apply," could be said to pertain to all opportunities in the city.

❧ JULIA O'CONNOR

At the end of World War I, the income of American workers fell, as the cost of living steadily rose. During 1919 the frustration of workers spawned some thirty-six hundred labor strikes from coast to coast. In New York City, harbor workers walked off the job; in Seattle, shipyard laborers conducted a work stoppage; in Boston, fishermen left the piers, elevated railroad workers deserted their trains, and policemen went on strike. It was in Boston, too, that under the leadership of Julia O'Connor, female telephone operators struck for better hours and higher wages.

Julia Sarsfield O'Connor was born on September 9, 1890, in Woburn, Mass., the second daughter and youngest of four children born to John and Sarah (Conneally) O'Connor, immigrants from Ireland. After attending parochial grammar schools in Woburn and public school in Medford, in 1908 Julia went to work in Boston as a telephone operator. In March 1912 she joined the newly formed Boston Telephone Operators Union, beginning an involvement with the labor movement that would last the next forty-five years. O'Connor quickly rose to prominence in the new female union, and became a member of the nine-woman committee that finally achieved recognition of their local by national union leaders.

In 1915 Julia O'Connor became the first working woman to serve as president of the Boston chapter of the Women's Trade Union

League (WTUL), and in 1919 she was a delegate to the First International Congress of Working Women. From 1914 to 1916 she also served as a workers' representative on the board appointed by the Massachusetts Minimum Wage Commission to determine a minimum wage for women retail workers. Following a near-strike in Boston in 1913, telephone operators across the country began to organize, but they were denied full representation in the International Brotherhood of Electrical Workers (IBEW), largely because of the male members' fears of "petticoat rule." When a separate department for the telephone operators was finally established within the IBEW in 1918, Julia O'Connor was elected as the president of the department, a position she would hold for the next twenty years.

During World War I, when telephone service came under government ownership, O'Connor served as the only representative of organized labor on the Ryan Commission, whose function was to advise Postmaster General Albert Burleson on wages and working conditions. In January 1919 O'Connor resigned from the commission in protest against Burleson's anti-labor attitudes. Three months later, in April 1919, she led the New England Telephone Operators Union in a six-day strike to force action on its wage demands. Completely paralyzing telephone service throughout New England, the strike was one of the few during the postwar outbreak of strikes to end on favorable terms for the workers. During 1921 Julia O'Connor traveled to Europe to observe postwar labor conditions in Great Britain, Ireland, France, Germany, and Italy, and sent back written reports that were published in *The Union Telephone Operator*. Upon her return to America, she became actively involved in the movement to end war and militarism.

The postwar climate of hostility to organized labor, combined with such technological changes as the mechanical dial system that replaced female operators, quickly reduced the size of the union organization as well as the influence of Julia O'Connor. In 1925 she married Charles Austin Parker, a reporter for the *Boston Herald*. After the birth of two daughters, Julia went back to work with the labor division of the Democratic National Committee, supporting Franklin D. Roosevelt in the campaigns of 1932, 1936, and 1940.

Under the New Deal's National Recovery Administration, she served as IBEW representative, testifying at hearings to determine labor standards in the telephone industry. From 1939 until her retirement in 1957, Julia O'Connor Parker was an organizer for the American Federation of Labor (AFL), and during the mid-1940s worked in the South and Southwest.

After the outbreak of World War II, O'Connor visited Great Britain for the U.S. Office of War Information to study production and labor conditions. When she returned to America, the AFL assigned her to the Boston regional office, where she took part in organizing Bridgeport Brass, General Electric, and the Fore River shipyards. Surviving her husband by twelve years, Julia O'Connor Parker died in Wayland, Mass., on August 27, 1972, at the age of eighty-two, after a long and influential career supporting the cause of working men and women.

¶ FREDERICK LAW OLMSTED

One would hardly suspect that a man of so little promise, so little formal education, and so little professional training as Frederick Law Olmsted would end up designing the visionary urban park system for Boston that would become familiarly known as "The Emerald Necklace." The city is forever indebted to a man who believed that well-designed parks, by improving the natural landscape, would have a civilizing effect upon the people who used and enjoyed them.

Frederick Law Olmsted was born in Hartford, Conn., in 1822, the son of a prosperous merchant. He intended to go to Yale, but a serious eyesight problem caused him to give up that plan in favor of studying civil engineering with a local clergyman. In 1844, after clerking in a New York City store and then serving aboard a ship bound for China, he settled down in Connecticut to the life of a scientific farmer. In 1850 he took a walking tour of England, during which he recorded his visits to many private estates and public parks. When he returned home, Olmsted was asked by the *New York Daily Times* to visit the South and report on his observations. After making three trips to the slave states, his reports were printed in the *Times,* and then published in a series of books. In 1855 he moved to New York City and became part owner of a publishing company that failed, leaving him without employment.

Falling back on his studies as a civil engineer and his success at farming, Olmsted accepted an appointment as superintendent of New York City's new Central Park project. He threw himself into his work, helped draw up an improved design, and assumed the additional title of architect-in-chief for this famous public park. The Civil War interrupted Olmsted's career in landscape design, however, and in 1861 he was appointed executive secretary of the U.S. Sanitary Commission, the forerunner of the American Red Cross. Resigning this position in 1863, he became manager of a California mining company for a time and then returned to New York to continue work on Central Park and to help design Prospect Park in Brooklyn.

It was about this time that a citizens' group in Boston petitioned the city council to reserve space in the growing city for a park system, to promote health and morality as well as to improve the appearance of the city. In 1875 the city created a three-member Parks Commission to establish such a park system and to solve the problem of drainage in the Back Bay. They called upon Frederick Law Olmsted, who began his work by constructing a series of channels and causeways at the point where the Muddy River meets the Charles, eliminating flooding and pollution, and turning the nondescript Fens into a lovely landscape. He then extended his plan for a string of sparkling ponds and sylvan parks for some five miles beyond the Fens, along the Jamaicaway to Franklin Park, the central jewel in the so-called Emerald Necklace—a term that Olmsted himself never used. Although the original design would have extended the string of parks from Franklin Park down Columbia Road all the way to Marine Park in South Boston, that part of the plan was never completed.

Olmsted's park system was one of the most extensive public projects undertaken in Boston until the days of the Big Dig. It had the practical effect of creating an attractive boundary for the city, while at the same time providing natural beauty for all citizens to enjoy. Olmsted himself felt that the amenities of civilized life were being threatened by industrial development, and hoped to design "breathing spaces" where people living in congested areas could enjoy fresh air and beautiful landscapes.

Frederick Law Olmsted's influence on the Boston environment continued even after his death in 1903. When he took the Boston assignment, he had moved from New York City and settled permanently in the town of Brookline, in a building that became both his home and his office. His son continued to maintain the family business in that town, and in 1900 created at Harvard the first formal training program in landscape architecture. In 1979, the National Park Service took over custody of the Olmsted documents and photographs, and turned the site on Warren Street into an educational and research institution.

❡ JOHN BOYLE O'REILLY

That a native of Ireland, a Fenian rebel, a convicted traitor deported to Australia, and an escaped criminal should not only find a haven in the Irish community of nineteenth-century Boston, but also become a literary favorite among the members of the city's Brahmin establishment, is only one more example of the way in which Boston has been able to absorb diversity and reshape it in its own image and likeness.

The son of an Irish schoolteacher, John Boyle O'Reilly was born June 28, 1844, in County Meath, on the outskirts of Drogheda, the town where Oliver Cromwell's troops massacred large numbers of Irish Catholics. As a young man O'Reilly traveled to England to find employment, enlisted in the British army, and worked to convert

Irish soldiers to the cause of Irish independence. When his activities were uncovered, O'Reilly was shipped off to a penal colony in Australia. He made a daring escape and eventually made his way to Boston, where he found work as a writer for the weekly Irish newspaper, *The Pilot.*

Although O'Reilly supported the Fenian movement, when he settled in the United States he soon developed an intense American patriotism, and criticized the violence that marked Irish nationalism. He called upon Catholics and Protestants in the United States to put aside their differences and work together. Because of his graceful writing style, his staunch patriotism, and his conciliatory attitude toward native Bostonians, O'Reilly soon became a favorite in literary and social circles. In 1872 he was invited to join the exclusive Papyrus Club; he was later installed as a charter member of the St. Botolph Club; and in 1881 he was elected to the Dartmouth College chapter of Phi Beta Kappa. In 1882 he published a poem titled "America," and delivered it personally before General Ulysses S. Grant at the reunion of the Army of the Potomac. In 1888 he published another poem, this time eulogizing Crispus Attucks, the black patriot killed during the Boston Massacre; the following year he was given the extraordinary honor of being asked to deliver the main address at the dedication of the Pilgrim Monument at Plymouth.

While establishing his literary reputation with Boston's Brahmin community, however, John Boyle O'Reilly was also concerned to demonstrate his commitment to the Catholic Church. He was on friendly terms with Archbishop John Williams, and helped found an organization of Catholic laymen called the Catholic Union. In 1876 O'Reilly accepted the position of editor of *The Pilot* when the archbishop took over management of the newspaper after its publisher, Patrick Donahoe, fell into economic distress following the Great Fire of 1872. As editor of *The Pilot,* O'Reilly charted a new and more idealistic direction for the weekly Irish Catholic newspaper. Although he continued to denounce England and agitate for home rule in Ireland, he urged Irish Americans to moderate their activities on this side of the Atlantic. He spoke out strongly in the columns of the paper for the neglected interests of Native American Indians, and became a vigorous advocate for the civil rights of African Americans. He often pointed out the tragic similarities between the discrimination practiced for so long against Irish Catholics and the kinds of oppression visited upon African Americans, Native Americans, and other minorities in the United States.

The sudden and unexpected death of John Boyle O'Reilly in 1890 at the comparatively young age of forty-eight was termed by Baltimore's Cardinal Gibbons a "national calamity," and messages of condolence came in from such prominent figures as Oliver Wendell Holmes, Jr., and President Grover Cleveland. His passing was described by the historian Mark Schneider as a lost opportunity for productive dialogue between Irish Catholics and African Americans in Boston at a time when virtually none existed.

℣ BOBBY ORR

On May 10, 1970, the Boston Bruins won their first Stanley Cup in twenty-nine years, with Bobby Orr beating goalie Glenn Hall of the St. Louis Blues to score the winning goal in overtime. The image, captured by the *Boston Herald* photographer Ray Lussier, of Orr literally flying through the air after being upended by the opposing defenseman Noel Picard, is considered one of the greatest sports photographs of all time. It confirms the belief of most Boston hockey fans that Bobby Orr is the finest hockey player in Bruins history.

Bobby Orr was born on March 20, 1945, in Parry Sound, a small rural town in Ontario, Canada. His father, Doug, had been a good enough hockey player to be considered for the National Hockey League, but was called to serve in the navy during World War II. Bobby himself began skating at the age of four on the nearby Sequin River, and was playing organized hockey at the age of five. By the time he was twelve, he was playing at advanced levels against youngsters four years older. Bobby would practice his skating and stick-handling for several hours during the day, and then worked on his shots at night in the family garage. In 1960 he was playing on a Parry Sound All-Star team that traveled to Ganonoque, Ont., to play in a tournament. Scouts from the Boston Bruins who were in the stands were sufficiently impressed by the young skater that they signed him to a Junior-A contract, even though he was still a schoolboy.

When the National Hockey League expanded from six to twelve teams during the 1967–68 season, Bobby Orr moved up to the Bruins and launched the start of a new era in Boston hockey. The game had never seen a player as talented and as charismatic. He was the player everyone wanted to be, the hero of every young boy, the dream date of every girl. Bobby Orr not only changed the manner in which hockey was played, according to the sports historian Richard Johnson, but with his grace, style, and precision on the ice he also opened up the game to millions of new fans, players, and spectators. When CBS began providing national telecasts of the NHL during the late 1960s, it was Orr's Boston Bruins team that captured the imagination of the American public.

Sparked by the arrival of this new sensation, the Bruins shook off a decade of mediocre performances and in only two short seasons became a real contender for the Stanley Cup. Bruins fans were finally rewarded for years of faithfully selling out the Boston Garden. Tickets for the 13,909 seats that had remained full during the years of disappointing hockey were now the toughest to obtain in the history of Boston sports. The 1970 season for the Bruins was marked by trauma as well as triumph. The team suffered a serious loss during the preseason, when the veteran defenseman Teddy Green suffered a fractured skull in a stick fight in a game with the Vancouver Canucks. But the team regrouped and rebounded. With Phil Esposito as center, John Bucyk as captain, Gerry Cheevers in the goal, and Bobby Orr as defenseman, they played through the regular season with grit and determination. The climax came in May, when the Bruins won the Stanley Cup for the first time in almost three decades. Bobby Orr captured the Norris Trophy as the best defenseman, and at the same time led the league in scoring—an unheard-of achievement for a defenseman. This feat won him the Hart Trophy as the league MVP, as well as *Sports Illustrated*'s "Sportsman of the Year" award.

The success of the Boston Bruins and the popularity of Bobby Orr produced a hockey mania that marked the advent of the greatest period of growth in the history of the game. In suburban Boston, hockey became the growth industry of the 1970s as public and private rinks sprouted up and players of all ages competed for ice time as early as 4:30 in the morning. Parents paid hundreds of dollars to outfit their kids with skates and equipment, and spent even more sending the youngsters to summer hockey camps.

Bobby Orr retired from hockey in 1978 because of knee injuries, and the Boston Bruins officially retired his number. The following year Orr was inducted into the Hockey Hall of Fame. He continued to make his home in Boston, where he has made a name for himself as a sports consultant, a member of the board of several major corporations, and an active participant in numerous charitable and humanitarian enterprises. He is recognized as an outstanding athlete whose professional skills and personal integrity did much to enhance the reputation of Boston on and off the ice.

ꡄ MARY KENNEY O'SULLIVAN

In 1999 the Massachusetts state legislature authorized the creation of a special work of art honoring six outstanding Bay State women, to be displayed in the State House on Beacon Hill. Mary Kenney O'Sullivan was among those prominent women, a fitting tribute to a daughter of impoverished Irish Catholic immigrants who became a national trade union official and an untiring crusader for the rights and welfare of working women.

Mary Kenney was born on January 8, 1864, the second of Michael and Mary (Kelly) Kenney's four children. Her parents, who had emigrated from Ireland in the 1850s, were married in Concord, N.H. Working as a railroad machinist, Michael Kenney and his family ended up in Hannibal, Mo., where his nine-year-old daughter excelled academically at a convent school, but was frustrated that the fourth grade was "as far as any children of wage earners were expected to go."

To Mary's dismay, after her brief schooling she was apprenticed to a local dressmaker, dashing all hopes that she might somehow escape life in a sewing shop, a factory, or a mill. Her father's death a short time later left Mary and her siblings with the task of providing for their invalid mother. Now in her teens, she went to work for a printing and binding company where her intelligence, industry, and personal charm—she was taller than average, with golden red hair and bright blue eyes—led to her eventual rise to the position of plant forewoman.

In the late 1880s Kenney moved to Chicago, where she found in the labor movement the perfect outlet for her ambition and her intelligence. As a result of her energetic work on behalf of women's rights in the workplace as well as for the crusade to win women's suffrage, she was selected by Samuel Gompers to serve as the AFL's first female "general organizer." Under her direction, the female garment workers were able to achieve greater recognition from the male unionists and their employers.

Coming to Boston with Gompers's approval, she was successful in 1892 in organizing Massachusetts women working in the printing, shoe, and carpet industries. During the summer of that year, she met John F. O'Sullivan, a former seaman and streetcar driver who was labor editor of the *Boston Globe*. After delaying their wedding for nearly two years, they finally took their vows on October 10, 1894. Mary and Jack made their home in Boston, living for a time in Denison House, a settlement house in the South End's congested immigrant district. Here, Mary addressed the plight of poor Irishwomen laboring in the factories. She organized the Union for Industrial Progress to publicize and curb the abusive practices of sweatshops. Her firsthand experience of these labor conditions led Kenney to found a summer camp in Winthrop, where young Boston Irish working women could escape the unhealthy slums and factories on weekends.

Mary Kenney O'Sullivan suffered a great loss in September 1902, when her husband, Jack, stepped off the wrong side of a train in Lynn and was struck down by another train. With three young children to support, the widow refused to wallow in her grief; instead she plunged back into activism with greater energy than ever. Among the many causes she took on was the Improved Dwelling Association's Ellis Memorial, a model tenement for poor Irish and other immigrants in South Boston. In the building's basement, she herself taught English to children of immigrant parents and gave instruction in sanitary housekeeping to their mothers. She was also one of the chief figures in settling the "bread and roses" Lawrence textile strike of 1912, her round-the-clock efforts on behalf of the female factory workers ending with sizable wage increases for the strikers.

At the same time O'Sullivan was active in union causes, she was also pushing for women's right to vote, organizing and delivering powerful speeches in all parts of the Commonwealth. Haranguing male opponents of suffrage, she enlisted recruits from the various wards of Western Massachusetts, her supporters turning out at mass rallies to wave signs and placards demanding the ballot. When women from Boston Irish neighborhoods and Brahmin brownstones alike walked to the voting booth for the first time in 1920, Mary Kenney O'Sullivan could take a large measure of responsibility for the accomplishment. O'Sullivan died of heart problems in 1943 in her West Medford home, and was buried in St. Joseph's Cemetery in West Roxbury.

¶ THEODORE PARKER

As Unitarianism supplanted Puritanism in Boston during the early part of the nineteenth century, it incorporated a measure of rationality and objectivity that some felt deprived the Christian message of its emotional content and mystical inspiration. Theodore Parker, a controversial clergyman once dubbed "Roxbury's Friar Tuck," was one of those scholarly intellectuals who sought to develop a new and more transcendental faith, based on the kind of intuition that would bring man immediately in touch with God.

Theodore Parker was born in Lexington, Mass., in 1810, the grandson of John Parker, captain of the minuteman company that famously defended that town against the British regulars on the morning of April 19, 1775. Son of a farmer, young Parker was largely self-educated until he went to Harvard and graduated from the Divinity School in 1836. The following year he became minister of the Unitarian church on Spring Street in West Roxbury.

A close friend and associate of Ralph Waldo Emerson, William Ellery Channing, and Bronson Alcott, Parker often walked the short distance to Brook Farm from his church in West Roxbury, and frequently traveled to Concord to meet with Emerson, Alcott, Margaret Fuller, and other members of the Transcendental Club when they were first publishing their journal *The Dial.* An immensely popular preacher, lecturer, writer, and essayist, Parker compiled one of the largest personal libraries in the Boston area ("a river of books that flooded his house from attic to cellar"), and mastered foreign languages ranging from Dutch, Danish, and Russian to Coptic, Chaldaic, and Arabic.

Parker became skeptical of the prevailing orthodoxy of Unitarianism, whose emphasis on rationalism he felt did not adequately reflect the mystical and individual encounter between man and God. He came to believe that religious truths were derived from individual intuition and personal feeling, rather than from divine revelation and theological study. He wanted to make Unitarianism a more idealistic faith that would ask its members to make a moral commitment to social justice. His demand for a new kind of theology, based on the immanence of God in nature and in human experience, created intense controversy in religious circles and caused the leaders of the Unitarian clergy in Boston to withdraw from him, even though he remained a member of their association until his death.

Resigning his West Roxbury pastorate in 1845, Theodore Parker became a minister of a new free church in Boston, where he proceeded to use his pulpit to support William Lloyd Garrison and the abolition movement, attack both the slaveholding aristocracy of the South and the merchant-manufacturing establishment of the North, and denounce the mainline Protestant churches of the North for having become "the sworn ally of slavery." He published inflammatory pamphlets denouncing the Fugitive Slave Act of 1850 and took an active role in public demonstrations against the apprehension of fugitive slaves in Boston. Although he was in Europe at the time of John Brown's abortive raid on Harpers Ferry in October 1859, he wrote back to America his approval of what Brown had attempted, and warned that this was only the beginning. Theodore Parker would not live to see the final outcome, however, for his health rapidly deteriorated, and he died in the city of Florence, Italy, in 1860.

Committed to the perfectibility of humankind and the inevitability of progress, Parker was described by the historian Henry Steele Commager as possessing "sweetness, gentleness, and love for his fellow men, a nobility of mind and a greatness of spirit."

❧ FRANCIS PARKMAN

It is one of the great ironies of the academic world that Francis Parkman, one of the most distinguished American historians, acclaimed throughout the world for the excellence of his research and the clarity of his style, was named a professor of horticulture at his alma mater, Harvard College.

Francis Parkman was born in Boston on September 16, 1823, son of a prominent family of wealth, social standing, and culture. As a boy, he spent much of his time at his grandfather's home on the border of the Middlesex Fells, a rough and rocky woodland where he developed a lifelong fascination for the American forest. In 1844

Parkman graduated from Harvard College and entered Harvard Law School. He received a law degree, but never bothered to take the bar examination.

It was while attending law school that Parkman set out from St. Louis, Mo., on a journey over the famous Oregon Trail. The twenty-three-year-old Bostonian disciplined himself to endure hundreds of miles of hiking and horseback riding, observing the Sioux, the hunters and trappers, and the pioneers in their wagons along the way. He published a record of his experiences in *The Oregon Trail,* which appeared in 1849.

Two years later, Parkman published his *History of the Conspiracy of Pontiac,* and then began work on what would eventually become an eight-volume history of the great imperial struggle between the English and the French for dominance of the North American continent. The first volume of the series, *The Jesuits in North America,* appeared in 1867; the last, *A Half Century of Conflict,* came out in 1892. The third volume in the series, *The Discovery of the Great West,* was published in 1869 to critical acclaim both in the United States as well as in Europe. Parkman later revised this particular work several times, and in 1879 changed the title to *La Salle and the Discovery of the Great West.* Like most of the other American historians of the period, Parkman's narrative followed what he viewed as the inevitable victory of the Protestant Anglo-Saxon people over the heathen savagery of the Native Americans and the authoritarianism of the Roman Catholic French. Parkman approached the writing of history in a community of Harvard-educated gentleman-scholars like George Bancroft, William Prescott, and John Motley, who were inspired by the Unitarian principle of encouraging good scholarship and good literature, convinced, as the historian David Levin puts it, that "the historian is a man of letters."

At the outset, Francis Parkman estimated that his history of the French in North America would take about twenty years to complete, but a series of physical ailments prolonged his work. A mysterious malady affected his nervous system, causing such a serious weakness in his eyesight that for most of his research in historical documents he had to employ copyists and assistants to locate the sources and then read the materials to him while he fixed the details in his mind. By this laborious method, wrote G. H. Farnham, "he acquired perfect possession of the materials needed for a volume." To accomplish the actual writing, Parkman designed a special frame with parallel wires to guide his hand as he wrote; later he was forced to dictate each day's production to his assistants.

Another consequence of Parkman's nervous illness was an inability to concentrate on a single objective for more than short periods of time. It was when he was forced to leave his historical research that Parkman turned to the study of horticulture. He developed several new species of roses and published a book that became a standard in the field. He was named professor of horticulture in the agriculture school of Harvard, served as president of the Massachusetts Horticultural Society, and became one of the founders of the Archaeological Institute of America before his death in 1893 at the age of seventy.

❡ ELIZABETH PALMER PEABODY

Modern-day American parents who look forward to the day when they can pack lunches for their five-year-old children and send them off to kindergarten for a few hours have a Boston woman to thank for that brief but welcome interlude of peace and quiet in their busy lives.

Elizabeth Palmer Peabody was born May 16, 1804, the eldest of seven children. Her father was a dentist in Salem, Mass., who taught her Latin and inspired her to go on to master ten languages. Her mother, a schoolteacher, developed in Elizabeth an abiding interest in theology, philosophy, history, and literature. Elizabeth herself became a schoolteacher in her teens, first in Salem, later in Maine, and still later in Brookline, Mass., where she became acquainted with such prominent intellectuals as William Ellery Channing, Bronson Alcott, and Ralph Waldo Emerson. During the 1820s and

1830s Channing became a sort of mentor to the young woman, introducing her to the works of the great European philosophers who influenced American Transcendentalism. In 1837, Peabody took her place alongside Margaret Fuller as one of the two female charter members of the Transcendental Club.

In the heady atmosphere of Boston during the 1830s, Elizabeth Peabody encountered other creative figures who helped shape her own ideas and ambitions. Her ideas about education, for example, were influenced by those of Horace Mann, who started the Boston public school system (and who later married her sister Mary), as well as by Bronson Alcott, whose progressive theories about education were put into effect at nearby Brook Farm. She developed a close relationship with Ralph Waldo Emerson, who had tutored her in Greek, and maintained a friendship with Nathaniel Hawthorne, whose Salem family she had known from childhood, and who married her sister Sophia.

In 1840 Elizabeth Peabody moved to Boston, where, in the front parlor of 13 West Street, she opened what one biographer has called "the most unusual and influential bookstore in American history." Specializing in foreign books and periodicals, her store became a headquarters for local Transcendentalists. On Wednesday evenings, Margaret Fuller would hold her famous "Conversations" there, and throughout the week figures such as George Ripley, his wife Sophia, Theodore Parker, and Emerson himself would discuss ways to save *The Dial* or methods to enhance the academic curriculum at Brook Farm. As a publisher, Peabody's output included a pamphlet on emancipation by her friend William Ellery Channing; several anti-slavery books; three of Hawthorne's children's books; and Henry David Thoreau's radical essay on "Civil Disobedience." For a brief period of time, Peabody also published *The Dial* when the original publisher failed in 1842. Elizabeth Peabody thus established herself as the first woman publisher in Boston and, it appears, in the nation.

It was the education of young children, however, that continued to be the focus of Elizabeth Peabody's efforts. She was convinced that absolutely essential to the creation of an ideal society was "educating its children truly." After the Transcendental movement faded away, she closed her bookstore in 1850 and went off to teach school at various locations, and eventually to write some ten books about the goals and purposes of education. In 1859 she heard about the kindergarten movement that had been founded in Germany by Friedrich Froebel. A year later, she started in Boston the first formally organized kindergarten in the United States. Although her kindergarten attracted positive responses, she was anxious to learn more about the system at firsthand. In 1867, with money saved from her lectures, she paid her way to Europe and traveled extensively to observe kindergartens conducted on the Froebel model. Upon her return to Boston, she established and edited a journal called the *Kindergarten Messenger.*

As Elizabeth Peabody passed into old age, her increasing stoutness, her failing eyesight, and her careless dress often caused new acquaintances to overlook the significant influence she had on American life. As a result of her own considerable intelligence, as well as her wide range of associations with leading American intellectuals, she was able to transmit to others a remarkable and original vision. Peabody died in 1894 at her home in Jamaica Plain at the age of ninety, and was buried in Sleepy Hollow Cemetery, Concord. Two years later, as a tribute to her lifelong dedication to education, a group of her friends established in Boston a social settlement called Elizabeth Peabody House.

❡ THOMAS HANDASYD PERKINS

In the early nineteenth century, Boston was home to a group of wealthy entrepreneurs who came to be known as the Boston Associates. Partners in industry and colleagues in business, they further integrated their interests through kinship and marriage. Among the Commonwealth's new commercial elite, the name of Thomas Handasyd Perkins was one of the most prominent and highly respected.

Thomas Handasyd Perkins was born in Boston in 1764, and later recalled being lifted on the shoulders of a family retainer on March 6, 1770, when he was five years old, and taken down to see the victims of the Boston Massacre. Six years later, he listened to the reading of the Declaration of Independence from the balcony of the Old State House. Three-quarters of a century later, he still remembered both events vividly, and recorded them for his children who, in turn, passed them along to their children. Perkins grew up in Boston, where his widowed mother ran the family store. He later joined his elder brother, James, in operating a commission business at Cape Francis, Santo Domingo, dealing in flour, horses, fish, and slaves.

Thomas returned to Boston in 1787, and married the daughter of Simon Elliot, a State Street tobacconist and snuff dealer. After his marriage he went into business with his new wife's uncle, a "convivial Irishman" named James Magee, who served as ship's captain for America's first millionaire, Elias Haskett Derby. They hunted seals on the Falkland Islands and otter on the northwest coast of North America, and then sold the pelts in China in exchange for tea, silks, and porcelain. Perkins and his brother took great risks and made great profits. In the opium trade, they beat the British, who controlled the product from India, by trading in the less refined but more potent drug that came from Turkey.

His long handsome face marred only by a brilliant red birthmark, Thomas Handasyd Perkins was a striking figure. After the Revolution he became a member of the Massachusetts Federalists, but in 1800, pleading "private concerns," turned down an opportunity to serve in the state legislature. The defeat of John Adams and the Federalists by Thomas Jefferson and the Democratic Republicans in the presidential election later that year, however, shook him out of his political indifference. "He thought the Devil's reign had begun," recalled his daughter Eliza. Perkins now became actively involved in state politics. Although the Federalists could not prevent Massachusetts from voting for Jefferson again in 1804, the following year they managed to keep control of the state Senate, to which Perkins was elected. For most of the next eighteen years, he rarely took part in public debate; but his opinions were marked by decision. "What he said was to the point; his language was good; and when he was strongly moved, he spoke with power," an early biographer wrote. Many of his supporters hoped that Perkins might become Secretary of the Navy, but he declined the honor, pointing out dryly that he already had a larger navy of his own.

Perkins and the other members of the Boston Associates were given to good living, festive dinners, and excellent Madeira wine. But like most of his colleagues, he also enjoyed lending his name, as well as his money, to good causes like the Massachusetts General Hospital, the McLean Asylum, and the Bunker Hill Monument, for which he built the first American railroad to transport the granite from Quincy to Charlestown. In 1830 he became president of the city's prestigious private library, the Boston Athenaeum, and in 1833 he donated his Pearl Street home to Dr. Samuel Gridley Howe's new school for the blind, which eventually became known as the Perkins Institution for the Blind.

Each of Perkins's two sons died at an early age, so it was left up to his eldest daughter, Eliza, to continue the family business and hold the Perkins empire together. Perkins himself resisted formal retirement, long past the point when he had accumulated a grand fortune far beyond his needs. He built a summer home for Eliza and her husband, Samuel Cabot, on the "Brooklyne Farm" property in Brookline, with its spectacular greenhouses and enchanting garden decorated with blue Chinese tiles he had brought back to America in his own ships. Perkins stayed on with the firm, he explained, so that he could give "continuance and support to my sons-in-law, Mr. Cabot and Mr. T. B. Gary." Thomas Handasyd Perkins died in 1854, at the age of eighty-one, after a lifetime of productive labor and community service.

◗ KING PHILIP

Almost from the time of their arrival along the New England coast, English settlers had pushed steadily westward and southward toward the Connecticut Valley. When the Pequot Indians tried to drive them back in 1636, a combined colonial military force defeated the warriors and massacred their women and children. The English continued their inland march into Indian lands, until in June 1675 the execution in Plymouth of three Wampanoag Indians became the signal for Metacom, the sachem of the Wampanoags—known to the English as King Philip—to launch a series of assaults on English settlements. Intended to reclaim the Indians' lands and drive the white settlers back into the sea, these attacks touched off a bloody conflict that became known as King Philip's War.

Meeting in Boston, local colonial leaders formed the New England Confederation, creating a large military force out of the militia companies of Boston and surrounding towns. Despite their numbers, however, the colonists were unable to capture King Philip or pin down his highly mobile fighting forces, who engaged in frustrating hit-and-run tactics. Philip and his warriors continued to lay waste to one English settlement after another. In July, Middleborough, Dartmouth, Plymouth, and Mendon were attacked. In August, it was Brookfield; in October, settlements in Springfield, Hatfield, and Northampton came under fierce attack. During the winter months, Pawtucket, Lancaster, Medfield, Groton, Longmeadow, Marlborough, Simsbury, and Providence were subject to terrifying Indian raids. So successful were the Indian assaults that other Native groups in the northeast—Nipmucks and Pocumtucks in Massachusetts, Narragansetts in Rhode Island, Abenakis in Maine—either joined Philip's campaign of terror or launched their own attacks against the English settlements. By August 1676 twenty-five English towns, more than half of the colonial settlements in New England, had been ruined, and the line of English inhabitants had been pushed back almost to the coast.

Gradually the English fought back, bringing together militia forces from Massachusetts Bay, Plymouth, Connecticut, and New Haven in a combined effort to stem the tide. Fearing attacks by Indians in their own immediate area, Boston authorities rounded up Christian Indians in the region during the fall of 1765. Despite their professed loyalty to the English, they were imprisoned on Deer Island in Boston Harbor, where many died from malnutrition and exposure during the long winter. Although the militia still found King Philip and his mobile warriors difficult to engage in open battle, the colonials waged a war of attrition designed to deprive the Indians of food and shelter. Slowly the Indians' numbers were reduced; their crops were burned; their villages destroyed; their families massacred; their survivors allowed to die of exposure or sold into slavery. Early in 1676, Canochet, sachem of the Narragansetts, was ambushed and killed by Pequot warriors who had allied themselves with the English. King Philip went into hiding at Mount Hope, but his location was betrayed by one of his followers. He was found and killed by English soldiers, and his severed head was staked on a pole in Plymouth for public viewing.

The cost of King Philip's War to white settlers was enormous, nearly forcing them to abandon their settlements in New England. For the native American Indians, however, the cost was much greater and the results more decisive. In addition to the destruction of their villages and the deaths of thousands of their people, the Indians also suffered the loss of their tribal lands and the erosion of their native culture. The conflict also marked the end, for all practical purposes, of attempts by English settlers like John Eliot to convert the Indians to Puritan Christianity and educate them in the ways of white civilization. By the time the fighting had ended, only a tiny number of copies of the much-celebrated Indian Bible could be found in all of America.

¶ JOSIAH QUINCY

On August 26, 1976, the Quincy Market Building, remarkably restored and refurbished, was triumphantly rededicated, 150 years to the day it first opened. With Mayor Kevin White supervising the ceremonies, and with the members of the Ancient and Honorable Artillery standing at attention, a seven-foot granite marker was formally unveiled. The marker, set in the ground outside the west wing of the building, bore the inscription: "HONORABLE JOSIAH QUINCY, MAYOR."

Josiah Quincy was born in 1772, in the town of Braintree, Mass., a young cousin of Abigail Adams and a frequent family visitor. He was such a high-spirited and energetic boy that when he was six his family sent him to Phillips Academy in Andover for proper discipline and rigorous schooling. He entered Harvard College in 1786, where he applied himself diligently to his studies and graduated in 1790, the youngest in his class, with high honors. He studied law, was admitted to the bar, and in 1794 opened his own law office in Boston.

Early on, Josiah Quincy found himself more attracted to a life in politics and public service than to the practice of law. In keeping with his conservative political principles he joined the Federalist party, and in November 1804 was elected to the U.S. House of Representatives, where he became minority leader. An affirmed enemy of Thomas Jefferson, Republicanism, and Southern slavery, Quincy opposed the purchase of the Louisiana Territory as well as the Embargo Act of 1807 that he feared would force a war with Great Britain. Reelected to three consecutive terms, he retired from Congress in 1813 when, with the outbreak of war with Britain, he felt that his principles were being ignored and his policies ridiculed.

Eager to reestablish his roots in Boston, Quincy became a member of the Massachusetts Senate, joined the Massachusetts Historical Society, supported the Boston Athenaeum, and became an Overseer of Harvard College. In 1822 he resigned from the state legislature and became a Justice of the Suffolk Municipal Court. He also chaired a legislative committee to study the causes and remedies for pauperism in Boston. This committee was eventually responsible for creating a new Charles Street Jail, for building a House of Industry to replace the old almshouse, and for creating a House of Reformation for the more humane treatment of juvenile offenders.

When Boston became a city in 1822, Josiah Quincy ran for mayor. He failed in his first attempt, but in 1823 was elected to the first of six consecutive terms as Boston's chief executive. Determined to institute much-needed urban reforms, he seized the reins of government and almost single-handedly proceeded to transform an old town into a new city. He reorganized and professionalized the police department and established a new fire department that used hoses instead of buckets. He filled up the Mill Creek, drained the old Town Dock, and brought the sewers under control. He had the streets cleaned and the refuse collected, and initiated a massive effort to bring a supply of pure water to the city. Perhaps his most notable achievement, however, was commissioning Alexander Parris to design a new granite market hall directly behind Faneuil Hall. Two stories high and more than 500 feet long, flanked by two granite warehouses, the central structure had a classical portico at each end, with a great dome gracing the center.

In 1827 Quincy lost his bid for reelection as mayor of Boston, but he did not remain at leisure for long; in January 1829 the Board of Overseers elected him Harvard's fifteenth president. During the next sixteen years, he revamped the curriculum, expanded the college's financial resources, constructed Harvard's first law school, built a new college observatory, and erected four additional buildings on the campus. On August 27, 1845, at the age of seventy-three, he retired from the college presidency to complete several books, the best-known of which was his two-volume *History of Harvard University.* He died in Boston in 1864 at the age of ninety-two.

As a successful city manager, Josiah Quincy was a municipal visionary, committed to a comprehensive program of urban renewal at least a century ahead of his time. He was a devoted and indefatigable public servant, as well as a humane and effective city planner who certainly earned the sobriquet "The Great Mayor."

❧ PAUL REVERE

"Listen, my children, and you shall hear / Of the midnight ride of Paul Revere . . ." How many schoolchildren first heard the name of Paul Revere as they memorized the opening lines of Longfellow's famous poem for a history class or a school pageant? This Boston patriot's midnight ride, however, was only one small part of a long, busy, and illustrious career in Boston.

Paul Revere was descended from a French Huguenot family with a substantial homestead near Bordeaux. His father, Apollos Rivoire, was sent to Boston to learn the goldsmith's trade. In 1729 he married a local resident named Deborah Hitchborn and changed his French name to the English form of Paul Revere so that the "bumpkins" could have an easier time pronouncing it.

Mr. Revere had a son, his third child, who was also named Paul Revere, born December 21, 1734. He was educated at North Grammar School on North Bennet Street, and then served an apprenticeship with his father. Talented in drawing and engraving, he was soon able to forge silver into practical objects such as spoons, bowls, tea sets, and even dental wiring. He also developed into a superb artist, turning out many beautiful silver pieces which were later donated by the Revere family to Boston's Museum of Fine Arts. One of his many skills was engraving copperplate for printing. His humorous, anti-English political engravings enhanced his popularity in a town that was chafing under British taxes, and led to his membership in such rebellious patriot organizations as the Sons of Liberty, the Long Room Club, and the North End Caucus. As tensions grew between the colonies and England, Revere took on the role of courier, riding to New York with the news of the Boston Tea Party, and then to the Continental Congress in Philadelphia, carrying copies of the Suffolk Resolves. His short ride to Lexington on the night of April 18, 1775, eventually brought him national fame, thanks in great part to the popular verse of Henry Wadsworth Longfellow.

Once hostilities began, Paul Revere sought to join the Continental Army, but received little encouragement, perhaps because he was considered too valuable in other capacities. As Sir William Howe led his transports out of Boston Harbor during the evacuation of the occupying British in March 1776, his troops stopped at the fort on Castle Island to set explosive charges and light a series of fires that left the whole island ablaze as the armada sailed away to Halifax. It was Paul Revere whom General George Washington subsequently engaged to do most of the repair work on the ruined structure, and

whom he appointed commanding officer at Castle Island for the duration of the war. During the spring of 1779, Revere also found time
to salvage twenty-one cannon from the British man-of-war *Somerset,*
which had gone aground on Cape Cod. After the fighting was over
and independence had been secured, Revere returned to his business
activities in the town.

Paul Revere was married twice and raised sixteen children—eight
by each of his wives—although at one time he had written to his
cousin, John Rivoire, "I begin to think I shall have no more children." At the age of thirty-five, he bought a home at North Square,
where he lived for thirty years. His neighbors included ship chan-
dlers, mast-makers, government officials, and prosperous merchants,
who had easy access to Clark's Wharf only a short distance away.
This house, despite substantial repairs and replacements over the
years, is now said to be the "only original colonial dwelling in America situated in the heart of a large city."

Revere was a remarkable man of many abilities. He was the first
president of the Massachusetts Charitable Merchants Association,
formed in 1795. In 1802, he provided some 6,000 feet of rolled copper—the first ever produced in America—which he applied to the
dome atop Charles Bulfinch's new State House on Beacon Hill. The
30-foot-high cupola, with a diameter of 50 feet, had been constructed from wood and covered with lead. When that surface began
to deteriorate, Paul Revere & Sons covered it with rolled copper. Not
until 1874 was the expensive 23-carat gold leaf added to the copper-
sheet base. Revere and his company also supplied copper sheeting
for the USS *Constitution,* as well as turning out bolts, spikes, pumps,
cogs, sheaves for blocks, and other fixtures for "Old Ironsides."
When Revere's base of operations grew too large to accommodate his
business activities in the town, in 1804 he established a new foundry
along the Neponset River in nearby Canton. It was first known as
Paul Revere & Sons, then the Revere Copper Company, and later
Revere Copper and Brass, Inc.

On May 10, 1818, the new bell that he had cast for King's Chapel
two years earlier to replace the old one that had cracked tolled the
mournful news that Paul Revere had died at the age of eighty-three.

Although by this time there was almost no space left in the Old
Granary Burying Ground on Tremont Street, enough room was
found to bury Paul Revere alongside many of his patriot colleagues
from Revolutionary days. A majestic equestrian statue of Paul Revere, modeled by the famed sculptor Cyrus Dallin, was cast and put
into place in 1940. It stands in the tree-shaded Paul Revere Mall in
Boston's North End, only a short distance away from the Old North
Church, whose lanterns sent the silversmith on his famous ride into
history.

¶ HENRY HOBSON RICHARDSON

It is often said that the architectural designs of Charles Bulfinch
transformed Boston from a modest seaport town into an active federal metropolis at the beginning of the nineteenth century. If that is
true, then Henry Hobson Richardson may well be responsible for
most effectively expressing the vigorous and expansive spirit of
Boston's Gilded Age at the end of the nineteenth century.

Henry Hobson Richardson was born September 29, 1838, in St.
James Parish, La., the eldest son of a prosperous cotton merchant.
Educated in New Orleans, where he displayed an early interest in
mathematics and drawing, Henry was prevented by his stammer
from attending West Point to work on an engineering degree. Instead, he went north to Massachusetts, to Harvard, where he was
elected to the elite Porcellian Club and was a popular member of the
class of 1859. After graduation he became a student of architecture at
the Ecole des Beaux Arts in Paris. He studied with Louis Jules André,
who helped him get work with local French architectural firms until
he could return to America at the end of the Civil War. Selecting
New York as the city with the best opportunities, he settled in
Brooklyn, but developed close ties with friends in Boston who sent
work his way. In 1866 he won a competition for a design for the First
Unitarian Church in Springfield; he later was selected to build an

Episcopalian Church in West Medford; in July 1870 he was chosen to design the Brattle Street Church in Boston. By 1874 Richardson was spending so much time in Boston that he moved his family to Brookline and settled in a home he eventually expanded into his office.

The rapidity with which Richardson's practice was growing brought him offers of work in Chicago, Pittsburgh, and Cincinnati, and he completed work on the structure of the New York State Capitol. But it was an invitation in 1872 to construct the new Trinity Church in Boston that eventually won the thirty-four-year-old Henry Hobson Richardson nationwide and lasting fame. Building on filled-in land in the newly developed Back Bay area, he drew upon early French and Spanish Romanesque styles to create a massive structure of colored granite, with small windows and rounded arches, and a single tower adapted from the Old Cathedral at Salamanca rising some 220 feet above Copley Square. The interior of Trinity Church was even more impressive than its formidable exterior, with John La Farge's stained-glass windows sending brilliant patterns of light over the colorful murals and terra cotta walls.

Although he began his career as an ecclesiastical architect, Richardson gradually branched out into more utilitarian applications of his art, creating buildings in a grandiose style that reflected his own corpulent physique and exuberant tastes. His libraries throughout Greater Boston—the Woburn Library (1877), the library at North Easton (1877), and the Crane Memorial Library in Quincy (1880)—were only a few of the many structures that display his use of thick stone walls and textured materials. His two Harvard buildings, Sever Hall (1878) and Austin Hall (1881), also provide examples of the architect's characteristic arched porches and lofty wings. And his series of picturesque railroad stations designed for the Boston & Albany Railroad, at Auburndale (1881), Chestnut Hill (1883), and South Framingham (1883), effectively combined both style and function in extraordinary fashion.

As he aged and grew even heavier, Richardson suffered from poor health. He died of Bright's disease on April 27, 1886, leaving an architectural legacy that was enormously influential not only in

Boston, but throughout the nation. Architects everywhere sought to re-create what had come to be known as the Richardsonian Romanesque style in monumental stone churches, libraries, courthouses, and commercial buildings, as well as in more prosaic structures such as railroad stations, prisons, waterworks, and pumping stations. The Romanesque style was eventually eclipsed by the revival of the neo-Classical style, but its monuments dominate many cityscapes. Celebrating its 125th anniversary in the year 2002, Trinity Church still stands as Boston's greatest work of architecture, and a tribute to the vivid artistic imagination of Henry Hobson Richardson.

¶ LEVERETT SALTONSTALL

Something of a dramatic intersection of the Yankee Brahmin and the Irish Catholic took place in Boston during the 1938 gubernatorial race. James Michael Curley, the perennial Democratic candidate, announced that his Republican political rival, Leverett Saltonstall, would never dare bring his "South Boston face" (long and craggy, with a protruding chin) into the predominantly Irish Catholic district. In open defiance of this challenge, "Salty" not only campaigned in the blue-collar neighborhood, proudly displaying his South Boston face, but actually defeated Curley and became Governor of Massachusetts.

Leverett Saltonstall was born on September 1, 1892, in the Boston suburb of Chestnut Hill, the son of Richard Saltonstall, an attorney, and Margaret Brooks. Few Bay State families have as long and distinguished a pedigree as the Saltonstalls. In 1630 Richard Saltonstall came to Massachusetts Bay with John Winthrop and the first wave of Puritans, and settled in Watertown where he became an officeholder and magistrate. Over the succeeding generations, eight Saltonstalls have served as governors of the Commonwealth, and in 1838 another Saltonstall went to the U.S. Congress from Massachusetts.

Young Leverett graduated from Harvard College in 1910 (the tenth Saltonstall in his direct line to do so), went on to the Law School, and received his L.L.B. in 1917. After seeing active service in France during World War I, he returned to join his uncle's law firm in Boston, and in 1926 became a partner in the firm of Gaston, Snow, Saltonstall & Hunt. During this same period Saltonstall entered local politics and showed a facility for walking around his district, meeting all kinds of people, shaking hands, and discussing the issues of the day. He became assistant district attorney for Middlesex County, and in 1923 began what would become thirteen years of service as a Republican in the Massachusetts House of Representatives, serving from 1929 to 1936 as Speaker of that body. In 1938 he defeated James Michael Curley in the race for governor, and was reelected in 1940 despite a Democratic sweep of the state in that year's presidential election by the popular Franklin D. Roosevelt. By the time he was again reelected in 1942, he had served longer as governor than any man in the previous ninety years. Saltonstall's term of office brought him into the World War II years, and he was active in establishing an industrial defense committee to expedite the production of war goods; a committee on public safety for defense purposes; and a committee to plan for the state's postwar readjustment. By the time he left the governor's office, the state debt had been reduced to $4 million, and the state treasury showed a surplus of over $19 million.

In 1944 Saltonstall won, by an impressively wide margin, the U.S. Senate seat vacated by Henry Cabot Lodge, Jr., who had entered military service. He did not speak much from the floor, but exerted considerable influence in committee meetings because of his extensive knowledge and his careful preparation. He became an expert in military matters, serving on the Naval Affairs Committee and, after 1947, on the Armed Services Committee. He was instrumental in the formation of the Central Intelligence Agency, and supported such Roosevelt-Truman international policies as the Bretton Woods agreement and the Marshall Plan. After his reelection in 1948, he turned his attention to his constituents, opposing the construction of the St. Lawrence Seaway as a threat to the local economy, and supporting measures helpful to the New England fisheries. He established good relations with John F. Kennedy when he became junior Senator from Massachusetts in 1953, and collaborated in the establishment of the Cape Cod National Seashore Park.

In addition to his concern for military preparedness and foreign affairs, Saltonstall also supported many civil rights measures, and voted to limit the filibuster whenever it was used to block the passage of civil rights bills. He was concerned about education, helped shape the details of the National Science Foundation, and served as a regent of the Smithsonian Institution. Leverett Saltonstall decided not to seek reelection to the Senate in 1966, and retired to his working farm in Dover, Mass., where he died on June 17, 1979, hailed as "New England's favorite son."

¶ PRESTON "SANDY" SANDIFORD

During the 1930s and 1940s, the intersection of Massachusetts and Columbus Avenues in Boston's South End marked the exciting center of a local "Harlem," where some of the nation's leading black jazz musicians like Duke Ellington, Fats Waller, and Lester Young ("Prez") could be found. But there were many fine local musicians who were also an important part of Boston's jazz scene, artists like Preston "Sandy" Sandiford, who gained national attention with his reputation both as a teacher and as a performer.

Preston Springer Sandiford was born June 25, 1911, the son of Preston and Helen Springer Sandiford, teachers who had immigrated from Barbados, in the West Indies, and settled in Cambridge. Young Preston began playing the piano when he was five, and after graduating from Boston English High School went on to the New England Conservatory of Music. The Conservatory was too expensive for his family's limited budget, however, and so he left the school and took private instruction instead. When he was fifteen, Preston had landed his first professional job, with the saxophonist Benny

Waters, and the following year he joined the Musicians Union and began working at downtown cafes and neighborhood roadhouses. He became well known as a skillful accompanist for singers, and one of his more colorful jobs was as a pianist for the famous stripper Sally Keith, who twirled her tassels at the Crawford House in Scollay Square.

By the time Preston was nineteen, he had begun writing and arranging music, as well as fronting a band that was in demand in many of the city's hotels, clubs, and lounges, and that soon attracted the attention of music publishers from the West Coast. Preston preferred to remain in Boston, however, where his band was hired to play for black dances and for shows called "Battles of Music," held at Roxbury's Ruggles Hall, which regularly pitted Sandiford's local band against out-of-town bands headed by Duke Ellington, Fletcher Henderson, Don Redman, and Billy Carter. Preston, now known more familiarly as "Sandy," also toured with various shows, and was increasingly sought after as a pianist and arranger by singers and dancers. In 1928 he arranged and staged a number of shows in New York City, including *Showboat* and *Shufflin' Along,* as part of an all-black vaudeville project for the WPA. Three years later, in 1931, he played for a large stage production called *HiDeHo,* which featured sixteen chorus girls, eight showgirls, and three comedians.

Sandiford stayed in New York for a while, where he teamed up with a drummer named Eddie Deas; he also toured with a band called the "Boston Brownies," and became a close friend of the jazz pianist Art Tatum. After two years, however, Preston decided to return to Boston, where he continued to play with his own orchestra in the various clubs and lounges, and also made inroads into the Back Bay set. Although Ruby Newman's band remained the society orchestra of choice in those days, Sandiford managed to play for several Christmas parties and debutante evenings on Mount Vernon Street and Beacon Hill as a result of his personal friendship with the Sears and Cochrane families. Sandy Sandiford's orchestra remained one of the premier swing dance bands in the Boston area until the early 1960s. He was a close associate of Duke Ellington's saxophonist, Johnny Hodges, and turned out musical arrangements for a number of major performers of the period such as the singer Eddie Fisher, and the comedian Jimmy Durante. During the 1940s and 1950s, he also wrote a number of successful commercial jingles, the most famous of which was the beer commercial, "Time Out for Dawson's," that ran for sixteen years.

In his later years, Sandiford concentrated more on his teaching, attracting musicians from many parts of the country to hear him play and to study with him. Dave McKenna, a popular local recording artist, worked with Sandiford, as did the multitalented Quincy Jones, who in his autobiography recalled the importance of coming to Boston to learn from an "old master." Sandiford continued active in union affairs, and was president of Local 535 of the Boston Musicians Union for more than ten years, until it merged in the 1970s to become Local 9-535. He remained an active musician, playing with the Mary Karl orchestra and teaching at his studio at 162 Boylston Street, until his death on June 6, 1988, at the age of seventy-seven.

❡ JOHN SINGER SARGENT

The inspiring murals of the artist John Singer Sargent in such notable Boston institutions as the Boston Public Library and the Museum of Fine Arts have been admired by visitors from all over the world. More than anything else, however, these works have forever categorized Sargent, in the minds of many people, as a distinctly Boston artist.

John Singer Sargent was born not in Boston, but in Florence, Italy, on January 12, 1856. He did not set foot in the United States until he was twenty years old. His mother was an amateur painter who had persuaded her husband, a Philadelphia physician, that the European climate would improve her delicate health. Educated at home, and conversant in several languages, John Singer Sargent remained an expatriate for most of his life, visiting America only on rare occasions.

When the Sargent family moved to Paris, young John studied with local painters and then, at the age of twenty-two, prepared to submit some of his works to the annual showing of the Paris Salon. In 1881 he was awarded a medal for one of his early portraits, and the following year won great acclaim for *El Jaleo,* the dramatic painting of flamenco music and Spanish dancing that would later hang in Isabella Stewart Gardner's palazzo in Boston's Fenway. In 1884, however, Sargent scandalized art critics with his portrait of Virginie Gautreau, which came to be known as *Madame X.* The woman's heavily powdered skin, bare shoulders, and distinctively haughty manner created such a furor that he gave up hopes of establishing himself as a painter in Paris. Four years later, he was to paint a daring portrait of Isabella Stewart Gardner that was considered so questionable that it was never publicly exhibited during her husband's lifetime.

In 1886 Sargent moved to London, where he established his reputation with *Carnation, Lily, Lily, Rose,* a charming painting of two young girls lighting Chinese lanterns in a garden. His ambition to become a successful portrait painter was further advanced when he came to America in 1887 to paint the wife of a wealthy New York banker. Doors were opened to more commissions, and Sargent soon found himself in great demand. Theodore Roosevelt, Woodrow Wilson, John D. Rockefeller, and Isabella Stewart Gardner were among the famous personalities who chose Sargent as their portraitist. In 1907, however, Sargent announced that he would no longer paint portraits, and returned to his earlier interest in landscapes and outdoor figures. During World War I he went to the Western Front and painted pictures of Allied soldiers on the battlefield. After the war, he painted a pair of murals for the Widener Library at Harvard University, symbolizing the involvement of the United States in the Great War.

Increasingly, John Singer Sargent turned to murals as the way to secure his artistic renown. He devoted a great deal of time to a series of murals he had promised for the Boston Public Library at Copley Square. The works were painted on canvas in his studios in London or in Boston and then shipped to the library, where they were attached, section by section, to the walls. His murals, titled *The*

Triumph of Religion, which fill the third-floor hall leading to the Special Collections Room, took some thirty years to complete before the last section was shipped to the library in 1919.

In 1916 Sargent also accepted a commission to paint the rotunda over the main staircase at the entrance to the Museum of Fine Arts on Huntington Avenue. Drawing upon ancient Greek mythology, his paintings depict Apollo and Athena, as well as other gods and goddesses, in their various attempts to preserve Art and Culture from the ravages of Time. On April 14, 1925, John Singer Sargent attended a farewell dinner in London the evening before he was scheduled to depart for Boston to personally supervise the installation of the last section of his murals at the Museum of Fine Arts. That night, at the age of sixty-nine, the great artist died peacefully in his sleep.

¶ ELEONORA RANDOLPH SEARS

At a time when most wealthy, well-bred Boston women were expected to devote themselves to domestic or charitable pursuits, dress appropriately, and conduct themselves with quiet and dignified propriety, Eleonora Sears broke all the rules, achieving both fame and notoriety as an outstanding American female athlete. During the early part of the twentieth century, this well-known member of Beacon Hill society established herself as a woman of remarkable talent and single-minded determination.

Born on September 28, 1881, Eleonora Randolph Sears was a member of a Boston family whose lineage went far back into American history. Her father, Frederick Sears, was heir to a great shipping fortune that was established by his ancestor, Joshua Montgomery Sears, in the West Indies trade during the early part of the nineteenth century. Eleonora's mother was a great-granddaughter of the Virginia statesman and third President of the United States, Thomas Jefferson. Growing up among the fashionable estates of Boston's North Shore, Sears became skilled as a horseback rider, tennis player, runner, long-distance walker, and swimmer. At a time when most men had never driven an automobile or flown an airplane, Sears did both, racing cars with her friends and becoming the first Boston woman to fly an airplane.

Although she excelled at many events, Sears thrived at racquet sports, finishing as a national runner-up in women's single tennis in 1911, 1912, and 1916. She also managed to capture four national doubles tennis titles between 1911 and 1917, as well as winning a national mixed doubles title in 1916. As a senior player in 1939, at the age of fifty-six, she again captured a national title, winning the Women's Veteran Doubles Championship. So talented was Sears that, after taking up squash at the age of thirty-seven, she won the first women's National Single Championship; she went on to help found the United States Women's Squash Racquets Association in 1928. All this was accomplished because she blithely ignored the posted signs that barred women from the squash courts at the Harvard Club.

For six decades, Eleonora Sears was known throughout Boston for her accomplishments and her eccentricities. Her colorful exploits were reported not only in the sports pages, but also in the society columns of the city's more than half-dozen daily newspapers. An outstanding beauty in her day, blue-eyed and blonde, Miss Sears, according to Cleveland Amory in his *Proper Bostonians,* "wowed Back Bay society in the 1900s, danced the meanest Portland Fancy in town, and was at various times rumored to be engaged to any number of eligible bachelors." She threw fabulous parties at her palatial Beacon Hill studio, where on one occasion she invited members of the cast of the visiting Ice Follies to mingle with members of Boston's social elite. She was even known to purchase tickets for extra theater seats so that members of her party would have somewhere to put their coats.

It was as a walker, however, that Eleonora Sears made perhaps her most enduring reputation as a female athlete. Among her feats was her highly publicized annual 56-mile walk from Newport, R.I., to Boston. In 1940, at nearly sixty years of age, Sears hiked 50 miles nonstop, leaving Boston at 4 o'clock in the morning, and swinging into Providence at 8:30 that same evening, followed along the route by her chauffeur in a long black limousine.

Clearly Eleonora Sears was well ahead of her time. Not only did she challenge and overcome the athletic barriers that had been erected against the women of her time, but she also achieved her success with an unmistakable grace and style. Despite her strenuous efforts as an athlete, she still maintained a careful decorum that allowed her to be received into the best private homes and the most exclusive clubs in Boston. She was not out to promote a cause or to dramatize an issue; although her attire was often masculine in cut and contemporary in design, and she was known to wear jodhpurs when playing polo, she insisted on wearing skirts when she skated, played tennis, or conducted her walks. She engaged in sports simply because she wanted to do it, loved to do it, knew she was good at it, and had the money to do it.

Following her death in 1968 at the age of eighty-six, Eleonora Sears was honored with enshrinement in both the International Tennis Hall of Fame and the Horseman's Hall of Fame. She is remembered as a pioneer who helped set the stage for the social acceptance of women's sports, and as someone who might be seen as the precursor of the era of Title IX.

❡ SAMUEL SEWALL

It was customary for Puritans to keep a strict daily accounting of their faults and failings, as well as their deeds and accomplishments, in order to better assess their position in the eyes of the Almighty. Many of these accountings took the form of personal diaries in which individual introspection was mixed with social observation. One of the best of these colonial diaries was that of a prominent judge and civic leader named Samuel Sewall, whom Henry Cabot Lodge once referred to as the "Puritan Pepys" because of the acute insights he provided concerning the private lives and family customs of the Puritan Commonwealth in which he lived.

Samuel Sewall was born at Bishop Stoke, Hampshire, England,

on March 28, 1652, when Oliver Cromwell was Lord Protector of England. Samuel's parents, Henry Sewall and Jane Dummer, had previously traveled to New England during the 1630s out of "dislike to the English Hierarchy" and settled in the town of Newbury. In 1646, complaining that "the Climat" was not agreeable, the couple returned to England, had five children, and then came back to America in 1661, made their home in Boston, and had three more children. Samuel was their second child.

At the age of fifteen Samuel Sewall was admitted to Harvard College, where he received his A.B. in 1671 and his M.A. in 1674. The next year he married Hannah, the daughter of John Hill, a silversmith and the mint-master for the Massachusetts Bay Colony, who brought Samuel into his business. In 1677 Sewall became a member of the South Church, just before the birth of John, the first of his fourteen children, and the following year was made a member of the General Court. While managing the Boston printing press from 1681 to 1684, he was regularly elected to the Court of Assistants, a post that gave him membership on the Board of Overseers of Harvard College.

Following the popular revolt against Governor Edmund Andros in April 1689, Sewall was named a member of the Council under the new Province Charter of 1691, and was reelected each year until his retirement in 1725. In May 1692 Sewall was appointed a Commissioner of Oyer and Terminer for the Salem witchcraft proceedings. At the end of that year, he was made justice of the Superior Court of Judicature; he became Chief Justice in April 1718, and served in that capacity until he retired in 1728. At various times, he also held a number of important Boston municipal offices, including moderator of the town meeting, town auditor, overseer of the poor, and school inspector.

Perhaps the main reason why Samuel Sewall has become such a well-known figure in the colonial history of the Massachusetts Bay Colony is not his work as a lawyer, his wisdom as a judge, his talents as a politician, or even his renown as the father of fourteen children, but his perceptive observations as a writer. His work *The Selling of Joseph: A Memorial* (1700) was the first antislavery tract to be published in America. But it is Samuel Sewall's *Diary* that provides what the historian Judith Graham calls "a superb record of the social history of his time." Not only did he comment on such important public matters as judicial proceedings, witchcraft trials, town meetings, church services, and marriage ceremonies, but he also provided fascinating details about private dinner gatherings, family purchases, daily household routines, feeding the chickens, illnesses and plagues (December 26, 1696: "We bury our little daughter . . ."), relations between husband and wife, and fights among the children ("Joseph threw a brass knob and hit his sister Betty on the forehead . . ."). At times, the Judge comes across as petty, petulant, and a little ridiculous, but at other times he assumes an air of great dignity, as seen in his entry of January 14, 1697, when he asks his pastor to read aloud his public repentance ("I take the blame and shame") for the part he played in the Salem witchcraft trials.

After his wife Hannah died in 1717, Samuel married Abigail (Melyen) Woodmansey Tilley in 1719, who died within a few months. In 1722 Sewall was married a third time, to Mary Shrimpton Gibbs, who survived him. Samuel Sewall died in January 1730, at the age of seventy-eight, and was buried in Boston's Old Granary Burying Ground.

❧ ROBERT GOULD SHAW

When the Confederates found him after the battle, the Yankee colonel was dead. He lay face down, a bullet in his breast, sand in his mouth, his saber in his hand. If he had been commanding white troops, the Southern officer later explained, he would have been given an "honorable burial." But since he was commanding a regiment of Negro troops, the body of Robert Gould Shaw was dumped unceremoniously into a common ditch along with the bodies of his men.

Born in Boston on October 10, 1837, Robert Gould Shaw was a

member of one of the city's most prominent families. His father, Francis Shaw, retired from business in 1843 at the age of thirty-two, moved to West Roxbury near Brook Farm, and devoted the rest of his life to family, literature, and philanthropy. As young Robert attended school, his parents became increasingly active in the antislavery movement.

After a disappointing year at St. John's College in Fordham, N.Y., Robert joined his parents on an extended tour of Europe, and spent a happy two years at boarding school in Switzerland. It was during this period that he read *Uncle Tom's Cabin* and began reflecting on the issue of slavery. After returning to America in May 1856, Shaw entered Harvard College as a freshman, but found the academic demands more than he bargained for. He never moved into the top half of his class, although he took an active part in sports, social activities, and theatrical productions as the division over slavery moved the nation closer to civil war.

After the Confederate attack on Fort Sumter in April 1861, Shaw joined the 7th New York National Guard and marched to the defense of Washington. After the 7th was disbanded, he secured an officer's commission in the newly organized 2nd Massachusetts Infantry—the so-called "Harvard Regiment." In the months that followed, Shaw went into battle, saw friends killed and wounded, was wounded twice himself, and survived the Battle of Antietam in September 1862. He rejoiced, along with the members of his family, when President Lincoln issued his Emancipation Proclamation, which went into effect in January 1863.

Almost immediately, Governor John Andrew of Massachusetts secured permission to organize an African American infantry regiment. Appreciating the fact that the 54th Regiment would "elevate or depress the estimation in which the character of the Colored American will be held throughout the world," he offered command of the regiment to Robert Gould Shaw. He saw Shaw as a gentleman of "the highest tone and honor" who would create "a model for all future colored regiments." With some initial reluctance, Shaw left his post as captain with the 2nd Massachusetts to become colonel of the new 54th Regiment. After a period of recruitment and training at

Camp Meigs at Readville, Mass., by May 1863, the 54th Regiment received its colors from the Governor of Massachusetts, marched proudly through the streets of Boston to the waterfront, and boarded the transport that took them to South Carolina.

On July 18, 1863, the 54th Regiment was ordered to take part in the assault on Charleston, a city guarded by heavily fortified islands. The Massachusetts regiment's specific objective was to capture Fort Wagner on Morris Island. With Colonel Shaw at the head of his men, the troops charged across 600 yards of open sand in the face of withering fire from the Confederate fortifications. Shaw fell mortally wounded; a third of the officers and half the enlisted men were killed or wounded; the attack failed. But the men of the African American regiment had become heroes, and to his friends and relatives back in Boston, Robert Gould Shaw appeared as the ultimate patriot.

In September 1863, after Fort Wagner was finally recaptured by Union troops, plans to recover Colonel Shaw's body were overruled by his father, who insisted that his son remain with his men "on the field where he has fallen." To provide a tribute to Shaw and the valiant men of the 54th Regiment, Bostonians engaged the sculptor Augustus Saint-Gaudens to create an appropriate memorial. The high-relief bronze, standing atop Beacon Hill directly across from the State House, was dedicated in 1897. On September 24, 1999, Colonel Shaw's ceremonial sword was moved from Boston's Old North Church and presented to the Museum of Afro-American History as a permanent tribute to the gallant 54th Regiment.

❧ Louise Stokes

On February 20, 2002, a former track star named Vonetta Flowers, from Birmingham, Ala., won a gold medal in the women's bobsled race at the Winter Olympics at Salt Lake City, becoming the first female African American athlete to be crowned an Olympic champion

in a winter sport. This was an honor and opportunity that was denied a young black female athlete from an earlier generation, Louise
Stokes, who was never allowed to compete in the Olympics because
she was female and because she was black.

Louise Stokes was the oldest of six children of William Stokes, a
gardener, and his wife Mary Wesley Stokes, a housekeeper. Louise
went to Malden High School, where she was a member of the girls'
basketball team. With the coaching of William Quayne, a postal
worker, Stokes began to run competitively. In the summer of 1931,
Stokes won the Curley Cup at the annual track meet sponsored by
Boston's Mayor James Michael Curley, setting the New England
women's 100-yard-dash record with a time of 12.6 seconds. In December 1931, at a Young Men's Hebrew Association indoor meet in
Roxbury, she tied the women's world record in the standing broad
jump with a leap of 8 feet $5\frac{1}{2}$ inches. The following month, at a national field meet at Princeton, N.J., Stokes won the National Junior
Championship in the 40-yard dash.

Despite these awards, little public notice was taken of the young
woman's accomplishments; at the time, most male athletes questioned whether females should be competing in track-and-field
events at all. Louise Stokes kept pursuing her athletic goals, however,
encouraged by William Quayle, who discussed the possibility of
making the Olympic team. In June 1932, at a Boston Park Department meet at Fenway Park, Stokes captured the New England regional crown in the high jump, and came in second in the 100-yard
dash. A month later, she traveled to Northwestern University for the
Olympic trials. The trials that year were dominated by the colorful
Mildred "Babe" Didrikson, who qualified in three major events, but
Stokes finished third in the 100-meter dash, which earned her a place
on the women's relay team that would compete in the 1932 Olympic
games at Los Angeles.

Sensitive to the possibility that black athletes might dominate the
American team, members of the Olympic Committee maneuvered
to keep several African American athletes from competing. According to a report in the *Boston Chronicle*, "too many Negroes had already got too much glory from the Olympics." Louise Stokes was

replaced by a white woman from the West Coast, and was never allowed to take part in the track meet in Los Angeles.

Despite her keen disappointment, Stokes accepted the decision quietly and continued to compete. In February 1935, she set a New England record in the 40-yard dash, and became the New England Amateur Athletic Union Senior Champion. Five months later, at Chicago's Soldier's Field, she won the 50-meter championship. In 1936, Louise Stokes again looked forward to the Olympics, this time to be held in Berlin, Germany, although her hopes were somewhat dimmed when she heard that Avery Brundage, the American Olympic Committee president, had recently described women track athletes as "ineffective and unpleasing." In the 1936 Olympic trials held at Brown University, Stokes won both the preliminary and semifinal heats in the 100-meter dash. In the final heat, however, she broke stride and finished a disappointing fifth, relegating her to a spot on the relay team.

At this time, Olympic athletes were required to come up with a certain percentage of the finances necessary for travel. Recognizing that Louise Stokes had no resources of her own, the members of her church, as well as the citizens of Malden, were able to raise the necessary $500 to send the young athlete to Berlin. Once again, however, Stokes was denied the opportunity to participate in the international games. Apparently feeling that after Jesse Owens's stellar performances a victorious black female athlete would further embarrass Adolf Hitler and the other Nazi officials, the American Olympic Committee replaced Stokes with a white runner.

Louise Stokes received a hero's welcome when she returned to her hometown of Malden. A parade in her honor brought her to Fenway Park where more than six thousand spectators listened to her give a short speech and watched her display mementos of her travels through Europe. Although she never complained publicly about her shameful treatment, she was deeply hurt by the experience at the Olympics and gave up running altogether. She went to work as an elevator operator; in 1941 she founded the Colored Women's Bowling League. Three years later, she married Wilfred Fraser, a cricket star from the Caribbean, and gave birth to a son, Wilfred

Fraser, Jr. She later took a position with the Massachusetts Department of Corporations and Taxation, retiring in 1975, three years before her death.

In 1972 the City of Malden named a field house after their star athlete, and on September 13, 1987, a statue of this pioneering athlete was dedicated in the courtyard of Malden High School in honor of Louise Stokes.

❧ LUCY STONE

At the height of the modern feminist movement during the 1960s and 1970s, when young women were deciding either to hyphenate their names with their husbands' or retain their birth names after marriage, a number of "Lucy Stone Leagues" appeared in many parts of the country, recalling the long-forgotten activities of a female activist more than a hundred years earlier who established a series of memorable "firsts" for American women.

Lucy Stone was born August 13, 1818, on a farm near West Brookfield, Mass., the eighth of nine brothers and sisters. Even as a young girl, Lucy resented the inferior position of women in American society, and determined to go to college to study Hebrew and Greek in order to disprove what she considered inaccuracies in the Bible's teachings concerning the subservience of women to men. In 1843 she enrolled at Oberlin College in Ohio, noted for its liberal antislavery views as well as its acceptance of women as students. At Oberlin, Lucy was satisfied that the Bible's teaching on the inferior position of women had been misconstrued. In 1847, at the age of twenty-nine, Lucy Stone graduated from Oberlin College with honors—the first Massachusetts woman to be granted a college degree.

Shortly after graduation, Stone accepted a position as a lecturer with the Garrison-dominated American Anti-Slavery Society. Before long, however, her strong commitment to women's rights began to clash with her responsibilities toward the abolition of slavery. "I was a woman before I was an abolitionist," she explained. "I must speak for the women." Her employers finally agreed that she could lecture on women's rights on her own during the week, as long as she talked for the Anti-Slavery Society during the weekends. As an impressive public speaker, Lucy drew large audiences, some members of which were openly hostile to her liberal views and ridiculed her as "shrieking Lucy." The notoriety of her public appearances also caused her church to expel her for conduct "inconsistent with her covenant engagements."

Although she had earlier decided against marriage so that she would never have to call any man her master, Stone was successfully courted by Henry Brown Blackwell, a merchant who was both antislavery and profeminist. At their marriage ceremony on May 1, 1853, they read a manifesto against the prevailing marriage laws. After the ceremony, Lucy announced that she would keep her own name, calling herself Mrs. Stone. A number of Lucy Stone Leagues were established in various parts of the country by sympathetic feminists, who became known as "Lucy Stoners." Although Lucy decided to remain at home to care for her daughter, who was born in 1857, she insisted that a woman could have a husband and children and still have outside interests. She continued to support the feminist cause, praised the Emancipation Proclamation, and worked for the passage of the Thirteen Amendment.

When the Civil War was over, in 1866 Mrs. Stone helped organize the American Equal Rights Association to agitate for both Negro and women's suffrage. Before long, however, a bitter controversy divided women's rights advocates. Mrs. Stone felt that, in the aftermath of the Civil War, the fight for Negro suffrage should be won first, before taking up the struggle for women's suffrage. Along with her husband, Henry Blackwell, and the African American spokesman Frederick Douglass, Lucy Stone insisted that "this hour belongs to the Negro." Another group of women's rights advocates, led by Susan B. Anthony, Elizabeth Cady Stanton, and Sojourner Truth, were outraged that people like Lucy Stone would support immediate suffrage for African American men while putting off suffrage for women.

In 1869 Mrs. Stone and her family moved permanently to the Boston area, settling in Dorchester, where she became the leading spirit of the New England wing of the suffrage movement. She served on the executive board of the American Woman Suffrage Association (AWSA), which was less radical than the National Woman Suffrage Association (NSWA). She made perhaps her greatest contribution in founding the weekly newspaper *The Woman's Journal.* After 1872, along with her husband, Mrs. Stone assumed editorial responsibility for the publication, and for the next forty-seven years *The Woman's Journal* was regarded as "the voice of the woman's movement."

After 1887 Mrs. Stone's health declined, and she was forced to limit her speaking to small groups. In 1893, at the age of seventy-five, Lucy Stone passed away at her Dorchester home. Her funeral brought great numbers of admirers from all over the country to pay their respects. At her request, her body was cremated at Boston's Forest Hill Cemetery—making Lucy Stone the first person to be cremated in New England.

❧ GILBERT STUART

Anyone in possession of a U.S. one-dollar bill will immediately recognize the face on the engraving as that of George Washington, and many Americans will probably know that the likeness was taken from a famous painting by an artist named Gilbert Stuart. Although Stuart was not born in Boston, he eventually became such a colorful and familiar part of the local scene that he was virtually adopted as a native son.

Born in Narragansett, R.I., in 1775, the son of a snuff-grinder, Gilbert Stuart set out to be a painter, and during the Revolutionary period traveled to London to live and work with the American artist Benjamin West. The young man became a member of the Royal Academy, largely on the strength of his elegant painting called *Por-*

trait of a Gentleman Skating, which was exhibited in 1782. Unfortunately, Stuart's taste for high living, together with difficulty in completing commissions, forced him to flee from his creditors, first to Ireland and then to the United States.

Gilbert Stuart arrived in Boston in 1806 and established a permanent residence on Essex Street. In a very short time he was accepted as a part of the town's fashionable society, whose members took pleasure in his lordly airs, his liberal use of snuff (rumored at a half a pound a day), and his taste for fine Madeira wine, which, according to historian Van Wyck Brooks, he poured from a half-gallon pitcher. Stuart found himself quite at home with the leaders of Boston's political circles as well as with the great East India merchants and their families.

Stuart's ruddy face, his delightful personality, and his store of amusing anecdotes put his portrait sitters at ease, and even the crusty Puritan John Adams conceded that he would be happy to sit for Stuart from one year's end to another. Local residents took pride in the way Stuart reflected the sophistication of Beacon Street in the salons and drawing rooms of Europe, while enjoying the stories they heard about the flamboyant artist who sipped claret while he mixed his paints, and who, on one occasion when one of his sitters nodded off to sleep, painted him with ass's ears.

Gilbert Stuart achieved perhaps his most enduring fame for his portraits of such prominent mercantile families as the Appletons and such distinguished national political figures as John Adams, Thomas Jefferson, and George Washington. Actually, he did three paintings of Washington from life. The first (called the Vaughn type) is a bust showing the right side of Washington's face; the second (called the Lansdowne type) is a full-length study. The third (unfinished) is often referred to as the Athenaeum head, and is now shared by Boston's Museum of Fine Arts and the National Portrait Gallery in Washington. This painting was commissioned by Martha Washington, and has been immortalized by the engraving on the one-dollar bill.

Stuart was unable to overcome lifelong financial difficulties stemming from prodigal living, and as he grew older and his income dropped off, he often resorted to copying his popular Washington portrait in an effort to make ends meet. Bostonians might have enjoyed his company and basked in his artistic reputation, but they did little to support him in his declining years. Stuart died on July 9, 1828, at the age of seventy-three, poor and destitute. And when he was buried in the Central Burying Ground on the southwest corner of the Boston Common, there was not even a marker erected over the grave of this memorable Boston artist.

❡ JOHN L. SULLIVAN

"George Washington might be the greatest American, Daniel Webster might be New England's greatest orator, and Longfellow her most notable poet," writes R. F. Dibble. "But who. cared? High above them all towered John—'*our* John'—begotten, born, nourished, reared, educated, and trained in Boston—her pet, her darling, her pride—her newest and greatest celebrity—*her* champion!" That was the way many Bostonians felt about the athlete known as the "Boston Strong Boy."

John Lawrence Sullivan was born in 1858 on Harrison Avenue, in Boston's South End. His father was a hod carrier who had come from Tralee, County Kerry; his mother had emigrated from Athlone, County Roscommon. After attending public schools, he completed his formal education at Boston College, which was still at its original South End site. While serving short stints at a variety of trades, Sullivan began to gain attention by engaging in sparring exhibitions at local theaters. Boston did not permit bare-knuckle boxing but the city did grant entertainment licenses for "sparring" with gloves.

In April 1880 Sullivan scored a major exhibition victory by defeating the English heavyweight champion, Joe Goss. Indeed, his victory was so impressive that the Boston *Pilot* prophesied that the twenty-two-year-old fighter would someday be ranked "among the leading heavyweights of the country." Five feet ten inches tall, weighing 190 pounds when he was in peak condition, Sullivan had powerful arms and shoulders, a deep heavy chest, and short sturdy legs. Where other boxers would begin a fight slowly and tentatively, Sullivan would rush out at his opponent, swinging ferociously, and never let up. "He is a fighting man," remarked John Boyle O'Reilly admiringly.

After a year spent barnstorming all over the country, winning a series of victories over local fighters or itinerant boxers, by 1880 John L. Sullivan was eager for national recognition. He was finally able to secure a match with the American champion, Paddy Ryan, in a bare-knuckle match originally slated for New Orleans in February 1882. Because prizefighting was illegal in Louisiana, however, the promoters moved the match to nearby Mississippi City, where Sullivan knocked out Ryan and claimed the championship. Boston hailed the victory of the "Boston Strong Boy," local newspapers carried all the details of the match, and Sullivan himself was given a public reception on his return to his home city. That summer he was the principal attraction at the annual picnic of the Irish Athletic Club, and Patrick Maguire's influential newspaper, *The Republican,* hailed him as the "Terror of Terrors."

For the next ten years, John L. Sullivan fought his way through small towns and whistle stops all over the United States, defending his championship in the ring and in the barroom, offering $50 to any man who could go four rounds with him. Sullivan also embarked on a tour of England, Ireland, France, and Australia, counting crown princes and dukes among his admirers, and achieving the reputation of a popular folk hero. On August 8, 1887, four thousand people crammed into the Boston Theater, with Mayor Hugh O'Brien and members of the Boston Common Council in attendance, to see Sullivan presented with a magnificent gold belt, studded with 397 diamonds, proclaiming him champion of the world.

Sports reporters in New York City, however, ridiculed the idea that Sullivan should call himself world champion, insisting that their fighter, Jake Kilrain, was the only real champion. Bostonians responded angrily, and local promoters worked to set up a championship match between the contenders. Two years later, on August 8, 1887, before four thousand rabid spectators, Sullivan defeated Jake Kilrain for the heavyweight championship under a blazing sun at Richburg, Miss., in a grueling bare-knuckle match that lasted seventy-five rounds. For the next three years Sullivan continued to dominate the field until September 1892, when he lost his crown to the boxing skills of young James Corbett. By that time, at the age of thirty-four, Sullivan had become overweight and out of condition, slowed down from too much eating and drinking and too little exercise. He had also squandered his earnings, and ten years after his last fight was forced to file for bankruptcy.

Although the "Great John L." never regained the championship, he was still a hero to the Boston Irish who had seen one of their own rise from poverty and obscurity to become world-famous as a great athlete and a credit to his people. His death in 1918 pushed the war news from the headlines. As testament to the high regard in which he was still held in Boston, the Mayor of Boston himself, James Michael Curley, served as a pallbearer at the funeral of the "Boston Strong Boy."

❡ CHARLES SUMNER

In 1845, a thirty-four-year-old Harvard lawyer named Charles Sumner was invited to give the annual Fourth of July address at Tremont Temple before a gathering of political officials and military representatives. Speaking on "The True Grandeur of Nations," Sumner stunned his audience by denouncing the evils of war, the wastefulness of national defense, and the uselessness of military academies. As the generals and admirals walked out of the hall, Mayor Samuel Eliot announced angrily: "That young man has cut his own throat!" Despite this controversial debut, Charles Sumner went on to become a famous orator and a powerful member of the Senate of the United States.

Born in Boston in 1811, Charles Sumner attended the Boston Latin School and then went on to Harvard College, where he mastered grammatical style and classical languages and became known as one of the best "declaimers" in his class. At the Harvard Law School, he discovered his "true profession," devoting himself to the study of law. After being admitted to the Massachusetts bar in 1834, he entered into a partnership with George Hillard, but spent much of his time writing scholarly articles on legal issues. His early writings show an interest in various "mild reforms" that would allow ethics and principles of justice to be applied in the legal process.

In 1837 Sumner traveled to Europe to study Continental jurisprudence and to meet with prominent lawyers and judges in England. On his return to Boston he became increasingly dissatisfied with his law practice. At a time when Samuel Gridley Howe was working with the blind, and Horace Mann was working to create a public school system, Sumner felt inclined to involve himself in social reforms. After his controversial Fourth of July address in 1845 on behalf of world peace, he took an active role in local abolition activities. In 1849, in an effort to desegregate the public school system of Boston, he represented young Sarah Roberts in a case that was argued before the Supreme Judicial Court of Massachusetts. Appealing for "equality before the law," Sumner made the case that both white children as well as black children suffer from attending separate schools.

In 1851, supported by a local coalition of Democrats and Free-Soilers, Charles Sumner was elected to the United States Senate, and carried his unrelenting antislavery views into the Congress. On May 20, 1856, during a heated debate over the Kansas issue, he delivered an impassioned speech, "The Crime against Kansas," in which he roundly denounced the "slavocracy" of the South. Three days later, he was badly beaten at his Senate desk by an irate congressman from South Carolina. Although Sumner did not return to his seat for more than three years, spent traveling abroad in search of medical treatment, he was reelected by the Massachusetts legislature. His empty seat in the Senate chamber was regarded as a public rebuke to his Southern colleagues.

From the very start of the Civil War in April 1861, Senator Charles

Sumner was a staunch supporter of President Lincoln and the Union cause, but he was also ceaseless in his demand for emancipation—satisfied only with the passage of the Emancipation Proclamation in January 1863. As chairman of the Senate committee on foreign relations, he was invaluable to the administration in warding off trouble with both Great Britain and France. Once the war was over, he was a strong advocate of a congressional plan of Reconstruction, and a persistent advocate for equal suffrage rights for freed African Americans. He was an early opponent of the Reconstruction policies of President Andrew Johnson, and became one of the leading congressional figures demanding Johnson's eventual impeachment.

In the years leading up to his death in 1874, beset by domestic sorrows and personal illness and dissatisfied with the nation's failure to provide adequate recompense to freed slaves, Charles Sumner became highly sensitive to criticism and increasingly intolerant of dissenting views. But during his years in public service, he was known for skillful and perceptive leadership in such matters as complicated tariff measures and civil-service reform, as well as for his staunch support of the rights of the enslaved and oppressed.

❧ KIP TIERNAN

Kip Tiernan likes to tell the story of a little girl walking along a beach, who picked up one of a huge number of beached starfishes and tossed it back into the water. A man passing by snorted, "Don't you know there are thousands of these starfishes? It's a waste of time, and it won't possibly make a difference." The little girl looked up at the man and said, "Well, mister, it sure made a difference to *that* one!" Tiernan is a Boston woman who has devoted her life to the principle that saving one person can make a big difference.

Kip Tiernan was born in 1927 in West Haven, Conn. She lost both parents by the time she was eleven and was raised by her grandmother. After being expelled from a Catholic boarding school at the age of sixteen, she worked for some local newspapers before moving

to Boston to study music and enjoy the local jazz scene. After struggling with alcoholism, she began working in advertising. In August
1968 she attended a Catholic meeting on poverty at St. Phillips–
Warwick Church, which was involved in the civil rights and antiwar
movements. It was at that moment, she has said, that she was converted to the cause of the poor.

In 1974, after reading an article about homeless women, Kip went
into downtown Boston, where she watched groups of women wan-
dering about aimlessly without food, shelter, or any visible means of
support. She noticed that at the back of food lines at shelters and
soup kitchens were many of these women dressed up as men in an
attempt to get something to eat. They were dressing as men, Tiernan
realized, because nowhere in the city were there any facilities for
homeless women. She made up her mind to meet that glaring need
and start a shelter exclusively for women. She wrote letters to a variety of local human service organizations, asking them for assistance,
only to be told that she was wrong—there were no homeless women
in Boston. The Boston Redevelopment Authority, however, finally
agreed to rent Tiernan an abandoned family supermarket on Columbus Avenue in the South End. Not wanting to give her project
an institutional name, she decided to call it "Rosie's Place," and after
a period of renovation, the shelter opened officially on Easter
Sunday, 1974, because, as Tiernan expressed it, "I believe in resurrec-
tions."

Four years later, Kip Tiernan purchased her first building on
Washington Street, where Rosie's Place provided homeless women in
the city of Boston with emergency food, shelter, clothing, advocacy,
and both transitional and permanent housing. In 1986 Rosie's Place
moved to its current home at 889 Harrison Avenue, ironically the
site of St. Phillips Church, where Kip Tiernan had her original conversion to the cause of the poor. At this shelter, students from local
colleges and volunteers from all over the Greater Boston area cook
and serve meals, respond to guests' needs and requests, assist with
cleaning, and help with various office projects. Because of a strong
desire to insure the independence of Rosie's Place, Tiernan has steadfastly refused city, state, and federal money for her undertaking, pre-

ferring to depend on volunteer support, individual contributions, and money from foundations.

After establishing Rosie's Place, Tiernan opened Open Space, a clearinghouse support system for women in the ministry, and in 1976 worked with Fran Froehlich, a former member of the Sisters of Providence, to create the Poor People's United Fund to raise money for grass-roots community groups. By the early 1990s, Tiernan had decided to transform Rosie's Place from a drop-in shelter for women into a more wide-ranging program to change the conditions that were keeping these women poor and homeless in the first place. This program ultimately included opening a grocery store, establishing a women's craft cooperative, and designing a children's educational curriculum to be used in the schools. Rosie's volunteer Board of Directors began lobbying the state legislature for more humane ways of distributing food stamps, and eventually established the first low-income food co-op in the Commonwealth. In 1990 Tiernan established the Ethical Policy Institute, a multi-disciplinary community of people engaged in political analysis, economics, and community activities.

Irreverent, incendiary, and indefatigable—a far cry from the genteel upper-class lady reformers of the nineteenth century who served the needs of poor immigrants—Kip Tiernan spares nothing and no one, including herself, in her ceaseless crusade to provide for the needs of poor and homeless people who have been denied access to justice. With her trademark battered canvas tennis hat perched on the back of her head, legs planted firmly on the ground, hands on her hips, she greets visitors to Rosie's Place in her gravely voice: "Whose side are you on, kid?"

❦ WILLIAM MONROE TROTTER

In the late nineteenth century, the residents of Boston's small and self-contained African American community lost any semblance of political self-expression when their West End neighborhood was redistricted by local Democrats. As they prepared to move to new homes in the lower South End, the only way they retained any political visibility was through the influence of local church leaders or the efforts of the publisher William Monroe Trotter and his newspaper *The Guardian.*

William Monroe Trotter was the son of a Mississippi slave named James Trotter, who moved his family north to Cincinnati around 1854 and who fought in the Civil War with the 55th Massachusetts Regiment. After the war, James moved to Boston permanently, worked at the post office, and turned Democrat. He was appointed by President Grover Cleveland to a federal position in Washington, D.C., but after his service he returned to Boston, where he started a prosperous real estate business. Growing up in the Hyde Park section of Boston, young William Trotter proved to be an outstanding student and an active member of his local Baptist church. He attended Harvard, graduating magna cum laude in 1895 and becoming the first African American student elected to Phi Beta Kappa. In 1899 he joined a white real estate firm in which he prospered, and the same year he married Geraldine Pindell, who became his closest friend and collaborator.

Despite his own financial security and his comfortable relations with Boston's white community, William Monroe Trotter was acutely conscious of the various forms of discrimination facing most black people in the north. Greatly influenced by his forebears in the black abolition movement in Boston, Trotter felt compelled to promote civil rights, and in 1901 started a newspaper called *The Guardian.* Using his weekly editorials and so-called indignation meetings, Trotter pressed for greater political and civil rights for African Americans. Much like William Lloyd Garrison, Trotter was a difficult man to work with, and often alienated his own friends and supporters. He demanded things be done his way or not at all, and saw himself as the center of a national civil rights movement based in Boston. In 1903 he engaged in public disputes with Booker T. Washington, and two years later split with W. E. B. Du Bois over the operations of the Niagara movement. In 1909 he challenged the new National Association for the Advancement of Colored People

(NAACP) by putting forth his own organization, the National Independent Political League (NIPL). His league never matched the influence of the NAACP as a national organization. This was particularly true after 1913, when Trotter made headlines after an impolitic exchange of views with President Woodrow Wilson.

William Monroe Trotter fought on, however, returning from a tour of the Midwest in 1915 to campaign against the showing of D. W. Griffith's film *The Birth of a Nation* in Boston. When the United States entered World War I in 1917, Trotter joined with most other black leaders in supporting the war, but he also demanded that the federal government pay greater attention to civil rights. Once the war was over, Trotter became more of a local figure than a national activist, generally displaying a skepticism toward Du Bois's Pan-Africanist ideas or Marcus Garvey's black nationalist programs. Trotter favored a more integrationist approach to civil rights, insisting his people were not African but American—his preferred terms were "colored Americans" or "Negro Americans." Through the columns of *The Guardian,* Trotter championed the causes of local African American organizations, campaigned for sympathetic political candidates, and reported on police brutality and racial violence in the city.

Trotter's influence declined during the 1920s as activities within Boston's small black community were overshadowed by events taking place in New York, Chicago, and Washington. As the NAACP established itself as a major national organization, *The Guardian* lost circulation and support. In 1922, however, Trotter was among those who protested a decision by the president of Harvard University to exclude black freshmen from college residence halls. "If President Lowell is responsible for race exclusion in the freshman dormitory," he wrote, "he is making Harvard turn from democracy and freedom to race oppression, prejudice, and hypocrisy." After the death of his beloved wife in 1918, Trotter grew increasingly isolated and depressed, and in 1934 he either fell or jumped to his death. The passing of William Monroe Trotter deprived Boston's black community of a voice that had never ceased calling for equal rights and equal opportunities for all Americans.

Lucy Stone

Dorothy West

❧ *Ted Williams*

❧ *John Winthrop*

¶ FREDERICK TUDOR

From the earliest times, New Englanders seemed to display a uniquely Puritan work ethic that drove them to an unrestrained pursuit of wealth, profit, and advancement. Generally referred to as "Yankees," they carried over their initial activities as enterprising merchants and sea captains to equally successful ventures as bankers, industrialists, and real estate speculators. There are perhaps few more representative examples of the indefatigable Yankee entrepreneur than Frederick Tudor.

Frederick Tudor was born in 1783, the son of a prominent Boston judge. His older brother, William, was a merchant, a member of the state legislature, and one of the prime movers in 1804 in annexing Dorchester Neck to Boston, forming what would become the territory of South Boston. William also helped found the Boston Athenaeum in 1808, started the *North American Review* in 1811, and coined the phrase "Boston, the Athens of America." Frederick Tudor, however, was an enterprising young man who was much more interested in making money than writing literary articles. At the age of twenty-two, Frederick proposed the risky venture of shipping blocks of ice from his father's pond in the North Shore town of Saugus to the West Indies. Most people thought that the young man was either mad or stupid to think that a cargo of ice could withstand a voyage through tropical waters—a view that seemed confirmed when a shipment of 130 tons of ice Tudor sent to Martinique in 1805 failed to survive the journey.

Frederick Tudor did not give up, however. For years he sought new ways of using doubled-sheathed vessels and sealed cargo holds to preserve his perishable product. After experimenting with all sorts of fillers with which to pack the ice, he finally settled upon sawdust as the most efficient form of insulation. All the while, he slowly expanded his business to include such Southern ports as Charleston, Savannah, and New Orleans.

In addition to dealing with the technical problems of packing and shipping, young Tudor also had to create profitable markets for his new product. As a salesman, he had to persuade potential customers of the pleasures of drinking cold beverages; as a distributor, he had to instruct purchasers how to store ice properly in hot weather. He proved highly successful in both endeavors, and in May 1833 Tudor made his first venture all the way to India, crossing the equator twice as he traveled the Pacific Ocean, and still arriving in Calcutta with almost two-thirds of his cargo of 180 tons of ice safely intact.

Between 1836 and 1850, according to Samuel Eliot Morison's *Maritime History of Massachusetts,* the lucrative Boston ice trade was extended to every large port in South America and the Far East. For several generations after the Civil War, until cheap methods of manufacturing ice were invented, the export of ice taken out of North Shore ponds continued to be a mainstay of the New England economy, and long before his death in 1864, Frederick Tudor was memorialized in Boston lore as "The Ice King."

❧ JOHN A. VOLPE

There are probably no more impressive examples of the traditional "rags-to-riches" story than the ways in which impoverished immigrants took full advantage of the opportunities offered by America to achieve fame and fortune. Certainly that was the case with John A. Volpe, who became a self-made millionaire, a federal Cabinet member, ambassador to Italy, and the first Italian American governor of the Commonwealth of Massachusetts.

Born December 8, 1908, in Wakefield, Mass., John Anthony Volpe was the son of Vito and Filomena Volpe, who emigrated at the turn of the century from their native village of Pescosansenesco, in the Abruzzi region of Italy. When the family moved to Malden, John attended the local public schools. He planned to enroll at MIT to study engineering, but was forced to go to work as a hod carrier when his father's plastering business failed. In 1930 he worked his way through Boston's Wentworth Institute, but two years later found himself unemployed as a result of the Great Depression. The following year, he borrowed $500 on his life insurance policy and started his own business, which gradually became one of the most successful construction companies in the country.

With the outbreak of World War II, Volpe shut down his company for the duration and signed on as a lieutenant commander in the Seabees. Once the war was over, he reopened his construction company in Malden and also became active in state Republican party politics. During 1951 he worked for the election of Dwight D. Eisenhower as president and Christian A. Herter as governor. After his election, Governor Herter appointed Volpe as Massachusetts Commissioner of Public Works, a position he held from 1953 to 1956, after which he joined the Eisenhower administration briefly as the first head of the Federal Highway Administration, launching a $50 billion federal interstate highway program.

In 1957 Volpe returned to construction work and state politics, and in 1960 was elected to a two-year term as governor of Massachusetts, the only Republican to win major office in a year that saw Democrats sweep the state on the tide of John F. Kennedy's presidential election. John Volpe thus became the state's 57th chief executive, and the first of Italian heritage. Although he was narrowly defeated in 1962 by the Democratic challenger Endicott "Chub" Peabody, Volpe was elected to the governor's office two more times—in 1964 and in 1966, when he became the Bay State's first governor to be elected to a four-year term. In the 1966 contest, he achieved a stunning 500,000-vote victory over his Democratic opponent, Edward J. McCormack, Jr.

In 1968, halfway through his term, Volpe resigned the governorship to accept the Cabinet post of Secretary of Transportation at the start of the Nixon administration. He had originally been considered as Nixon's vice-presidential running mate, but lost out to Spiro Agnew, the former governor of Maryland. Before assuming his Cabinet post, Volpe sold his $1 million stock holding in his construction company to avoid the appearance of conflict of interest, turned over control of the company to his brother Peter, and ordered that his firm not bid on any U.S. Transportation Department contracts as long as he was Secretary. After President Nixon was reelected in 1972, Volpe was eased out as transportation secretary and named ambassador to Italy—only the second U.S. ambassador to be sent to the country of his ancestors. A devout Roman Catholic who attended Mass daily and spoke fluent Italian, Volpe traveled to Rome early in 1972 and remained there until 1976.

A highly respected and much loved figure throughout Massachusetts, John Volpe was the recipient of many awards and honors. He received an honorary LL.D. degree from Boston College in 1967, and in 1973 Logan Aiport's new International Terminal was named in his honor for his accomplishments in the field of transportation. In September 1991 the federal transportation research and development center in Cambridge, Mass., was renamed the John A. Volpe National Transportation Systems Center. John Volpe died in November 1994, at the age of eighty-five, at his home in Nahant, Mass. "He served the Commonwealth and the country well," commented his former gubernatorial rival, Endicott Peabody.

℣ JOHN COLLINS WARREN

Starting with Dr. Joseph Warren, the Boston physician who was killed on June 17, 1775, while rallying American troops during the Battle of Bunker Hill, the Warren family has played a preeminent role in the town's medical and humanitarian history. Dr. Joseph Warren's brother, John, also a physician, became a leading surgeon in Boston, promoted the idea of vaccination for smallpox, and gave a course of lectures in anatomy that in 1782 led to the establishment of a medical department at Harvard College.

John Collins Warren, the son of Dr. John Warren, was born in Boston in 1778. After graduation from Harvard in 1797, he studied medicine with his father and then went abroad to pursue advanced studies in London, Edinburgh, and Paris. When he returned home,

he acted as an assistant to his father, helped organize the Massachusetts Medical Society, and was among those who started a medical
journal that would eventually become today's *New England Journal
of Medicine.* Upon the death of his father, John Collins Warren was
appointed full professor at Harvard, where he taught from 1815 to
1847. Together with Dr. James Jackson, a physician who had come
down from Newburyport to practice in Boston, Warren revolutionized medical education and practice and became a prime mover in
establishing the Massachusetts General Hospital.

In 1810, Drs. Warren and Jackson circulated a letter among the
town's wealthy residents outlining the need for a hospital to care for
"lunatics and other sick persons" for whom no facilities were available. The following year, the state legislature voted to incorporate
such an institution, provided that private supporters raise $100,000
within five years. After a vigorous program of fund-raising and door-
to-door appeals the necessary funds were raised, and on July 4, 1818,
town and state officials gathered to witness the laying of the corner-
stone of the Massachusetts General Hospital. With its main building
on Allen Street designed by Charles Bulfinch in the Greek Revival
style, its massive Ionic columns topped by a shallow dome, the new
hospital stood on the banks of the Charles River in Boston's West
End, intended as a truly "general" hospital that would serve "the
whole family of man."

Despite his numerous public activities, John Collins Warren also
remained active in the medical field. He was the first surgeon in the
United States to operate on a strangulated hernia, and was the
author, among other works, of *Surgical Observations on Tumours*
(1837), a landmark treatise in the history of the subject. While studying abroad, Warren visited the Scottish surgeon Joseph Lister, and
was so impressed by his use of carbolic acid as an antiseptic in his operating room that he brought the idea back to the MGH in Boston.
It was Dr. Warren, too, who invited the dentist William T. G. Mor-
ton to demonstrate his use of ether as an anesthetic at the Massachusetts General Hospital on October 18, 1846, and it was Warren who
performed the surgery to remove the tumor from the patient's jaw
after the anesthesia had been administered. Warren bequeathed his

own body to Harvard Medical School for dissection as an example to the public of the importance of donated cadavers to medical education. To further meet the needs of medical students, he established an Anatomical Theater and Dissecting Room at the Harvard Medical School, which the Harvard Corporation later named the Warren Anatomical Museum in his honor.

John Collins Warren's son, Jonathan Mason Warren, carried on the family medical tradition, becoming a doctor and acquiring the title of an "artist with a knife" because of his skill as a pioneering plastic surgeon. Jonathan's son, J. Collins Warren, who also went into medicine, held the post of Mosley Professor at the Harvard Medical School from 1899 to 1907 and became a specialist in the field of bacteriology.

❧ MERCY OTIS WARREN

For a long while there was a tendency among historians to assume that because for the first two centuries of the nation's history American women were denied both civil and political rights, and because their activities were confined to an exclusively "domestic sphere," they had been unable to generate any ideas worthy of serious consideration. In more recent times, however, the discovery of women's history has revealed in the writings of women like Abigail Adams and Mercy Otis Warren that colonial social conventions failed to suppress the working of perceptive and imaginative intellects that had much to say about the nature of human society and the future of the American Republic.

Born in Barnstable, Mass., on September 14, 1728, Mercy Otis was one of thirteen children of James and Mary Otis, members of an old Cape Cod family. Mercy's father was a farmer, a merchant, and a lawyer, who served as a county judge and a colonel of the local militia. In keeping with the custom of the period, his daughters received no formal education, but Mercy was allowed to sit in on her brothers' tutorial sessions. In addition to browsing through her family's substantial library, the young woman was also exposed to a great deal of political discussion and debate. On November 14, 1754, at the age of twenty-six, Mercy was married to James Warren of Plymouth, a merchant and farmer, and a Harvard graduate, with whom she had five sons.

As tensions increased between the American colonists and the British authorities, Mercy Warren was drawn into public affairs, especially since her brother, James Otis, had become a noted Patriot figure because of his famous speech against the writs of assistance. As such leading rebel figures as John Adams and Samuel Adams came to her Plymouth home to talk politics with her brother and her husband, Mercy began to turn her own hand to composing poems and satires in support of the Revolutionary cause. Her first play, *The Adulateur,* which appeared in a Boston newspaper in 1772, depicted Governor Thomas Hutchinson as an autocratic tyrant in a mythical country. In subsequent plays published in Boston—*The Group* (1775); *The Blockheads* (1776); *The Motley Assembly* (1779)—she satirized the loyalist Tories of Massachusetts as elitist bumblers and humbugs. In 1790, after the war was over and independence secured, she published *Poems, Dramatic and Miscellaneous,* which dealt with the broader themes of freedom and human liberty.

After the Revolution, the Warren family went into something of a political decline. Mercy's husband, James, lost his seat in the state legislature and her sons, despite her attempts at intercession, failed to obtain political appointments. Perhaps as a reaction to her spirited opposition to the ratification of the new Constitution, as expressed in her *Observations on the New Constitution* (1788), Mercy and her husband were later accused of having been sympathetic to the leaders of Shays's Rebellion in the western part of Massachusetts, although there no evidence of such support in her correspondence. Conservative Federalists in Boston were further antagonized by Mrs. Warren's defense of the French Revolution.

During the post-Revolutionary period, Mercy Otis Warren continued to work on her major literary effort, a three-volume *History of the Rise, Progress, and Termination of the American Revolution,* which she had started in the late 1770s and completed in 1805. While there is nothing particularly informative about the historical information contained in the work, it is a valuable exposition of the opinions of a Massachusetts Jeffersonian Republican who had more confidence in the ability of the people to govern themselves than most Boston Federalists of the period. Unfortunately, it caused a break in Mercy's friendship with John Adams, whom she had accused of having forgotten the principles of the American revolution. Although a reconciliation was finally effected in 1812, Adams was still sensitive to Mrs. Warren's criticisms. "History," he complained rather grumpily to Elbridge Gerry, "is not the Province of the Ladies."

Mercy Otis Warren continued to write, to converse, and to maintain a wide and lively correspondence well into her eighties, until her death in Plymouth at the age of eighty-six, having survived her husband by six years. Something of an early feminist, at least by the standards of her time, she deplored the fact that women were not given the opportunity of a formal education and were prevented from participating in public activities. Although it may be true that most of her plays and other works possess small literary merit, they nevertheless offer striking testimony to the energy and imagination of a woman who had never been allowed to receive a formal education, who had never seen a play actually performed on a stage, and who had never traveled farther away from Plymouth than Boston.

❡ EDWARD WEEKS

At the height of New England's literary renaissance, in 1846 a number of the local literati decided to found a journal to demonstrate to the English-speaking world the superior thoughts and ideas of American writers. Ralph Waldo Emerson worked with Oliver Wendell Holmes to found the *Atlantic Monthly*—so named by Holmes, who published his popular column "The Autocrat of the Breakfast Table" in the new journal. Almost a century later, Edward

Weeks joined the line of outstanding editors whose influence kept
the magazine in the forefront of American literary publications well
into the twentieth century.

Edward Weeks was born in 1898, in Elizabeth, N.J., of English
and Dutch ancestry. He wanted to attend Princeton, but was not
admitted. He entered Cornell instead, intending to become an engineer, but withdrew in 1917 when the United States entered World
War I, to volunteer as an ambulance driver in the French army at the
age of nineteen.

Weeks returned from France in 1919 and entered Harvard College,
studying English under Dean Le Baron Russell Briggs, and earning
extra money freelancing for the *Boston Evening Transcript.* After
graduation, he spent the summer as a harvest hand in Kansas, then
worked his way to England on a Scottish cattle boat. He studied at
Cambridge University for several years before returning to the
United States and settling in New York's Greenwich Village. There
he began to work as a bookseller for the new publishing firm of Boni
and Liveright. In 1924 Weeks was offered a job in Boston by Ellery
Sedgwick, the eighth editor of the *Atlantic Monthly,* whose first
editor, James Russell Lowell, had pledged to create an indige-
nous American magazine "free without being fanatical," and one
that would open its pages to "all available talents of all shades of
opinion."

In 1928, when Theodore Dreiser's novel *An American Tragedy* was
brought to trial by jury for containing language liable to corrupt the
morals of young people, Weeks set out, almost single-handedly, to
change the Massachusetts obscenity law—which was so obscurely
worded and so vaguely written that it allowed policemen virtually to
walk into any bookstore and take offending books right off the
shelves. After failing in two attempts to change the law, Weeks took
the advice of Lemuel Shattuck, chairman of Ways and Means, and
went on an ambitious speaking tour to influence the votes of legislators and members of local communities. His campaign was successful, and in March 1930 the state legislature voted to substantially
modify the obscenity law.

In 1938, at the age of forty-one, Weeks succeeded Sedgwick as
editor-in-chief of the *Atlantic Monthly.* He remained editor for

twenty-eight years, longer than any man in the history of the magazine. In the process, he made the *Atlantic Monthly* into one of the most influential publications in American history and one that was read throughout the English-speaking world.

Edward Weeks had come to Boston after a considerable apprenticeship in the practical aspects of publishing. As a bookseller working the bookshops of New York, he learned how books moved *after* they were written, edited, and published. He also learned about the country by traveling, by talking before clubs and civic groups, by teaching at Bread Loaf, and by getting to know the writers who wrote the books and the kinds of people who read them. Weeks lectured in almost every part of the world, served on the Board of Overseers at Harvard University, and held memberships on the boards of numerous committees and civic organizations. Building on this broad experience, Weeks encouraged the *Atlantic Monthly*'s readership to follow his lead as he attracted a list of contributors that included such great names as André Malraux and Jean Paul Sartre; Walter Lippmann, Archibald MacLeish, and Edmund Wilson; John Steinbeck and Ernest Hemingway; George Bernard Shaw and William Butler Yeats. In addition to highlighting such well-known literary figures, however, Weeks also took special pains to encourage unknown writers, and solicited over-the-transom submissions that led to launching writers as different as Mazo de la Roche, Geoffrey Household, and Joseph Wambaugh.

In 1966, Edward Weeks retired from his editorship of the *Atlantic Monthly* and became senior editor of the Atlantic Monthly Press. According to James Alan McPherson, Weeks "defined the twentieth century not only in terms of events but through people he himself had known, and the way in which events had touched them."

❧ DOROTHY WEST

During the 1920s and 1930s, members of Boston's African American society mostly lived in the city's South End. Much of their social life centered around club meetings and elegant gatherings, usually at the homes of prominent clubwomen in the area. But their ranks included a small intelligentsia of professional women, such as social workers, as well as creative writers like Dorothy West, who described in her novel *The Living Is Easy* (1948) the experiences of southern black visitors to Boston.

Dorothy West's birth date is often mistakenly given as 1912, but the City of Boston records show that she was actually born in 1907. Brought up in Boston, she was the only child of Rachel Benson and Ike West, and lived a fairly privileged life, attending the prestigious Girls' Latin School, taking dancing lessons, and spending her summer vacations in the family cottage in the well-to-do African American vacation community of Oak Bluffs on Martha's Vineyard. She showed an interest in writing at an early age, and when her short story "The Typewriter" won second place in the June 1926 contest sponsored by *Opportunity*, a journal published by the National Urban League, she left Boston and traveled to New York with her cousin Helene Johnson, who was the same age as she. Once in New York, Dorothy took bit parts on the stage, and during the daytime worked as a relief investigator in Harlem, an experience that was later reflected in her story "Mammy."

Living in New York at the high tide of what is called the Harlem Renaissance, by 1932 Dorothy West had become part of a group of black intellectuals and artists that included Langston Hughes, Wallace Thurman, Zora Neale Hurston, Claude McKay, and Countee Cullen. She traveled to the Soviet Union with the "Black and White," a project to make a film about race relations in Alabama. The film failed to materialize, and when she learned that her father had died, West returned to the United States.

After her return home, West founded a new magazine called *Challenge*, with the apparent intent of recapturing, during the mid-1930s, the vitality that had characterized the Harlem Renaissance before it went into a decline during the dark years of the Great Depression. During its three years of existence (1934–1937), with Richard Wright as associate editor, *Challenge* featured some prestigious writers and published some stimulating articles, such as Wright's "Blueprint for Negro Writing," but it was also criticized for its moderate political stance. This criticism from the left made it more difficult for West to attract young talent, and the magazine was forced to cease production.

From the time of her literary debut in 1926, Dorothy West continued to turn out short stories focusing on the dramatic personal and family struggles of black men and women to achieve mobility and status in a predominantly white society. These pieces appeared in *Opportunity,* the *Daily News,* and the *Saturday Evening Quill,* Boston's highly regarded black literary magazine. Perhaps the best known of West's works, and certainly the most widely reviewed, was her full-length novel *The Living Is Easy,* dedicated to her father and published in 1948. In this work, West provides the first study of Boston's African American community, drawing the portrait of a middle-class woman named Cleo whose ambition takes a cruel toll on her family. Equally disdainful of poor southern blacks and upper-class northern liberals, Cleo is implacable in her determination to achieve middle-class financial success and social status. Reissued in recent years, West's novel has received a more understanding audience among modern American feminists, who are more sympathetic to its strong and aggressive central female character.

After 1958, Dorothy West, who never married, resided on Martha's Vineyard, where she wrote a weekly social column, turned out occasional vignettes for the island newspaper, the *Vineyard Gazette,* and occasionally appeared in brief television interviews. Miss West died in April 1998, and her papers, including both personal correspondence and story manuscripts, are housed in the libraries of Boston University, Atlanta University, and Yale University. An oral history of Dorothy West may be found at the Schlesinger Library at the Radcliffe Institute.

❧ PHILLIS WHEATLEY

During colonial times, some of the most respected families of Boston were slaveholders. Although the town itself never had a formal slave market, it was not unusual for residents to purchase slaves from the West Indies to serve as maids and house servants. The Reverend Cotton Mather's congregation made him the gift of a slave; Peter Faneuil ordered a slave from the West Indies; and Paul Revere received a bequest of a slave from his grandmother.

In July 1761, Mrs. Susanna Wheatley, the wife of a prosperous tailor with a large house on King Street, purchased a sickly eight-year-old African girl from Senegal who had been transported to Boston as a slave. By the time of her arrival, there were about 1,000 slaves in the town, whose total population was some 15,000 persons. The young girl took the name of Phillis Wheatley, and within two years she had learned English from the family with which she lived and worked.

By the age of twelve, Phillis had begun to write poetry, and in 1767 she published her first poem, "On Messrs Hunley and Coffin." After an attempt to publish a book of her poems in Boston proved unsuccessful in 1772, efforts were begun to find a publisher in London. To allay suspicions that a young slave girl could not possibly have written the poems by herself, John Wheatley and seventeen other prominent Bostonians, including Governor Thomas Hutchinson, signed a public statement vouching for her authorship.

In the spring of 1773, Phillis Wheatley sailed to London in the company of John Wheatley's son, Nathaniel, where she met a number of important people and was treated with great courtesy. In September 1773, shortly after she had returned to Boston, her collection of poetry on various religious and moral themes was published. Phillis was given her freedom in the fall of 1773, but continued to live with the Wheatley family for some years, while continuing to write. She received a personal note from General Washington for whom she had written a complimentary piece of verse.

In 1778 Wheatley married John Peters, described as a "respectable colored man of Boston," and had three children, all of whom died at a young age. Wheatley's own poor health continued to deteriorate, and she died in 1784 at the age of about thirty-one. Phillis Wheatley went down in history as the first African American in North America to publish a book of poetry.

❡ TED WILLIAMS

Although he has not played in a major league baseball game for more than forty years, Ted Williams will always hold a special place in the hearts of Boston sports fans. The "Splendid Splinter," as he came to be known, the swaggering young ball player who never wore a necktie, will forever remain in the opinion of many as the greatest pure hitter in baseball. Red Sox fans will always remember the smoothness of his swing, the graceful arch of his body, the powerful snap of his wrist, the crack of the bat, and the elegant follow-through that sent the ball soaring into the air.

Theodore Samuel Williams was born on August 30, 1918, and grew up in San Diego, Calif., where his father, Sam Williams, ran a photography shop while his mother, Mary, was a well-known worker for the Salvation Army. Because of their activities, Williams's parents were not around much, so he found surrogate parents among his friends, neighbors, and teachers. He became particularly attached to the director of the nearby North Park playground, who taught him to play baseball.

While Ted was in high school he played outfield, pitched for the varsity as a freshman, and hit an amazing .583 as a junior. In addition to regular high school games, he played in postseason tournaments, American Legion contests, and pickup games with Navy and Marine teams in the seaport town of San Diego. It was not long before baseball scouts began to take notice of young Williams's hitting and pitching abilities. In 1936 Eddie Collins of the Red Sox, on a scouting trip to the West Coast, was so impressed by Ted's "sweet swing" that he persuaded the Red Sox to sign the seventeen-year-old schoolboy to a contract. During his years in the minor leagues the rookie showed steady improvement and compiled a .366 batting average, with 43 home runs while he was with Minneapolis.

In 1939 he came up to the majors, joining the Red Sox, and proceeded to set a major-league record as a rookie with a .341 batting average and 31 home runs. In 1941, the twenty-two-year-old Williams, having perfected his swing, had a remarkable year at the plate, and by the time of the All-Star break at mid-season, he was already hitting .405. He won the All-Star game in Detroit for the American League by hitting a dramatic two-out, three-run homer in the bottom of the ninth inning. He entered the last day of the season with a 3.995 average, which would have been rounded off to .400. Sox manager Joe Cronin offered to hold Williams out of the lineup on the last day's doubleheader with Philadelphia to preserve the magic number. Williams refused to sit out, however, and had an incredible day, slamming six hits in eight trips to the plate, ending the season with a batting average of .405.

Ted Williams had another great season with the Boston Red Sox in 1942, before going into the Air Corps during World War II. In 1946, along with many other Red Sox players, Williams returned to civilian life and to his career in baseball. The Red Sox won 61 games with only 16 losses that year at Fenway Park, and finished the season in first place with a 12-game lead. In a September game against Cleveland, Williams hit an inside-the-park home run to left against the new "Williams shift," which moved all the outfielders to the right whenever he was up and the bases were empty. The final World Series against the Cardinals was very exciting, going all the way to the seventh game. But Ted Williams's only World Series proved to be very disappointing: the great slugger managed only five singles and one run batted in.

Through the late 1940s and 1950s, the Boston Red Sox usually started out strong, but always faded toward the end of the season. In 1950, the team batted an impressive .301, but ended up in third place—four games behind the Yankees. That year, disaster struck Williams in the All-Star game, when he crashed into the wall making a difficult catch and shattered his left elbow. In 1952 Ted Williams returned to military service during the Korean War, and flew 39 missions in Korea. Upon his return during the 1953 season, he played in 37 games, hit 13 home runs, and ended up with a batting average of .407. In 1956, at the age of 39, Williams brought his average up to .388, with a figure of .453 in the second half of the season, and over .650 for the last ten days.

Ted Williams's last season was in 1960. That year the forty-two-year-old player batted .316, with 29 home runs in 310 times at bat, bringing his career batting average to .341. His last time at bat took place at Fenway Park, facing the Oriole pitcher Jack Fisher, who was born in Williams's rookie year. With the count at 1-1 in the eighth inning, Williams went into his swing and blasted a home run into the Red Sox bullpen for his 521st major-league home run. Later he recalled the reaction of the Boston fans: "They cheered like hell, and as I came around the cheering grew louder and louder."

In 1966, Williams was inducted into the Hall of Fame. From 1969 to 1971 he was manager of the Washington Senators, continuing on for another year after the franchise became the Texas Rangers. Plagued by ill health, he retired to Florida. In 1999 he appeared at the All-Star game at Fenway Park, where the game's current stars paid tribute to one of its masters. Ted Williams passed away on July 5, 2002, at his home in Florida at the age of 83.

¶ JOHN WINTHROP

In early April 1639, a line of vessels left the English Channel and set sail across the Atlantic Ocean, heading for America. In the lead was the flagship *Arbella,* followed by ten more ships carrying members of an English Protestant group called Puritans who were leaving a country where they could no longer enjoy religious freedom. At their head was a country squire named John Winthrop, who promised them that if they followed the ways of God and treated each other in a truly Christian manner, they would become a "City upon a Hill" that the whole world would look up to with great admiration.

Born in 1588, John Winthrop was a member of a prominent English family. He attended Trinity College at Cambridge for two years, and then married Mary Forth, a wealthy young heiress, with whom he had three sons and three daughters before her death in 1615. A second marriage ended with the death of his wife after only a year, but in 1618 he married Margaret Tyndal, a devout and intelligent woman, who bore him eight more children. Not long before his death, Winthrop married a fourth time. It was during his first marriage that Winthrop became seriously interested in religion and allied himself with the Puritan dissenters who wanted to rid the Church of England of beliefs and practices that they viewed as not sufficiently Protestant. After returning to college and receiving his law degree, Winthrop managed his family's estate, and in 1627 became a well-paid attorney at the Court of Wards and Liveries in London.

After King Charles I succeeded James I in 1625, the English government made it difficult for Puritans to worship freely, as well as to hold government offices. In 1629 Winthrop decided to resign his position in the London court, and began to speculate about finding "a hidinge place for us and ours." Winthrop and his Puritan friends took over control of a joint-stock company with a grant of land in America that they renamed the Massachusetts Bay Company. After Winthrop was voted governor of this company, the Puritans met at Cambridge, England, where they decided that only those investors who would actually go to America could take part in the enterprise. To make sure that their colony would be free from English interference, the Puritans took the original copy of their Charter with them to America.

On March 22, 1630, John Winthrop set out from the port of Southampton on his mission to the New World. Crossing the stormy Atlantic, the vessels reached the coast of Maine, and then moved southward along the shoreline until they put in at either Salem or Charlestown. When the water supply at Charlestown proved inadequate, Winthrop accepted the invitation of Reverend William Blackstone to move across the river to the Shawmut peninsula, where springs of fresh water were plentiful. Here Winthrop and many of his Puritan followers settled, calling the site Boston, after the town in Lincolnshire from which many of the colonists had come. For the next twenty years John Winthrop was the guiding force and moral inspiration for the Puritan commonwealth he had established on the shores of Massachusetts Bay.

A life of public service was not always easy for John Winthrop, who came under attack from both political rivals and religious critics on various occasions. In April 1634, for example, the citizens found out that Winthrop had failed to reveal that the Charter of the Massachusetts Bay Company called for annual elections. Showing their displeasure, they turned him out of the governor's office and replaced him with Thomas Dudley. Early in 1636, Winthrop was taken to task by a group of religious leaders, including the Reverend John Cotton, who accused him of having become too lenient in disciplinary matters and judicial decisions. It may be that this rebuke caused him to move against the teachings of Anne Hutchinson in such a vigorous manner.

Elected governor again in 1638, Winthrop protected the colony's Charter from attacks directed at it from England, but the following year he learned that he had suffered serious financial losses in England, which left him forever without sufficient personal income. Returned to public office again in 1642, he engaged in the famous controversy that resulted in the division between the magistrates (representing the interests of the Company) and the deputies (representing the interests of the towns), as two separate houses in the Great and General Court. After being out of office for the next three years, Winthrop was brought back in 1645, and continued to be elected governor of the Massachusetts Bay Colony each year thereafter until his death in 1649 at the age of sixty-one.

¶ CHARLES WYZANSKI

Ever since the ratification of the new Constitution of 1787, American jurists have been divided over the role of the government in determining the constitutionality of laws. Those who believe in strict construction argue that the federal government has no powers beyond those specifically granted in the Constitution. Those who believe in loose construction argue that in addition to certain expressed powers, the Constitution also provides many powers that are implied by the very nature of government. Judge Charles Wyzanski of Boston was one of those jurists who believed that the role of the legislative branch was to expand democracy and insure equal rights.

Charles Edward Wyzanski, Jr., was born in Boston on May 27, 1906, the son of Charles Edward Wyzanski, Sr., a real estate developer, and Maude Joseph. He was raised in the town of Brookline, attended Phillips Exeter Academy, and graduated magna cum laude and Phi Beta Kappa from Harvard University in 1927. He went on to Harvard Law School, where his teachers included such influential legal figures as James Landis, Zechariah Chafee, and Felix Frankfurter. After graduating in 1930, Wyzanski went to the United States Court of Appeals for the Second Circuit in New York, where he clerked first for Augustus Hand and then for Learned Hand. He returned to Boston in 1932 to work for the prestigious law firm of Ropes & Gray, but declined an assignment to prepare a brief challenging the state's recent anti-injunction laws. This refusal brought him to the attention of President Franklin D. Roosevelt, who appointed him solicitor of the Labor Department after he drafted a bill that became the legal foundation for the New Deal's Works Progress Administration.

In 1935 Wyzanski moved over to the Justice Department as special assistant to the Attorney General, and in 1937 he successfully defended the unemployment provisions of the Social Security Act and the authority of the National Labor Relations Act before the United States Supreme Court. In 1941 Roosevelt nominated Wyzanski to the federal district court in Boston, making him at thirty-five years of age the youngest federal judge ever appointed. Wyzanski highly valued the personal freedom and judicial independence provided by sitting alone as a trial judge, selecting his own cases, rather than sitting with other judges on a panel where cases were assigned at random. For this reason, he turned down a seat on the Court of Appeals for the First Circuit in 1959.

Wyzanski's independent spirit and sense of judicial activism became apparent in several of the highly publicized decisions he made in his long and controversial career. In 1953, in *United States v. United Shoe Machinery Corporation,* a leading antitrust case, Wyzanski ordered the breakup of the company after ruling that it had used its leases to maintain monopolistic power. In 1961, in *United States v. Worcester,* in a ruling severely criticized by civil libertarians, he reduced the sentence of a contractor convicted of income tax evasion on condition that he name those persons to whom he had paid bribes and illegal kickbacks. In keeping with his strong public-service tradition, Wyzanski was very active off the bench, frequently lecturing and writing about such topics as fair legal procedures, the importance of the democratic tradition, and the nature of the human condition. "A lawyer is or ought to be," he said, "the moral educator of the society." From 1952 to 1976 he served as a trustee of the Ford Foundation; from 1943 to 1949 and again from 1951 to 1957 he was a member of the Harvard Board of Overseers. His hobbies were collecting books and works of art, and he made a colorful figure as he strolled around American and European cities browsing through art galleries and bookstores, wearing a broad-brimmed hat and a loose floppy tie, and carrying a walking stick.

Perhaps his most controversial rulings came during the Vietnam War era, during a conflict he publicly denounced as illegal. In 1969, in *United States v. Sisson,* he ruled that a sincere, but not necessarily religious, conscientious objector could not be drafted for combat in Vietnam. In another case, he ruled that a high school principal could not dictate the length of a student's hair. And in 1973, he came out with his assertion that the Vietnam War had been conducted illegally following the 1971 repeal of the Gulf of Tonkin Resolution. That same year, after serving a chief judge of the Boston Court for six years, he took senior status on the bench. In response to the judge's liberal opinions and his judicial activism, in 1973 the Massachusetts House of Representatives passed a resolution in favor of his stepping down from the bench; but Wyzanski remained defiantly in his place. After a long and productive career trying to use his judicial powers to expand individual freedom, Charles Wyzanski died in Beth Israel Hospital in Boston on September 3, 1986, after suffering a cerebral hemorrhage.

❡ Carl Yastrzemski

During the 1950s, Bridgehampton, at the tip of New York's Long Island, was a small community of Polish Catholic farmers who grew potatoes, danced the polka, and loved baseball. Born August 22, 1939, Carl Yastrzemski grew up in this warm and tightly knit community, living a happy boyhood surrounded by loving parents and grandparents named Yastrzemski and Skonieczny. Carl's father, Michael, had been a semipro ball player; he gave his son a tiny baseball bat when he was eighteen months old and raised him to believe that one day he would play for either the New York Yankees or the Boston Red Sox.

Young Carl took to the game of baseball naturally, playing in the Little League and then the Babe Ruth League, trying out different positions, practicing his hitting, and in the process attracting the attention of professional scouts. After protracted negotiations with various clubs, Carl's father finally came to terms with the Boston Red Sox—$108,000, plus a two-year Triple A farm contract at $5,000, plus the remainder of his son's tuition at Notre Dame. He wanted to ensure Carl's future in baseball, but Mike Yastrzemski was also determined that his son get a college education. Even though Carl left Notre Dame after his sophomore year, when he moved to the Boston area and settled in Lynnfield, he enrolled at Merrimack College in Andover, from which he received his B.S. degree in business administration in 1966.

In the meantime, Carl had moved to North Carolina, where he joined the Raleigh Capitals and in 1959 was named the Most Valuable Player of the Carolina League. After a year with the Minneapolis Millers (in the American Association), he switched to the American League and became a member of the Boston Red Sox in 1961. Ted Williams's last season as an active player for the Red Sox was 1960 and, as successor to the legendary left fielder, it took the twenty-two-year-old Yastrzemski some time to develop his hitting style. For several years, Boston baseball fans consistently booed him whenever he walked onto the diamond, regardless of how he played. In an effort to increase his physical stamina and improve his game, "Yaz," as he was now called, embarked upon an ambitious exercise regime during the 1966–67 off-season, with the trainer Gene Berde of the Colonial Health Club. He emerged from the strenuous routine a new man, and in 1967, together with Tony Conigliaro, Jim Rice, Fred Lynn, and Dwight Evans, became an essential part of the team's most powerful batting order. In that year, Yaz won baseball's Triple Crown by leading the American League in home runs, batting average, and RBIs, led the Red Sox to the World Series, and was named the American League's Most Valuable Player.

The booing died down as Yaz became an accepted part of the ball club and a favorite with the team owner, Tom Yawkey. In 1975, less than a year away from his own death from leukemia, Yawkey gave up his own enclosed box seats at Cincinnati's Riverfront Stadium so that Yaz's mother, also suffering from cancer, could watch her son play in the World Series in comfort. In addition to his prowess as a hitter, Yastrzemski also developed into a first-class base runner as well as a skillful outfielder who exploited the home-field advantage of the famous Wall at Fenway Park. He mastered the art of altering his catching stance, depending on whether the ball ricocheted off the cement at the base of the Green Monster, or struck the deadening metal above.

Carl Yastrzemski was ranked first among active major-league players in games played, runs batted in, bases on balls, total bases, and extra base hits before he ended his twenty-three-year career with the Boston Red Sox in 1983. Six years later, in 1989, Yaz was elected to baseball's Hall of Fame.

❡ THOMAS YAWKEY

For nearly seventy years, the Boston Red Sox baseball team was associated with the name of one family—the Yawkeys. Tom Yawkey and his wife Jean established a long and highly personalized ownership that created a legacy not only of financial success but also of devoted sportsmanship. Although it has been more than eighty years since the Red Sox have been able to overcome the Curse of the Bambino and win a World Series, the fans keep coming back to Fenway Park in the hope that Tom Yawkey's dream will finally come true.

Thomas Yawkey Austin was born February 21, 1903, in Detroit, Mich., lost his father at an early age, and lived with his maternal uncle, William Hoover Yawkey, a wealthy business tycoon who was part-owner of the Detroit Tigers baseball team. When his mother died in 1918, he was adopted by his uncle, and later changed his name to Thomas Austin Yawkey. Tom Yawkey was active in high school athletics and attended Sheffield Scientific School at Yale to study chemistry, mining, and metallurgy.

Given his Yale education and his generous family inheritance (estimated at $20 million), Thomas Austin Yawkey could have lived the leisurely life of a country gentleman. Instead, he chose the raucous and often turbulent career of a sportsman-owner of a major league baseball team. Yawkey purchased the Boston Red Sox in February 1933, when he was only thirty years old, and immediately became something of a local hero when, between the 1933 and the 1934 seasons, at the height of the Great Depression, he put hundreds of union laborers to work rebuilding Fenway Park. During the same period, he also began making serious attempts to purchase many first-rate players in order to defeat teams like the New York Yankees, the Washington Senators, and the Detroit Tigers, and move into first place. Although followers of Boston baseball were delighted when Yawkey brought in such power hitters as Jimmie Foxx and Ted Williams, they rarely experienced the thrill of winning a pennant. Returning war veterans were excited when Yawkey's postwar Red Sox came close in 1946, but the club's defeat in the seventh game of the World Series with the St. Louis Cardinals brought another heartbreak to the hopeful Boston fans.

In 1948, and again in 1949, the Red Sox missed winning the pennant on the final day of the season, but Tom Yawkey never gave up. He loved the game, he loved the players, and he loved the Sox. He came regularly to Fenway Park to watch the game, dressed casually in khakis and a windbreaker, where he mixed easily with players and patrons and was often mistaken for a member of the grounds crew. In 1953 he accepted the leadership of the Jimmy Fund of the Dana Farber Cancer Institute, and since that time the Red Sox have raised millions of dollars for cancer research. Tom and his wife made additional contributions to the Fund as well as to other major charities.

When Tom Yawkey died of leukemia in July 1976, he left the Red Sox and most of his vast estate to his wife, Jean R. Yawkey, and to his charitable foundation. With no children of her own, Jean ran the Red Sox from 1976 to 1978 with the advice and assistance of a young man named John Harrington, who had left a job teaching accounting at Boston College to become treasurer of the team in 1972 and who had gradually become a close friend and confidant of the new owner. After Haywood Sullivan and Edward G. "Buddy" Le Roux became the second and third general partners in the organization, Harrington left briefly to work for the state, but was asked to return by Mrs. Yawkey and become her legal proxy in all matters relating to the Red Sox. In 1983, in a desire to secure a greater return on their investment, Le Roux and his supporters made a move to take over control of the team, but Harrington worked with Mrs. Yawkey and Haywood Sullivan to stave off the attempt. After a court ruling in her favor, Mrs. Yawkey bought out Le Roux's stake in the team.

Jean Yawkey continued to take an active and personal interest in the affairs of the Red Sox, with John Harrington as both her professional adviser and her personal friend. Although he had been named several years earlier by Mrs. Yawkey as the sole trustee for all Red Sox–related matters, it was only with her death in 1992 that he actually gained control of the team. Acting on behalf of the trust, the following year Harrington bought out Haywood Sullivan's general partnership and completed the process of taking over the organization. In July 2001, after thinking about the matter for several years, Harrington finally decided to sell the Red Sox, and in October made the public announcement that he was putting the team up for sale in accordance with the wishes of Mrs. Yawkey. It was purchased for the record-breaking sum of $700 million by a team of investors who will lead the Sox into a new era—one that fans hope will retain the best of the Yawkey years.

❧ LEONARD P. ZAKIM

As a major component of Boston's Big Dig highway project, plans were made for the construction of a massive fourteen-lane bridge across the Charles River. This impressive span would not only help relieve the city's traffic congestion but also dramatize a chapter of local history, with replicas of the Bunker Hill Monument on the bridge-tower spires, and cables that symbolize Boston's maritime heritage. When finally open to traffic, replacing the present six-lane I-93 upper and lower decks, the soaring $100 million bridge, designed by Christian Menn, will be the widest cable-stayed bridge in the world. In the spring of the year 2000, Governor Paul Cellucci and Cardinal Bernard Law announced plans to name the new bridge for Leonard P. Zakim, a man known for his tireless work in building bridges across religious, racial, and ethnic lines.

Lenny Zakim was a well-known local activist who spent most of his life trying to counter bigotry and bring together diverse groups of people. For some twenty years he was regional Executive Director of the Anti-Defamation League of New England. He frequently appeared on radio and television as a spokesman for the Jewish community, and often addressed audiences of high school students. He published numerous articles concerning the Middle East, Black-Jewish and Catholic-Jewish relations, anti-Semitism, violence, and hate crimes of every kind. He was the author of a Brandeis University publication on the process of coalition building, and published a book on anti-Semitism called *Lift Up Your Voice* in the fall of 1998. Zakim served on the Reebok Human Rights Advisory Board, the Massachusetts Martin Luther King Jr. Commission, and Harvard's national Black-Jewish working group. He received numerous awards and honors, including the Urban League's Community Service Award and the Catholic Charities Medal; and on a trip to Rome in November 1999 he was made a Knight of St. Gregory by Pope John Paul II in recognition of his work to establish greater understanding between Catholics and Jews in New England.

In addition to his scholarly and media involvements, Lenny Zakim was also active in grass-roots movements and associations. He was one of the initiators of the anti-bias educational project called A World of Difference Institute. Since its inception in Boston in 1985, it has been adapted in twenty-nine other cities and six countries. Zakim was also co-founder of the Team Harmony Foundation, along with former Celtics assistant coach and later Deputy Assistant Attorney General for the Department of Justice Jon Jennings. Jennings and Zakim founded Team Harmony in 1992 after the death of the Celtics captain Reggie Lewis, as a means of gathering students, of all races and backgrounds, to work together to fight hatred and bigotry. In November 1999 Zakim addressed more than twelve thousand students from all over New England at Team Harmony. Zakim made many trips to the Middle East, meeting with major political and religious leaders. In 1986 he traveled to Poland with Cardinal Bernard Law to participate in historic meetings on Catholic-Jewish relations. Two years later he returned to Krakow, where the Anti-Defamation League and the Polish Episcopate Commission co-sponsored the first Catholic-Jewish conference on Jews, Judaism, and anti-Semitism in Poland.

On December 2, 1999, Leonard Zakim lost a five-year battle with cancer at the age of forty-six, leaving behind a wife and three children. The number of dignitaries who attended his funeral at Temple Emanuel in Newton, including Elie Wiesel, Cardinal Bernard Law, Minister Don Muhammad, and Senators Edward Kennedy and John Kerry, was eloquent testimony to the great esteem with which he was regarded. After the governor recommended that the new bridge be named in Zakim's honor, representatives of Charlestown suggested that his name be combined with Bunker Hill in order to associate the area's historic identity with the magnificent new structure. Leaders of the Anti-Defamation League worked closely with Charlestown community representatives to agree that the span would be called the Leonard P. Zakim Bunker Hill Bridge, linking the colonial traditions of Charlestown with the name of Lenny Zakim, a man who spent his life building bridges uniting many of the communities that make up Greater Boston.

❡ ACKNOWLEDGMENTS

Jennifer Snodgrass, Editor for Reference and Special Projects at Harvard University Press, has been extraordinarily helpful in the editing of these brief biographical sketches of Eminent Bostonians. The gracefulness of her literary style and the unusual range of her personal knowledge about Boston have added immeasurably to both the clarity and the accuracy of the work. Annamarie Why has produced a most attractive publication with her creative design.

I am grateful to my secretary at Boston College, Rose De Maio, for her invaluable support, and to my undergraduate research assistant, Jane Kalista, for her professional and enthusiastic assistance on the project. Nancy Richard at the Bostonian Society, and Aaron Schmidt at the Print Department of the Boston Public Library, responded to my requests for photographs with their usual expertise and cooperation.

I wish to acknowledge the following institutions for granting permission to reproduce illustrations. Archdiocese of Boston: Richard J. Cushing, John Bernard Fitzpatrick. Boston College: Doug Flutie. Boston Public Library: Samuel Adams, Fred Allen, James Michael Curley, Mary Dyer, Isabella Stewart Gardner (painting by John Singer Sargent), Elma Lewis, Samuel Eliot Morison, John Boyle O'Reilly, Ted Williams. The Bostonian Society: Phillips Brooks, Edward Everett, John F. Fitzgerald, John Murray Forbes, William Lloyd Garrison, Julia Ward Howe, Henry Wadsworth Longfellow, James Russell Lowell, Cotton Mather, John Winthrop. Harvard University Division of Continuing Education: Allan Crite (photo by Jeffry Pike). Massachusetts Historical Society: Lewis Hayden. Perkins School for the Blind: Laura Bridgman and Samuel Gridley Howe.

Schlesinger Library, Radcliffe Institute: Julia Child (photo by Paul Child), Lucy Stone, Dorothy West.

And, once again, I am indebted to my relatives, friends, and colleagues, and to staff members at Harvard University Press, for the interest they have shown in my projects and the numerous suggestions they have made concerning those who should be regarded as truly Eminent Bostonians.

❧ Index